33621

Emily Reuwsaat
Ida Grove, Iowa
('45)

# MEET THE
# SOUTH AMERICANS

*Books by Carl Crow*

400 MILLION CUSTOMERS

I SPEAK FOR THE CHINESE

MASTER KUNG

THE CHINESE ARE LIKE THAT

HE OPENED THE DOOR TO JAPAN

FOREIGN DEVILS
IN THE FLOWERY KINGDOM

MEET THE SOUTH AMERICANS

*Harper & Brothers
Publishers*

# MEET
# THE
# SOUTH
# AMERICANS

By
CARL CROW

Drawings by
OSCAR OGG

BLUE RIBBON BOOKS   *Garden City*, New York

33621

# CONTENTS

[ v ]

*German Propaganda*

## *Preface*

MANY books will have to be written about South America, many visits made there before we come to know the continent as well as we know other parts of the world. This is my contribution toward a better understanding; offered with a complete consciousness of its inadequacy. The story of what I saw is all that I can tell. My own point of view is all that I can present. I see things that others do not see. Others see things I do not see. No one of us can do more than observe carefully and translate sincerely.

I do hope that this book will help to arouse more interest in South America; will cause more books to be written and read; will cause more people to visit this long-neglected area which is destined to be the continent of the future.

C. C.

May 15, 1941

South America

Scale of Miles

0   200   400   600   800   1000

MANHATTAN DRAFTING CO., INC., N.Y.

CHAPTER I

## We Explore South America

IT IS still something of a distinction to cross the equator though the feat is by no means so important as the crossing of the 180th meridian out in the Pacific. When that line is crossed you add one day or drop one day from the calendar just as you add an hour or drop an hour when on a transcontinental trip. In the course of my journeyings I have both added and dropped days and a careful calculation shows that I have actually lost three whole days out of my life which I can never regain except by traveling three times around the world from east to west.

You don't even set your watch when you cross the equator but every passenger is prepared for the event well in advance of its occurrence. Notices chalked up on the bulletin board advise the hour and minute when the line will be crossed. Someone usually manages to get a gullible passenger to go out and look for the line and others are warned to be prepared for the bump. The ship's whistle signals the accomplishment of the crossing. If it occurs at a reasonable time of the day, and even if it doesn't, passengers who happen to be in the smoking room have a gin and tonic, a planters punch or a Barbados rum swizzle. The smoking room is usually pretty well crowded. Someone always makes the crack that the ship will travel faster now on account of the fact that it will be going downhill. It is usually about this time that the often futile attempt to locate the Southern Cross is begun. If you do manage to locate it you always wonder why you went to so much trouble and who called the damn thing a cross anyway.

Sometimes there is a burlesque party at which Emperor Neptune and his consort hold court and those who cross the line for the first time are initiated after being tried on a charge of trespassing on the Kingdom of Neptune. This ceremony was originated centuries ago by sailors and allowed free play for the forecastle sense of humor. If ancient stories are to be believed, one of the favorite stunts was to "keelhaul" the neophyte with a rope tied around his middle. The victim would be hauled under the keel from one side of the ship to the other, scraping off barnacles on his journey. As a variation he was sometimes hauled along the keel from one end of the ship to the other. *Webster's Dictionary* says nothing about keelhauling as a social function but says it was formerly a mode of punishment used in the Dutch and English navies. The *Oxford Dictionary* just tells what the process of keelhauling consists of without offering any explanation as to who did it or why. That would give the men from Mars something to puzzle over and would doubtless lead to some curious speculations as to what kind of creatures we are.

That playful little prank set the pattern for Neptune parties which are not so popular as they formerly were.

Passengers on a luxury liner don't wear old clothes and Neptune parties are always boisterous and often rough. A passenger on an American steamer had his leg broken a few years ago and successfully sued the company. That has made the skippers cautious and some of them will have nothing to do with equatorial celebrations. For another thing the same people have been traveling to South America in the past few years and it is difficult to find enough neophytes to stage a party. There was no initiation when I crossed the equator on the Moore-McCormack's *Argentina* but Captain Simmons gave me a certificate anyway.

In the old days when one rolled down to Rio in the windjammers the crossing of the equator was indeed something of a feat. Under the most favorable circumstances it required many weeks from any port on the North Atlantic and ships were often delayed by calms. Long before Rio or Buenos Aires was reached the salt pork was rancid, there were weevils in the sea biscuits and the drinking water stank. One left the discomforts of the ship only to find equal discomforts and more dangers ashore. Rio was not the spotless city it is today. Mosquitoes abounded and when the city was not ravaged by yellow fever it waited with dread for a scourge of bubonic plague. Stories are still told both in Rio and Santos of ships which did not sail for years because it was impossible to find enough healthy seamen to man them.

Discomfort was then thrust on every traveler. Today one steps on a floating hotel with better food and better service than can be found in many a good hotel ashore. The Moore-McCormack boats which ply on the east coast leave the passenger no opportunity to get bored with the tedium of a long sea voyage with a few stops. The latest

Hollywood productions are shown on the movie program; there are floor shows and dances and cocktail parties, occasional lectures. If one wants to learn Spanish he will find a language school on board and after a course of twenty lessons will have the fundamentals of the most beautiful of spoken languages. There is also a dancing school where one can learn to dance the rhumba. Many young Americans take both courses and by the end of the voyage are prepared for either business or romance. The personable young man finds plenty of opportunity to practice both Spanish and dancing on the boat. The dancing pupils usually include quite a number of señoritas for while the rhumba and other exotic dances originated south of the equator they have been refined and perfected in the United States. This round of entertainment is not needed on the Grace boats which serve the west coast. They are seldom out of sight of land and there are frequent stops at interesting ports.

The ports of South America are no longer the pest holes that they were. As in many other parts of the world the residents of Rio for generations looked on the sting of a mosquito as one of the unavoidable irritations of life and the periodic holocausts caused by yellow fever as something beyond the control of man. But Dr. Oswaldo Cruz, a well-known Brazilian scientist, was inspired by reports of the famous experiments we carried on in Cuba. He studied the work of Dr. Walter Reed and then succeeded in inducing the Brazilian government to undertake an ambitious campaign of extermination. This was so successful in Rio that it was extended to other cities with result that the largest area of mosquito-free territory to be found any place in the world outside the Panama Canal Zone is very probably in Brazil. In Rio there is no market for mosquito netting.

There are good hotels in all of the large cities and passable ones in the smaller places though not many of them. In fact if a hundredth part of the tourists who formerly went to Europe should start traveling south of the Panama Canal every hotel in South America would be crammed to capacity, and the local residents would have to start keeping boarders or let visitors sleep in the streets. That wouldn't be so bad as it sounds for with a mild climate and no mosquitoes a nice grassy plaza might provide a very comfortable bed.

In anticipation of increased travel new hotels are being built, some with government encouragement or subsidy. Almost every large city has at least one hotel that was completed in the past few years. Architecturally the best are as good as any in the United States which is equivalent to saying that they are as good as any in the world. Above all one is amazed at their cheapness. There are a few exceptions but in most places hotel rates are just about half what one would expect to pay for similar accommodations in a reasonably priced establishment in any large American city. Indeed most people who live comfortably in hotels at home could take a six months' trip to South America with the satisfaction of knowing that they were saving money. The cost of the steamer ticket would be more than offset by the reduced living expenses. If one is inclined to put on weight a stay of that length would mean either an increased girth or a successful battle against temptation for the food of South America is good and plentiful.

Steamships and travel agencies and even some governments are actively promoting more tourist travel. Copy writers in advertising agencies handling these accounts have an easy time of it. They have a new story to tell and many pleasant things to say. Millions are being spent on new hotels. At the same time antiquated and useless passport, customs, quarantine, and police regulations make the entry into any port a tedious burden. I had always thought the customs examination in our own country was about the worst in the world but getting into New York is child's play compared to getting into Rio and in no port is it easy.

The passport examination at Rio is divided into three parts—that is one has to run the gauntlet of three sets of officials, immigration, foreign office and police. All that any of them did was to check the information on the passport against that on the ship manifest to see that the men in the purser's office had made no mistakes. Three sets of officials verified everything and found the data correct. And then, just to make sure that nothing had been overlooked a fourth official had a look at my passport again before I could pass down the gangplank.

There followed the weary wait for baggage. I could have carried all of mine, but there is an official regulation against that. I could not even carry off my brief case containing all of my papers. The business of portering is monopolized by a gang of Genoese who make the most of the infrequent arrival of ships. Their kinsmen are to be found in every port and railway station in Brazil and their tactics have been copied in all the other countries. It is a rather curious thing that the traveler does not have to fear overcharges in hotels and restaurants, does not have to protect himself against rackets that are designed to defraud travelers the world over. But throughout South America the man with a piece of baggage is marked for exploitation.

Porters fight for possession of his bags and then work every trick known to the craft to despoil him of his milreis or pesos. Taxi fares are immediately doubled or tripled if you carry a single piece of baggage.

My first experience in Rio set the pattern for all the rest. The porter with whom I had entered into definite contractual relations managed to shift me from one to another of his colleagues so that before I got through I had to pay three fees instead of one. The taxi driver shamelessly demanded forty milreis for transportation to the hotel. I made the trip several times daily after that and was never asked a third of that amount. I had the same experience in almost every other port. Two or three passengers may pile into a taxi and ride as or almost as cheaply as one. But put a single bag or a portable typewriter in the car and the fare skyrockets.

There are a number of dodges which the most seasoned and cagey traveler cannot escape. Having come to grips with water-front racketeers in many parts of the world I am usually able to take care of myself but I had to acknowledge not one but many defeats. At the Peruvian port of Callao the porters insist on acting in the capacity of customs brokers and pass your baggage through the examiners. Then when you are all through the policeman on duty demands a tip. At Barranquilla the porter rides to the hotel with you where all he can do is to lift the bags from the car and hand them to the bellboy. It then develops that the all inclusive price which had been agreed to in the presence of witnesses did not include the hire of the car. It was only for the porter who handled the bags and was ready to act as interpreter in case you wanted to have a chat with the chauffeur. I suppose that if one is inclined to seasickness and ends an ocean voyage in a slightly queasy condition these experiences with porters will drive all sad recollections from one's mind and the strange hotel appears as a refuge from a cruel and rapacious world. To give these rascals credit that is due them it should be said that ships arrive infrequently, tourists are few in number and there are many idle and profitless days. And reduced to terms of United States currency the amounts they manage to gouge out of their victims is very small indeed.

Customs examiners take their time about their duties. If a big ship arrives at Rio at noon some of the passengers will probably still be in the customs shed at five o'clock. At no other port are the proceedings any speedier. At all of them the customs officials appeared to be more interested in the strange new merchandise they find in the trunks than in the discovery of items against which duty can be assessed. In the baggage of a lady from Des Moines was a new make-up kit—at any rate it was new to the officials. All three of them looked at it and discussed it. One removed the top of the lipstick like an opium suppression official in China looking for smuggled dope. The brilliant red was shocking to him and he quickly replaced the top. Another sniffed at the face powder. Those of us who were watching felt sure that the lady had run foul of some regulation and would at least have to pay a very heavy duty. But they passed it back to her with a smile and then chalked up all her baggage as duty free.

They paid but scant attention to my four bags once they found that they contained nothing of any special interest. They had a look at the portable typewriter and then one of them helped me strap up the bags which is the first time a customs inspector ever did that. So far as I know, not one of the passengers on the *Argentina* had to pay a cent of duty but we all grew weary and irritable over the long wait. It would have been especially tough on an Englishman for he would have missed his afternoon tea.

Once his baggage is in the hotel and there is no further need to cart it about the traveler finds himself in a new world. He has little need to guard himself against overcharges and he can accept courteous attention without the suspicion that a tip will be expected. Most of the taxis are taxis in name only as few of them have meters, but this need cause no alarm. In most cases the driver without a metered car charges less than the others. I used them daily in a dozen or more cities and in only one instance was I overcharged. Most taxi rates are so low that the visitor fresh from New York could be charged twice the usual fare without having his suspicions aroused. Although drivers accept tips without any signs of surprise and with an appreciative word of thanks, they do not appear to expect them.

The prices of things are not, as in New York, regulated so as to make tipping easy. For example the price of a hair cut in the best places in Brazil is five milreis or approximately twenty-five cents. When I gave the barber a twenty-milreis note in payment for his services he handed me three five-milreis notes in change, and the transaction was closed. Now I know just what change a New York barber would have given me under similar circumstances. He would have given me one ten-milreis or two five-milreis notes and five of the little brass coins which represented one milreis. And he would have expected one or two of the smaller coins as a tip. The Brazilian barber obviously didn't expect anything more than payment for services rendered. I would not mention this trivial incident were it not for the fact that it was typical of all of the

South Americans who rendered me any personal service. This proud, self-respecting attitude on the part of workers who make but a fraction of the wages paid to Americans is in striking contrast to that of the tip-cadging unionized stewards on American boats.

These stewards provide my authority for the statement that the South Americans themselves show a noticeable restraint in the matter of tips. Their opinion is unanimous in a matter which is of great—one might almost say of primary—concern to them. One of my room stewards told me in some unnecessary detail how far the tips he received from Spanish-speaking passengers failed to measure up to any reasonable expectations. He concluded with the philosophical observation that the South Americans were not experienced ocean travelers and so didn't know what was expected of them. He thought they would eventually learn so that it would be both pleasant and profitable to have them on board instead of a pain in the neck as at present. That, of course, was an excellent build up for me as we were approaching the port of destination where tips, such as they might be, would be handed out.

There may be taxi rates some places in the world that are cheaper than those of Lima but I doubt it. The actual per mile rate is lower in Rangoon but the tiny vehicles will carry only one person with complete comfort if he is not too fat. The passenger cars which ply for hire in South America are all of standard American manufacture. For an ordinary trip around the city of Lima the fare is one half a sole or exactly eight and a half cents. As the geography of the place was confusing to me I had on a number of occasions to ask for help in giving directions to the driver and on every occasion my advisor, whether a Peruvian or a fellow countryman would confirm the fact that the fare was half a sole and wind up with the injunction:

"Don't pay one centavo more."

At first I assumed that the Peruvian drivers must be as voracious as the porters at Callao who are the worst I have ever encountered, and that this advice was offered for my own protection. But day after day I used the taxi and no driver ever tried to overcharge me even when I wickedly threw temptation in his way by pretending to be ignorant of the fare. It finally dawned on me that this ridiculously cheap taxi fare was one of those special privileges which the people of Lima enjoy and they are anxious to preserve. If people started paying more than the conventional half sole the drivers might wake up to an appreciation of the value of their services and then the fares would be raised. In spite of the advice of the local residents I was usually big hearted and rewarded the cheerful driver with a tip of one and a half cents, bringing my total payment up to the equivalent of a dime. One day I inadvertently mentioned this to a local resident and found that I had committed more than a social error,—I was disturbing the whole economic setup of the place.

Foreigners on the China Coast used to be the same way and many of them still are. Servants were satisfied with such low wages that the poorest white man could enjoy the comforts reserved for the rich in other lands. Everyone seemed to think that this was just too good to be true. And there was a general conspiracy to keep the servants in their place. One of the most heinous offenses one white man could commit against his fellow white man was to rouse the lowly ambitions of cooks or coolies or houseboys by liberal tips in hotels and restaurants or by paying his own servants anything above what was looked on as the standard wage. The privilege of getting those in a lower social scale to work for you at a ridiculously low wage is one that is seldom surrendered without a struggle. It is a privilege the South Americans have enjoyed from the beginning of their national life.

It is quite impossible for the layman to understand the reason for all of the formalities to which the traveler must submit in every South American country.[1] The number of passport inspections by the police, immigration, public health and other governmental departments is amazing. Peru carries its regulations to what appears to be absurdity. No visitor can secure a permit to visit Peru even as a tourist, unless he can present a satisfactory letter from the police department of his own city testifying to his good moral character and high reputation in the community. Unless he has a return ticket he must present a letter from a bank showing that he has money enough to pay his way while in Peru and eventually go home without becoming a charge on the community.

Having taken all these precautions the layman would think that the common or garden variety of tourist should be allowed to roam the country at will. But not so. He must surrender his passport before leaving the ship and must later call for it at the Palacio de Justice where a record is made of his local address, age, occupation, whether male or female, married or single. The passport is then returned and will be inspected by various officials on any journey into the country.

[1] Minor officials of two South American governments asked me what I thought about the possibilities of building up a tourist trade. I told each of them I thought they would have to simplify the passport and customs formalities and told them of some of my own difficulties. Each made the same comment. They said it was all my own fault, that if I had only let it be known that I was a writer everything would have been made smooth for me and I would have had no trouble at all.

As the date for the homeward journey approaches the traveler finds that while there has been a good deal of difficulty about getting into the country getting out of it is no simple matter involving as it does a good deal more than having a ticket or the price of one. First it is necessary to pay a visit to the Minister de Hacienda where all the vital statistics are again recorded, a document signed and a print of your right thumb made and kept in a permanent card index file. Just why you should be thumb printed as you are leaving the country and not when you enter it is a problem I made no attempt to solve.

If you are smart you will have kept the taxi waiting for after having gone through with this formality you go back to the Palacio de Justice where if everything is in order you are given a ticket that allows you to board the steamer or the plane for which you have bought a ticket. Just what would happen if everything was not in order I have no idea. But the Peruvians are a good-natured and tolerant people and I have an idea that the officials would find some way of cutting the red tape.

This sounds much worse in the telling than it actually is in the practice. In fact, I rather enjoyed it and in my rounds of the various offices met a lot of interesting people. One Peruvian gentleman in the Palacio de Justice was so mellow, so well read and had such a dry and salty humor that I was really sorry when he finally put his rubber stamp on my paper and I had no excuse to make further calls on him. However all of this does take time. If a hurried visitor wanted to spend two days in Lima he might well waste most of the first day getting permission to stay and the better part of the next day getting permission to leave. About the most he could expect to do in the way of sight-seeing would be to pop into the cathedral and have a look at the mummified body of old Pizarro lying there in his glass case. I did actually spend four hours getting permission to leave the country and then no one asked to see the precious document and I still have it.

It was worse in Colombia where I spent from ten o'clock in the morning until four in the afternoon getting permission to go on board the steamer. This was not because there was any difficulty about it. The official who was in charge of the office—the man with whom all travelers must deal—refused to speak anything but Spanish and as he did not approve the kind of Spanish I spoke put my passport at the bottom of the heap. Before he got around to it he went out for a much-needed shave. Finally the papers had to be approved by the port captain and he didn't get back from lunch until four o'clock.

It is the consensus of opinion among North Americans who have traveled much in South America that the passport regulations of the various countries could be efficiently enforced with about half the number of officials who are now employed and that if they ever expect to build up a big tourist business this will have to be done. A very careful calculation shows that I spent no less than seventeen hours getting visas, being fingerprinted, securing permits to enter a country and permits to leave it. This does not include a number of long taxi drives to the offices of consulates, police chiefs or port captains, nor the time spent in getting extra passport pictures, which are filed in archives of various governments. More than half of this time was spent in Colombia and Peru, two countries where the regulations are most vexatious.

While always expressing mild surprise that anyone should not know how to speak Spanish or Portuguese as the case may be, the South Americans have not exerted themselves especially in the study of English. There are without a doubt a great many more Chinese living in China who have a working knowledge of English than there are South Americans with a similar accomplishment. Even in remote cities of China and of Japan, the average hotel servant knows all the English he needs to know to carry out his duties. A half dozen or more New York hotels put on advertising campaigns in Spanish and Portuguese and I have an idea that visitors have no great difficulty in making their wants known.

But in all South America I did not find a single waiter, chambermaid or other servant above the rank of headwaiter or hall porter who spoke any English or had the faintest idea of what I wanted until I talked to him in his own language. Even then he frequently didn't know. There are two points of view on the subject and I have always felt that by compelling other people to learn English I was making a greater cultural contribution to the world at large than I possibly could by attempting to master the dozen or more languages with which I have at various times come into intimate contact. Confucius said that in speech as in writing, all that is necessary is that the meaning be clear, and when all one wants to do is to order something to eat or drink or inquire direction, one does not need a large vocabulary nor any expert knowledge as to how words should be used. One day after I had had what I thought was an especially successful conversation in Portuguese with a Brazilian policeman a friend who was with me told me that what I had actually said was:

"That Palace Hotel it is what?"

Anyway what I wanted to find out was the location of the hotel and I did this very successfully for the policeman pointed to the hotel which was just across the street.

That is more than a Paris policeman would have done. He would have answered my question literally and explained that the Palace Hotel was, as its name implied, a hotel.

There are some aids to those who are underprivileged in the matter of languages. The menu of the justly popular Pan-American Airways at Rio could be used even if it did not contain a word of text.

Perhaps it was because the Yankee officials of the Pan American Airways found the languages of South America puzzling that they adopted the device of a pictorial menu so that no matter how illiterate you may be in any or all languages you may point to an item on the menu with some general idea of what you are going to get. To the man in search of a meal in a strange land this is rather important. Years ago in Mexico City I ordered a meal from a Spanish menu and found myself with two kinds of bread. There is no danger of this at the Pan American restaurant. For example under the heading of "Aves" there is a picture of a rooster who does not look any too edible but at any rate you know that if you order anything under the *Aves* division you will get something in the poultry line. It will not surprise you when you find that *frango a Milanesa* is just plain old-fashioned fried chicken. The heading of *Ovos* is illustrated not only with two obvious eggs but with an indignant day-old chick trying to scramble out of an egg cup, and *ovos cosidos* turns out to be two soft-boiled eggs. Unlike food pictures appearing in the magazine advertising pages, there is nothing deceptive about these illustrations and the dishes are always much better than you have been led to expect.

My knowledge of languages is confined to a certain familiarity with the foreign names of food at which I am fairly expert. But breakfast was always a problem. Anyone who is content with the continental snack has easy going. All you do is to press a button or lift the hook off the service phone and after enough time has elapsed for the toast to get cold and the hot milk lukewarm a waiter will bring the stuff to your room. To get anything else requires detailed arrangements and as a daily routine I always consulted my dictionaries as soon as I was dressed, making sure that I had not forgotten the appropriate words. With this preparation I thought I got along very well although the conversation was always long and complicated considering the simple issues involved. But the waiter was never able to stand the mental strain for he invariably said with hopeful politeness *"señor, le mismo mañana,"* that is to say "the same tomorrow." I always felt that I should be firm and talk over each meal in detail but I always weakly agreed with the result that in Rio I always had eggs and ham *sur le plat*, in São Paulo *ovos cosidos*.

By dint of great effort I did manage to master enough Portuguese and Spanish numerals to put through telephone calls but always in the hope that someone at the other end of the line could speak English. Sometimes I was lucky and sometimes not. In São Paulo I called a man to whom I had a letter of introduction and finally got someone who spoke English. "Mr. Blank is not here," he said. "You will have to call him long distance." "Where shall I call him?" I asked. "New York," was the reply. I never knew whether he was a wag or just plain dumb.

Having worried along for about two months with taxi drivers whose knowledge of anything but Portuguese or Spanish was at best fragmentary and uncertain I just by accident got a driver in Lima who not only spoke a perfectly understandable English but gave me intelligent answers to all of my questions. A few days after that I regretted my carelessness in not taking his name and number for I wanted to do a little exploring and my customary guide and interpreter was not available. I explained to the porter at the Maury Hotel that I wanted a taxi with an English-speaking driver—a message beset with many difficulties as neither he nor any other employee of the hotel spoke any English. But I accepted his assurances that he understood and after he had done some telephoning the car arrived.

"Do you speak English?" I asked the driver.

"Oui, Monsieur," he replied cheerfully. That didn't sound very encouraging but his car was clean and he had such a pleasant smile that I climbed in.

"What is the name of this car?" I asked a little later just to make conversation.

"Dis car, I hav' not given the name. He is not the lizzie. He is an automobile."

"But what is the make of the car. Is it a Ford?"

"Mais non, he not ze Furd. He is ze Chevverloot. He is not ze petit Chevverloot. He is ze gross Chevverloot."

Assuming that I was curious about the makes of all motorcars we saw he kept up a running fanfare of names. Finally we were stopped by a traffic light alongside a big bus and this gave him an opportunity to give his English a real tryout.

"That is the dizzle engine," he said. "He is sehr strong, more than tiger Chevverloot. Mais he stench."

Just then this trait of the Diesel engine was fittingly demonstrated for there was an emission of gray smoke and the oil fumes filled our car.

"Voila!" cried the driver. "My dear fellow she stench like merry hell!"

How I wished that I could speak Spanish as fluently as he spoke English!

## CHAPTER II

## Mademoiselle from New Rochelle

WHAT appeared to be a very charming bit of South America sat directly opposite me in the dining saloon of the S. S. *Argentina*. She was all that I had ever imagined a señorita of dazzling beauty should be, coal-black hair, lustrous dark eyes, everything that one would presume those lucky devils, the movie directors, would look for in casting some romantic production with the scene laid south of the Rio Grande. Every time I looked at her, which was every time I lifted my eyes from my plate, I thought of castanets and strumming guitars and all the stage settings one more or less instinctively associates with these two musical instruments. I began to see that writing a chapter about the women of South America was not going to be such a difficult task after all and wondered whether or not the señorita spoke English. With luck I might have the chapter completely

outlined by the time we reached Rio. But it didn't work
out that way. Before the first stop at Barbados the captain
gave a cocktail party. It was my birthday. As I stepped
into his quarters I was very happy to see that the charming
señorita was one of the guests. I was still wondering
whether or not someone would act as an interpreter,
when she introduced herself in English.

"It is so nice to find a neighbor on board a big ship like
this," she said. "I was born and have always lived in New
Rochelle—on the Shore Road, near your home in Pelham."

There were several days of not unpleasant research shot
to—anyway I had to make a fresh start.

There were a number of genuine señoritas on board—
from Chile, Brazil, Venezuela, Argentina and one from
the small and isolated Paraguay, the sister of the president
of the country, who had recently been killed in an airplane
crash. Not a single one of them looked as much like I
thought a señorita ought to look as my New Rochelle
neighbor. Not a one of them would have attracted my
attention or the attention of anyone else as being noticeably
different in any night club of New York or in a crowd on
Fifth Avenue—or on any fashionable street in the United
States. That wasn't entirely because they were ship travelers who had embarked in New York and still had a lot
of the Yankee atmosphere clinging to them. My South
American shipmates constituted what is known in commerce as "a fair sample." They were just like their sisters
in the hotels and cafés of all the cities I visited later. They
didn't try to look like the glamorous South American
beauties of the movies but like well-dressed girls on Fifth
Avenue and succeeded very well. There were no mantillas,
no high shell combs. This female perversity in refusing to

conform to a standard and already popularized type is very confusing to the serious writer who is in search of facts. And what a lot of trouble the entertaining but irresponsible fiction writers have made for us writing their intriguing romances about the black-eyed señoritas who wear poinsettias in their hair!

They are responsible for the great brunette fallacy, the general belief that there are not enough blondes in South America to supply what might be called the normal demand. The actual figures, which I am happy to be able to present, are surprising. Brunettes constitute 60 per cent of the population, blondes 39 per cent and redheads 1 per cent. About 10 per cent of the brunettes have brown or chestnut hair, leaving just half with the ebony locks commonly attributed to all. These figures were not obtained as a result of my own observation nor from official census reports which in South America as elsewhere ignore such interesting vital statistics. But they came from a thoroughly reliable and dependable source. As a matter of routine research that would enable them to give their clients sound advice on the cosmetics market, the great J. Walter Thompson advertising agency made a thorough survey of more than a thousand women of all classes living in the city and suburbs of Buenos Aires. That is the unromantic way in which advertising men learn about women! Surveys made by advertising agencies in other cities were not so complete as this one but indicate that the percentage is about the same in all ten countries. Of course, as the executives of the J. Walter Thompson Company are careful to point out, no one can tell how many blondes are synthetic, but who would quibble over a technical question like that?

Neither blondes nor brunettes wear poinsettias in their

hair for such a noticeable display of color would be looked
on as evidence of extreme bad taste. The writers of romances would like to make us believe that they put flowers
in their hair and wear high-heeled red shoes but the fact
remains that they do not and so far as I have been able to
discover, they never did. Indeed the costumes of all the
señoras and señoritas are distinctly lacking in gay colors
without being somber. In the great fashion parade that is
held on Avenida Florida in Buenos Aires every fair afternoon or on Rio Branco in Rio one will note that practically
all of the gowns, even those worn by those of sub-deb age,
are black or white or gray or combinations of these three
colors. But there is nothing funereal about these parades
which every idle young man and old one is always on
hand to see. With such color limitations, costumes become
studies in black and white and there is never a vogue for
fashionable colors which leave the owner with an unwear-
able wardrobe when the vogue for the color passes.

The Parisian proprietor of a ladies' dress shop who established himself in Rio about twenty years ago gave me
what appeared to be a plausible explanation of this general
adoption of sober colors. He said that in the large colored
population in Brazil and of Indians in the other countries
there was a vulgar demand for bright and glaring colors,
just as there is among colored people everywhere. This
has led the high-class Brazilian lady, as well as the ladies
of other South American countries, to lean toward the
other extreme with the result she will reject many colors
which are fashionable in Paris and stick to black, white
and gray. He said that for a similar reason the South American man demands a hat with a brim so narrow as to appear
slightly ridiculous to others. The gaucho who spends his
days in the sun must wear a broad-brimmed hat. The

white-collar worker, who feels himself vastly superior to the gaucho, goes to just the opposite extreme. Thus the sombrero of South America is not the wide-brimmed ten-gallon hat of the Texas plains but a cute little affair that no self-respecting cowboy would wear. The Parisian, by the way, said he thought the average Brazilian making his first trip to the United States would be amazed at the colored livery worn by bellboys in some of the best hotels and would assume that the hotels were catering to the negro trade.

The explanation satisfied me until a better one was supplied by a charming Chilean lady, the wife of a British businessman. She said that the custom of observing periods of mourning after the death of a relative was practically universal in South America as indeed it is in all Catholic countries. But in South America all families are large, there are many relatives. According to a strict interpretation of the code, mourning must be observed for all of them—even those so remotely related as a husband's second cousin. The result is that a very large proportion of the population is actually in mourning at all times. Once in a while there might be a period when there were no deaths in a family and a lady would be allowed by the social code to change to a gayer costume. But unless something happened to the law of averages she barely became accustomed to it before having to go into mourning again. During the brief respite she would be uncomfortably conscious of the fact that in any social gathering she might very probably be the only woman in the room with a bit of gay ribbon at her neck. And so they just remain, so far as clothing is concerned, in mourning all the time, though I must say that no one would ever guess it.

That is understandable and is just what the Koreans did

many centuries ago. Their observance of periods of mourning was not in deference to social custom but in obedience to imperial mandates requiring every subject of the Hermit Kingdom to put on the long white gown of mourning and wear shoes made of sackcloth every time a member of the royal family died. There was no nonsense about it. Show proper respect or get your head chopped off. As successive emperors with fruitful concubines added to the members of the royal family the periods when there was no mourning to be done grew shorter and more infrequent and merchants who had stocks of indigo or of blue cotton cloth found it increasingly difficult to dispose of them. Old blue gowns just became heirlooms or museum pieces. Finally, by mutual consent, the Koreans adopted the compulsory mourning garb as a national costume which they now retain as insignia of their enslavement by the Japanese.

The Koreans never bothered to relieve the dull uniformity of their white gowns. But the South American ladies have made their habitual mourning costumes creations of style and beauty. Not being particularly observant about such matters I might have returned from my unsentimental journey without having noticed the lack of color in their costumes had it not been for the fact that the Paris dress shop proprietor and I had a drink together when we crossed the equator and fell into one of those chance conversations which are often so delightful.

After that my reportorial instincts were turned in a strange direction and I found myself unconsciously checking over the dresses of women to see how closely they adhered to the conventions. I remember quite distinctly one teatime period when I was loafing in the lounge of the Crillon Hotel in Santiago. As is always the case in that fashionable old hotel, the tearoom was comfortably filled with Chilean ladies who, unlike their sisters in more conservative countries, have no inhibition about gadding around without male escorts. A trio of newcomers arrived and there was that momentary hush that always occurs in any party of ladies when it is necessary to give a new arrival a more than casual inspection. As soon as the trio was seated it was obvious to me what had attracted such universal attention. One of the ladies, like all the rest, was smartly dressed in black and white but a quarter-inch red ribbon encircled the crown of her hat. It was the only bit of color in the entire room and there was no doubt about the fact that it did make the wearer very very conspicuous. Even I wondered what had inspired her to be so daring. Of course she may have been a North American tourist who either was ignorant of the conventions or scorned them.

The señoritas do not put poinsettias in their hair nor do they try to make their lips and fingernails simulate the scarlet bracts of that flower. In a women's magazine the other day I read the advertisement of a new lipstick of a particularly provocative shade called "the South American red" and the advertisement urged readers to "lend your face South American excitement." The advertisement was in the best copy writer tradition, an appeal to the exotic. Just why it should be I don't know, but in the clothing we wear, the merchandise we make, the trains we build and in many other ways we are the most colorful of nations and yet we maintain the pretense that we are merely following exotic styles. The truth is that we create colorful styles which others follow. The lipstick advertisement made an appeal that was based on an entirely false premise. A more accurate appeal could have been made south of the equator: "Lend your face North American excitement." That is what the señoritas do but with a certain restraint. Turning again to the survey of feminine tastes made by the J. Walter Thompson agency we find that 94.3 per cent of the women used lipsticks, most of which by the way are made in the United States. More than half used the light or natural shades. An even greater proportion used what are known as the mild shades of nail polish such as rose and natural. Only 4.2 per cent used ruby.

With such restraint in the use of color either in clothing or cosmetics it is not surprising that an American tourist lady should occasionally attract as much attention as a circus parade when she appears on the street in a candy-striped waist, or a plaid skirt or a green jacket. When a single band of red ribbon will attract so much attention, imagine what a red hat would do. In their assurance that no self-respecting woman would dress like that the South Americans assume that she must be a movie actress, or in any event wants to attract attention to herself. If she appears too old for such gimcracks, as is often the case, then her strange behavior can only be explained as an amusing eccentricity. If she wants to put on a show there are plenty of men and boys ready to crowd about and provide an audience. It has happened on a good many occasions that an adventure of this sort has ended by a jump into a taxi and a retreat to the hotel where the offending garment is packed away and not unpacked until on the homeward-bound steamer.

If there is any great increase in tourist travel to the South it wouldn't be a bad idea for our State Department to compile and publish a little manual for the ladies giving some hints as to what they should not wear. The purpose would be to prevent them going out on the streets in costumes calculated to provoke unpleasant incidents. If the State Department experts get out a manual of this sort they might add a word of kindly advice to husbands about taking wives into hotel bars where their presence may be misunderstood by all the young gallants in the place.

A great many observant travelers on their first visit to South America make what appears to them to be the astounding discovery that women there buy clothing in Paris. I did not make this discovery myself as everyone who had written a book about South America had beat me to it. All that I could do was verify the accuracy of the statement. But I was unable to get at all excited about the fact. All over the world women who can afford to do so, pay the price for a Paris label. Ladies in Shanghai bought their gowns in Paris and so did ladies of Rangoon if it was at all possible to manage it. But the number who could manage an annual trip to Paris with a sufficient number of bankers' checks or a letter of credit was in all cases very limited and that was also true in South America as well. Most of them had to content themselves with a copy of something on which some famous designer had placed his magic touch. As to gowns actually made in Paris there were undoubtedly a greater number of North Americans than of South Americans able to flaunt Paris clothes in the eyes of their sisters. This does not mean any difference in taste, but simply that there are more sugar daddies in North America who can be cajoled into paying the price.

At present, with Paris in the hands of the Germans, the señoras and señoritas buy the New York fashion magazines. They can at least look at the pictures and their reliance on these publications for news about fashions adds another incentive to the study of English. Our designers have not been slow about stepping into the gap left by the fall of Paris. On every hand one hears talk of Hollywood styles or New York styles and in Lima I attended a fashion show where New York creations were modeled. There must have been a lot of curiosity about what was going to be shown for the place was packed. Our designers did something that the Parisians had never done—they made generous use of Peruvian furs. Local newspapers said the show was a great success and predicted that New York styles would be followed.

My dress-shop acquaintance had been going to Paris every year to buy materials and pick up the latest style ideas and when I met him he was returning from his first visit to New York. He was free to admit that when it came to sport clothes we led the world but he was a little pessimistic about whether or not we would ever be able to do as good a job as Paris had done in designing more definitely feminine styles. He said we would probably never be able to do this because it is too easy for the American girl to get a husband simply by waiting for one to turn up. Matrimony is not so easy in France. The little French girl is barely in her teens before she is made acutely conscious of the fact that she will have to keep herself prettied up if she wants to get a desirable husband and the only way she can do this is by her own ingenuity. She is usually poor or, if she isn't, she has a thrifty mama who sees to it that nothing is wasted so she has to make the best of every scrap of material. As a result every French girl is a potential style expert and designer. There are many who are not pretty but none who is not attractive or who does not have what appears to be a genius for accentuating her best features.

As he told me all this it just happened that visual evidence of the point he was trying to make paraded on the deck. There were a couple of girls from Des Moines who had quite obviously set themselves the pleasant task of being the style leaders on the ship. In ways that are mysterious to men they carried enough baggage to come out with entirely new and different costumes every day —sport suits in the daytime, new evening gowns at dinner. We never thought the day had really started until they appeared on deck and we could see what the color scheme for the day was. Someone suggested starting a sweepstakes on it letting each ticket holder draw a color and winner take all. But nothing came of it.

The little French girl who came into view soon after the Des Moines beauties disappeared around the corner had no such equipment as this. The only changes she could ring in what appeared to be a shamelessly scanty wardrobe were accomplished by means of a single silk scarf and a pair of jeweled earrings. The whole outfit could have been stuffed into an overcoat pocket. One day she would wear the scarf as a turban and make a brooch out of the earrings. Another day the scarf became a belt and the earrings were in her ears. Or the scarf was draped around her shoulders and the earrings were in her hair. No matter what the arrangement she always stole the show, a fact of which the Des Moines girls were pleasantly unconscious.

My dress-shop shipmate may be right. I remember he said the famous great fashion creators of Paris didn't just sit down and smoke a cigarette and think up a new style. They usually got their ideas from some unusual garment or some new treatment of material which they saw on the streets of Paris and in many cases this was the result of the amateur efforts of some poor girl to make up the only materials she had. That was the reason Paris must always be the fountainhead of fashion. On several occasions he had brought Parisian designers to Brazil but after a few years they lost their cunning because they lacked the inspiration provided by the daily sight of cleverly dressed women parading the boulevards.

There is, however, still another reason why the American stylist will have difficulty in holding the South American trade unless he can orient himself to a new conception of what the female figure should be like. Or, it might be more accurate to say, can revert to earlier ideals. To put the matter bluntly the ladies south of the equator are more globular than those north of the equator and styles for the North American girl are not suitable for the South American. The slim girlish figure is neither present nor desired. Extra ounces have no terror. The South American mama doesn't warn her marriageable daughters to beware of the cookie jar and the candy box. The result is pleasing to the South American male. His tastes in feminine charm go back to our own horse and buggy days when according to Frederick Lewis Allen, a young gentleman in New York refrained from proposing to a lady with whom he was much smitten because, as he confided to a friend, he didn't believe "that bust could be real."

If my shy masculine hints have not revealed what I mean I may venture a bit farther and say that the one product of French manufacture most persistently advertised south of the equator is a bust developer. Shops give shameless show-window exposure to mysterious appliances which no male should be allowed to see—especially the young who have not been disillusioned. In the days when chorus girls wore tights and they put pictures of actresses in packages of Sweet Caporal cigarettes these deceptive contrivances were known as "symmetricals" used only by ladies of the stage. A Mae West revival might turn the tide and bring about a uniformity of pulchritude that would make the gowns of each continent uniform in contour. Until that comes about the señoras and señoritas have to make allowances for the fact that the American styles do not provide the necessary displacement. Mother nature appears to have gone to a lot of trouble to give her daughters an infinite variety of attractions. Without venturing to express an opinion on what may be a controversial subject I will say that after living several years in New England it was a relief to travel all about South America without seeing a single girl who was trying to look like Katharine Hepburn.

Until she is safely married and becomes a señora the señorita is shielded by the convent school and by her parents. It has been said that there is not an unmarried girl in Argentina who has her own latch key. With the possible exception of Chile there is no country where the boys and girls enjoy that free and wholesome association which is such a distinctive feature of life in the United States. There are no parties to be enjoyed except under the bored and watchful eye of a chaperon—or a crew of them if the party is too large for one of them to keep an eye on everything that is or might be going on. In fact parents seem to take it for granted that if every social gathering of boys and girls is not carefully watched something very dreadful is sure to happen. It is because of this that so little progress has been made in getting South American girls to qualify for the many scholarships offered by coeducational schools in the United States. The parents are simply afraid to send their daughter to a school where there is such a free and easy standard that she and a boy friend may stroll about the campus together without a chaperon. Only the Chilean girls have taken full advantage of the educational advantages we have offered. The girls of Argentina have been the most backward.

In what I must admit was very casual investigation I found insufficient data to support the stories that South American young men not only stare at beautiful ladies but that students jostle them on the street and if opportunity arises will pinch them in pinchable places. Avenida Florida, the fashionable shopping street of Buenos Aires, was supposed to provide the scene for these playful diversions. This is the street in which all vehicular traffic is barred from 4 to 8 P.M. so that for four hours shoppers can shop with a minimum of danger from the chauffeurs who range the streets. I walked from one end of Florida to the other on a number of sunny afternoons. No one could help noticing that threats of ogling, jostling and pinching had not deterred a great many well-dressed ladies from their usual promenade along a street which should be called the "Peacock Alley" of South America. In such a crowded thoroughfare jostling is inevitable and with so many attractive ladies about a certain amount of ogling was natural.

But I did not witness any face slapping nor did I hear any feminine squeals. Of course no one would maintain that the South American student, no matter what his birthplace may be, is a perfect little gentleman. His manners are not those of Eton or Harrow for his attitude toward women, like that of his father, are frankly predatory.

It is a very ungallant thought to entertain but it has occurred to me that some of our tourist ladies who have brought back most of the stories have exaggerated matters or possibly have done just a little bragging. Which reminds me that one of the stock stories North Americans tell is about the girl from Venezuela who returned from a visit to New York to complain about the rudeness of the men. She was beauty parlored and dressed in her best but in a walk down Fifth Avenue the women all had a good look at her but the men paid no attention to her. It was not like that in Caracas.

As an old Shanghai friend was fond of remarking, women are a peculiar race.

CHAPTER III

## *The Continent of the Future*

SOUTH AMERICA is still awaiting discovery. It is one of the few sections of the world which we do not know. No high school graduate can go to England or to many parts of Asia entirely unprepared for the sights he will see or unfamiliar with the characteristics of the people he will meet. Most newspaper readers could with a fair degree of accuracy, draw a map showing the location of the principal countries of Europe. Yet I doubt if one out of a dozen who are reading this book could from his own knowledge name the ten countries and the three colonies which comprise continental South America. I am sure I could not have done so two years ago.[1]

[1] The total population of the American hemisphere is approximately 277 millions being just a little more than one tenth of the world population

We are the most assiduous globe-trotters the world has ever known; but we have traveled toward the east or the west instead of the south. Hundreds have sailed up the muddy waters of the Whangpoo to see the sky line of Shanghai for one who has seen the unbelievably beautiful harbor of Rio de Janeiro emerging through the mists. Of the thousands who have sat at the sidewalk cafés of Paris only a handful know from their own experiences that the sidewalk cafés of Rio de Janeiro, Buenos Aires, or Lima are just as interesting and colorful. Several generations of white men were living in South America long before the first colony was founded at Jamestown, but through the intervening centuries they have remained neighbors with whom we did not get acquainted. We did not visit them and they did not visit us. In almost every community in the United States there are residents who were born in Great Britain and the principal countries of Europe, possibly a Chinese laundryman and a Japanese retail shop. These people help to give us mental pictures of the countries from which they came. But there are millions of us who have never even seen a South American.

The continent does not easily lend itself to description. Each of the ten countries and each of the three colonies is

---

of 2,640 millions. The population of South America is 90 millions. The population of the continent by countries is as follows:

| | |
|---|---|
| Argentina | 13,129,723 |
| Bolivia | 3,426,296 |
| Brazil | 44,115,825 |
| Chile | 4,634,389 |
| Colombia | 8,701,816 |
| Ecuador | 3,200,000 |
| Paraguay | 1,000,000 |
| Peru | 6,672,881 |
| Uruguay | 2,093,331 |
| Venezuela | 3,491,159 |

The three colonies, British, French and Dutch Guiana, have a combined population of about 1 million.

unlike any of the others. Considering their geographical propinquity there is a surprising absence of common interests. Aside from figures such as those showing area, populations, foreign trade or average annual rainfall few common denominators can be found. Nothing can be said about the climate, the people, the resources or the government of any of the countries or colonies that will apply with any degree of accuracy to any of the others. Each of the countries has a republican form of government yet in no two of them is the degree of self-government approximately the same. Some were ruled for years by dictators of the worst type, others boast that they are pure democracies. One has a record of orderly and undisputed elections over a period of more than a hundred years except for one interruption. In some there is complete freedom of press and speech. In others politicians who oppose the government are sent into exile and newspapers are suspended for offering mild criticisms. In each country the predominant religion is Roman Catholic but in no two does the church play exactly the same part in politics and education. The continent is often referred to as being a part of Spanish-America yet Spanish is the language of only about half the people.

Only by making a brief survey of each of the countries is it possible to visualize their great size, potential wealth and the dazzling opportunities for future development.

Argentina, with an area of a million square miles, is as large as that part of the United States east of the Mississippi River or about four times the size of the state of Texas. The population of 13 millions is the same as that of the state of New York or the population of the United States a hundred years ago. One fifth of the population is found in the city of Buenos Aires rated as the fifth or sixth largest city in the world.[2] As the native Indian tribes were practically exterminated by the early settlers and negro slaves were never brought in the population of Argentina, unlike that of its neighbors, is almost pure white. The wealth of the country which exceeds that of any other, is agricultural, the principal exports being meat and grain. The owners of the huge haciendas comprise the wealthiest class south of the Rio Grande.

Brazil, colossus of the South, is three times the size of Argentina, is larger than the United States. Its borders touch every other South American state except Chile and Ecuador. The population is 44 millions, made up of many races. The predominant white population consists of descendants of the original Portuguese settlers. The many negroes are descendants of the African negroes who were enslaved by Portuguese planters. There are also a number of descendants of Italian, Spanish, German and Japanese settlers and in the remote parts of the country many Indians. There is probably no other country in the world where the so-called "color line" is so completely disre-

[2] There are 17 cities in South America with populations of more than 200,000. Of these 6 are located in Brazil, 4 in Argentina, 2 in Chile, 1 each in Columbia, Venezuela, Uruguay and Peru, none in Ecuador, Bolivia or Paraguay. The cities are:

| | |
|---|---:|
| Avellaneda, Argentina | 230,775 |
| Bahia, Brazil | 363,726 |
| Bogotá, Colombia | 330,312 |
| Buenos Aires, Argentina | 2,364,263 |
| Caracas, Venezuela | 300,000 |
| Córdoba, Argentina | 288,916 |
| Lima, Peru | 370,000 |
| Montevideo, Uruguay | 682,664 |
| Pará, Brazil | 279,491 |
| Pernambuco, Brazil | 472,764 |
| Porto Alegre, Brazil | 231,628 |
| Rio de Janeiro, Brazil | 1,711,466 |
| Rosario, Argentina | 511,007 |
| Santiago, Chile | 829,830 |
| São Paulo, Brazil | 1,151,249 |
| Valparaiso, Chile | 263,228 |

garded. Unlike other South American countries the language of Brazil is not Spanish but Portuguese, a fact of which the Brazilians are inordinately vain. The principal source of wealth is provided by coffee for which the United States is the most important customer.

Bolivia, one of the smaller of the republics, is twice the size of Texas, but with half its population, that is about 3 millions. More than half of the Bolivians are Indians and a majority of the remainder are of mixed blood. About 80 per cent of the people live at an elevation of more than 10,000 feet. Most of the Indians exist on the small proportion of the land which can be cultivated. The tin mines of Bolivia are second in importance only to those of the Far East and provide practically all of the native export trade.

Chile is the long, lean country occupying the narrow strip of land between the Pacific Ocean and the Andes. With a coast line of 2,800 miles the average width of the country is less than a hundred miles. The area is a little larger than that of the state of Texas and the population of less than 5 millions is about the same as that of New Jersey. A very large part of the area is composed of the barren foothills of the Andes, devoid of vegetation but rich in minerals, principally copper. The mineral wealth of Chile is estimated to be twice that of all other South American countries combined. On the other hand its agricultural wealth is negligible and without great expenditure for irrigation projects the country could not provide foodstuffs for any great increase in population. It is generally believed, however, that Chile has great possibilities for industrial development.

Colombia is our nearest neighbor on the north, being separated from the Panama Canal by only a few miles of jungles. The area of 443,000 square miles is a little larger than the combined area of California, Oregon, Washington and Colorado and the population of 9 million is approximately the same as that of these four Western states. Curiously enough the natural products of Colombia are very similar to those of these states, comprising oil, a variety of minerals, livestock and fruit. It is the only country with ports both on the Atlantic and the Pacific. Almost three quarters of the population consists of people of mixed blood, white and Indian. There are about 2 million pure whites, less than a million pure Indians and about half a million pure negroes. Colombia ranks next to Brazil in the quantity of coffee produced.

Ecuador with an area of 167,000 square miles and a population of less than 3 millions is larger than the state of California and has about one half of its population. As is true of a number of its neighbors some of the boundaries of Ecuador are in dispute and there are no dependable population figures. It is estimated that about a quarter of the population is pure white, a quarter pure Indian and a half of mixed blood. The country is purely agricultural and as the area embraces high mountainous regions as well as extensive tracts lying a few feet above the sea level there is a surprising variety of products. Cocoa and bananas provide two of the important exports.

Paraguay, the pygmy of South American states, has an undisputed area of only 61,000 square miles and a population of one million. It is a few square miles larger than the state of Georgia, and half as populous. A territory of about 100,000 square miles has long been the subject of dispute with Bolivia and the scene of much bloody fighting. The majority of the inhabitants are of Indian descent with but little admixture of Spanish blood. The outstanding industry of the country is the cultivation and preparation of maté, or "Paraguayan tea," which might be called the national beverage of many of the neighboring countries. The Indian men lead such indolent lives and the women do such a large amount of work that Paraguay has been called "The Country of Women." While the official language of the country is Spanish the Indian dialects are more widely spoken.

Peru is approximately twice the size of Texas and is estimated to have about the same population, that is more than 6 million. No census of the country has ever been taken. More than half of the inhabitants are Indian, the largest indigenous group in South America. About one tenth of the population is made up of pure whites, some of whom are able to trace their ancestry back to the days of Pizarro. The remainder are of mixed blood in which there is every conceivable combination of whites, Indians, negroes and Asiatics. For many years Peru thrived from the guano deposits which had accumulated on outlying islands from the dropping of birds through the ages. Silver which formerly brought such great wealth to the kings of Spain is no longer of primary importance. Guano and silver have been supplanted by oil and copper as the principal sources of wealth. As the seat of the old Inca empire which was destroyed by the Spaniards Peru provides more spots of historical and archaeological interest than all other South American countries.

Uruguay, with an area of 73,000 square miles and a population of 2 million is almost exactly the same size as North Dakota and has three times the population. It is the most densely populated of all the South American countries. The encouragement of immigration has brought to the country a large number of settlers, doubling the population in the past thirty years. The immigration is largely made up of Spanish and Italians, with a small number of Germans. The wealth of the country, like that of its big southern neighbor, Argentina, is principally in grain and livestock.

Venezuela with an area of 400,000 square miles and a population of 3 million is eight times the size of North Carolina and has approximately the same number of inhabitants. Venezuelans of pure white blood of Spanish descent are very few in number. By far the greater part of the population is composed of persons of mixed blood, principally whites and Indians but with a generous admixture of negro blood. In isolated parts of the country there are a number of settlements of pure Indian tribes. The fertile plains were formerly covered with herds of cattle and horses but with the war of independence followed by a long period of civil wars the herds were killed off and have never been completely replaced. Coffee is now the most important agricultural crop. However, the spectacular development of the long-neglected oil fields has given the country a source of wealth far greater than any that could possibly be developed from coffee or cattle or any other product of the soil. Oil seepages are known to have existed in Venezuela before the birth of Columbus but it was not until about thirty years ago that any attempt was made to develop them. In 1925 the country was able to boast of a production of 20 million barrels for the year. The next year the production was tripled and the following year it was doubled. Since that time there has been a steady increase until now the annual production is about 200 million barrels, giving Venezuela the rank of third largest oil-producing country in the world. The government is supported by royalties from oil production to the extent that there are practically no personal taxes in the country.

The three colonial possessions in continental South America are British, French and Dutch Guiana, forming a tier of territories grouped on the northern border of Brazil. The total area of the three colonies is 168,000 square miles, the population less than a million.

The one outstanding impression one gets from a visit to South America is that of the dazzling opportunities that lie before the continent. The wealth which Pizarro filched from the Incas has become proverbial yet it was as nothing compared to the wealth as yet untouched in forests and fields. The great and growing cities give a false impression of the extent to which the different countries have been developed. Actually the surface has only been scratched. With a total continental population of less than a hundred million there is room for many times that number. With greater development of natural resources a population equal to that of the entire continent could easily be supported by either Brazil or Argentina, possibly by Colombia. Venezuela could support a population equal to that of Brazil. With the exception of Chile there are in all the countries great areas of uncultivated land and in none is the land cultivated by anything approaching efficient methods. Chile has already completed its agricultural era and is turning toward industrialization. With water power, coal and abundant minerals the progress of Chile is dependent only on the energy and ingenuity of the people.

If the continent were as densely populated as the United States it would have a population of 300 million people and there is no reason why it should not be even more densely populated. The agricultural resources alone are richer and more varied and the development of manufacturing has just begun. There is every reason to believe that in the not very distant future South America will be the most populous part of the hemisphere, that Argentina, Brazil and Chile may become world powers.

With its great tracts of undeveloped land and unexploited riches the continent stands today about where we stood a hundred years ago, but with some very important differences so far as the future is concerned. We had to await the development of machines such as railways, motorcars, refrigeration, and the great array of agricultural equipment. Each of these sent us farther forward and added to our prosperity by making possible the further development of natural resources. The South Americas do not have to wait for these things which are now commonplaces. While we were confined to the slow progress of the covered wagon they can go forward with the speed of the motorcar. The development of our manufacturing had to wait on the perfection of tools and processes. These are available now for the South Americans to use them. They do not have to go through the tedious process of developing from handicrafts to machine production but can start near the top.

They also have the benefit of our experience and the experience of others in all manner of social problems such as the relations between capital and labor. It may be significant that they have displayed what appears to be a greater degree of energy in attempts to solve these social problems than in the development of industries. Machinery for the solution of problems which are inescapable in an era of industrial development has been set up before the actual appearance of the problems.

In this land of limitless opportunities progress is dependent only on the people. There can be no doubt about the fact that they are thoroughly aware of the possibilities as well as the problems which face them. The present war has done much to destroy the old complacent reliance on easily earned incomes from inherited estates carelessly and inefficiently managed. The feudal period is coming to a close. The new era which is beginning promises to center the interest of the next century in South America which will be the continent of the future.

## CHAPTER IV

## The Ten Bad Neighbors

FROM the time that they threw off the rule of Spain and Portugal and set themselves up as independent self-governing nations the South American countries have not been good neighbors to each other. They were not, in fact, good neighbors during the colonial period before nationalism gave encouragement to the old envies and jealousies. They bickered and quarreled over real and imaginary issues just like our own colonies did until the common aims of defense against oppression and injustice brought them together. Desire for independence was common in South America but it was not achieved by a common effort. Some of the colonies revolted together, but in the main each one fought its own battles. Even those which fought together against the common oppressor laid the foundations for future quarrels which broke out when it came time to allocate the expense of the military campaigns. Some of these controversies over money dragged on for years and left lasting heritages of ill will. The differences which had existed in colonial days were stressed and exaggerated under the stimulus of the nationalism that developed with independence. While the issue of slavery eventually divided us into two hostile camps, a dozen petty issues made every new South American country jealous and suspicious of its neighbors.

An ever-present source of trouble and potential wars was found in boundary disputes. As a matter of fact the many wars between these countries were invariably fought for the purpose of defending their own or encroaching on the territory of a neighbor. There are few boundaries that have not been soaked in the blood-battles fought for the possession of territory—much of it of little or no conceivable value to its possessors. Many of the disputes were inherited from the days of Spanish rule for boundaries of the colonies were ill defined and after more than a hundred years there are still many which are in dispute. The original grants made to Pizarro and other conquerors or favored families carved up the continent in checkerboard fashion for all the boundaries followed lines of latitude or longitude. No attention was paid to the existence of natural geographical boundaries, such as mountains, lakes and rivers.

Simon Bolivar, the great soldier and statesman, hoped and believed that the different newly established states would find unity in some kind of a federation but instead they split up into smaller fragments. Colombia was formerly known as Great Colombia, a name justified by a vast expanse of territory which included not only Panama but Ecuador and Venezuela. The latter country was formed of provinces which seceded before the government of Great Colombia was completely organized. That was in 1829 and for more than a hundred years there were perennial disputes as to the possession of some mil-

lions of acres and it was not until 1941, as I was writing
this chapter, that a treaty was signed which it is hoped will
mean a final settlement. Ecuador followed Venezuela in
breaking off from Colombia and had barely become independent before it was attacked by Peru over a boundary
dispute which has never been completely settled.

The Bolivians, who found themselves landlocked, coveted the near-by ports of Peru and as the result of a successful invasion, the two countries became temporarily
united with Bolivian interests in the ascendancy. This
growth of power aroused the fears of neighbors and the
joint territory was invaded by the forces of Chile and
Argentina. The Peruvians had barely regained their independence before they attempted to pay off old grudges
and add to their territory by an invasion of Bolivia. These
are only a few of many clashes which occurred more than
a hundred years ago but the issues were never satisfactorily
settled and the hatreds engendered by the conflict of those
old days still exist.

There were many later boundary wars. In 1864 Peru
fought what is now a half-forgotten war with Spain and
her old enemies Ecuador, Chile and Bolivia came to her
assistance and for a brief interval all the old rivalries were
forgotten. Hostilities had been suspended but the treaty
of peace had not been signed before an old boundary dispute was revived between Chile and Bolivia. Peru attempted to settle the dispute and met the fate that so often
falls to peacemakers for Chile declared war on both countries. Possession of the rich nitrate deposits was the real
issue involved. The war was a long one and bitterly fought.
The Peruvian army was defeated and the country invaded. Chilean troops destroyed a great deal of property
and occupied Lima and were not finally withdrawn until

1884. The treaty which was signed at that time did not prove a very effective instrument and quarrels continued. The nitrate fields were given to Chile, a settlement which still rankles in the hearts of Peruvians.

The two countries, which are as close neighbors as New York and Pennsylvania, broke off diplomatic relations in 1910. It was not until twelve years later that they accepted an offer of mediation by the United States. In the meantime another war between Peru and Bolivia was narrowly averted in 1909 and a year later there was an equally narrow escape in a threatened war between Peru and Ecuador.

Bolivia has never been free from border wars for very long at a time. In addition to hostilities with Peru and Chile, Bolivia has never been on friendly terms with her small but provocative neighbor, Paraguay. In 1879 an attempt was made to reach a permanent settlement of long-standing differences between these two countries and a treaty clearly defining the boundaries was drawn up and signed by the diplomats. Each had been compelled to make some concessions in order to reach an agreement and as a result the treaty met opposition in both countries and was not ratified. Dispute over the boundary settlement made by this unratified treaty enlivened the politics of each country for almost fifty years. The long-deferred war finally broke out in 1928 when all the rest of the world was at peace and lasted for several years. The treaty of peace was not signed until 1938. There was a great loss of life on both sides.

Chile and Argentina bickered for years over possession of the Straits of Magellan and the southern tip of the continent, Patagonia. A treaty on this subject was signed in 1881 but like most other treaties intended to define boundaries it left plenty of scope for further controversies.

War was narrowly averted just at the beginning of the present century. A treaty of peace signed in 1902 contains provisions for limitations of armaments, each pledging the other to equality in naval strength. This treaty provision highlights and emphasizes the fact that the armies and navies maintained by the different countries are primarily kept for the purpose of protection against each other or, inversely, for use in the event that the old game of filching territory from neighbors should start again. Chile maintains a standing army of 40,000, Argentina 50,000, Brazil 112,000. The total armed forces of the ten countries number about 300,000 and in addition there are more than a million and a half in reserve. There is some form of compulsory military service in each country.

Long before Argentina had decided on what form of government she would adopt or which section of the country should be dominant in governmental affairs, she fought a successful war against Brazil to put a stop to the latter's plans for southward expansion. A few decades later an unsuccessful attempt was made to annex Uruguay, the small state which lies between the two giant countries Brazil and Argentina. Argentina armies actually held Montevideo in siege for nine years. Quarrels between Argentina and its other small neighbor, Paraguay, began as soon as Spanish authority was driven out. About the middle of the last century, when different provinces of Argentina were still fighting each other, the rulers of Paraguay kept their armies in active training by taking sides in the Argentine controversies. Rosas the tyrant dictator who held the balance of power in Argentina at this time decided to settle the matter once and for all by making Paraguay a province of Argentina. Some of the Argentine factions, through no love for Paraguay and no respect for her right, sided with the little country solely because they hoped for the downfall of Rosas. The result was that when the warring Argentine provinces were finally united (1862) the confederacy which was formed recognized the full independence of Paraguay.

That was the signal for a new dictator of Paraguay to start on an ambitious program of empire building for himself. The result was a fantastic, tangled and contradictory succession of events about which historians can write many pages. A Brazilian army invaded Uruguay and in reprisal a Paraguayan army invaded Brazil. The Argentine government refused a request to allow the passage of Paraguayan troops through its territory in order to attack Brazil and Paraguay declared war on Argentina. This led to a truce between old enemies for (1865) an alliance was formed between Argentina, Brazil and Uruguay for the purpose of making joint defense against the relatively tiny neighbor. The war continued much longer than anyone expected and did not end until five years later when the Paraguayan dictator was killed and his leaderless troops surrendered.

The above constitutes a very brief and sketchy outline of the principal conflicts that have occurred between the different countries. It will be noted that, almost without exceptions, each has at one time or another been at war with one or more of its neighbors. Brazil alone has never resorted to arms or threats in the settlement of boundary disputes, and there are no differences of opinion as to where Brazilian boundaries lie. The many controversies over boundary lines have all been amicably settled by negotiation. The wars fought by the other countries were not *opéra bouffe* affairs. A great many men were killed, a great deal of property destroyed leaving impoverished survivors with bitter memories. Little has been done to heal old sores but many things keep them open. The anniversary of many battles which should have been forgotten long ago are still celebrated as public holidays, wreaths placed on the statues of military heroes and speeches made which revive old grudges and perpetuate territorial ambitions. It is against this background of old prejudices and distrusts that the countries try to solve their economic problems and in doing so often create new frictions. The maintenance of the standing armies has in many cases prevented normal political development because control of the army has provided the means by which every dictator has risen to power.

Boundary disputes still flare up after more than a century of controversy, wars, treaties and agreements. While I was in Chile there was an exchange of notes between that country and Argentina over the question of possession of some territory in the extreme south that was supposed to have been settled by the treaty signed in 1902. When I was in Bogotá two months later the papers featured for several days stories of the movement of troops in Ecuador which some alarmists thought presaged an attempt on the part of that country to push the border farther north adding some territory to Ecuador at the expense of Colombia. Several fiery statements were made by public men in each country but after a few days the excitement died down. An area much larger than that of England is in dispute between Bolivia and Paraguay and a similar area between Peru and Ecuador. As I write this I see that the leading newspaper of Peru has published an editorial bitterly criticizing the government of the United States because of aid given to the navy of Ecuador. The argument is that by helping Ecuador we are siding against Peru in the century-old boundary dispute.

There is always the danger that when these controversies arise some hotheaded patriot will do something that the peacemakers cannot explain away. Unfortunately there are still a great many square miles of territory which map makers have to mark with shaded lines and designate as disputed. And in many countries it is possible to stir the people to a frenzy of excitement by merely spreading rumors that some neighbor is planning a territorial raid. The situation is not so bad as in the Balkans but follows the same pattern.

Even within the countries there are many provincial and sectional differences, many projects for public works held up because of the fear that some section will benefit at the expense of another. When the Portuguese colony became a republic it called itself "the United States of Brazil." But the states were never actually united until the administration of President Vargas compelled them to respect the federal authority. Each state had its own flag and was as touchy as a principality about the respect shown to the flag by neighbors. Individual states showed but scant respect for federal laws if they were counter to what was considered to be local interests.

One cannot remain in South America for very long without running into manifestations of the jealousies and envies which play such a large part in the life of every country. The Trans-Andean railway enterprise in which the two governments participated was constructed during one of those rare periods when Chile and Argentina had no serious controversies. A few years ago a glacier escaped from its ancient prison and completely destroyed a section of the railway in Argentine territory. Through traffic was then abandoned and has never been resumed. The Chileans bitterly complain that Argentina will not repair this section of the road because to do so would be of greater benefit to Chile than to Argentina. Passengers are compelled to leave the rail terminus and travel by bus.

The Peruvians are equally bitter about the failure of Colombia to complete its section of the proposed Pan-American highway. The Peruvians who talked to me about the matter so feelingly said the completion of the highway would mean a tremendous influx of American tourists who could drive their own cars all the way down to Lima at a fraction of the cost of a steamer trip. But, they said, the Colombians refused to do their part because they knew that tourists would not halt in their country but would speed on to Peru and spend their money and their time there.

Whether or not there is any truth in either of these allegations I haven't the slightest idea. But they do accurately depict the attitude of most South American countries toward their neighbors. I feel sure that any unflattering comments I may make in this book will be bitterly resented by the people of the country affected, cheerfully endorsed and applauded by all the others. Even the foreign residents of these countries absorb the local prejudices. One of my fellow countrymen who had spent the better part of a lifetime living in Lima was as bitter as any Peruvian when discussing the iniquities of Chile, Bolivia and Ecuador. The most blasting of many dissertations I listened to on the characteristics of the Argentines came from a British resident of Brazil.

This jealousy and distrust and prejudice manifests itself in romance as well as business and politics. Having met a number of fellow Americans who were married to Brazilians, Chileans or other charming representatives of the South American countries, I hastily concluded that there must have been a great deal of intermarriage in the different countries themselves just as there has been in all parts of the United States. Much to my surprise I found that this was not true. Argentines do not marry Chileans, Chileans do not marry Peruvians, Peruvians do not marry Ecuadorians and so one might go on and list every possible marital combination. Of course there are exceptions to this rule but they are so rare that they attract a great deal of attention and often unfavorable comment. This limitation of marriages within national boundaries is partly due to the fact that the South Americans do not visit each other and a very large part of them never leave the boundaries of the country in which they are born. When the hot sun of the summer season makes the flat city of Buenos Aires uncomfortable a great many make the overnight boat journey to Montevideo or to other beaches farther up the coast of Uruguay. A smaller number cross the Andes to holiday at Santiago in Chile where there is the most famous roulette establishment in the continent. That is about all the tourist travel there is. There is practically no business travel.

But the fact that boys and girls from different countries meet infrequently is not the only impediment. In spite of the fact that they speak the same language and, in the main, come from the same racial stock the nationals of each country look on all the others as "foreigners" and on each is focused all the old prejudices and suspicions. If a young South American marries a girl from some other country and takes her to his home to live the chances are that she will have as difficult a time breaking into the local social circles as a newcomer into an inhospitable New England community. A young Peruvian who was married to a charming Chilean girl was a shipmate of mine and told me about the many difficulties he had encountered. Each family opposed the match and it was a long time before the consent of the girl's parents could be obtained. When they were married and he brought her to Peru to live she was very unhappy because everyone made her feel that she was an unwelcome stranger. He finally solved the problem of his own marital happiness by going into business in Chile which was the home of his wife, and as he was successful and prosperous the Chileans had to treat him decently even if he did come from a country with which they had often been at war.

If there were more marriages between representatives of different South American countries it would not only help to create a better understanding between the countries but perform another very useful function. The populations of the countries are small and in each the so-called "ruling class" is composed of a small number of old families. This limits the possible selection of a mate to a dangerously small number. For example the total population of Chile is about 5 millions. Owing to geographical barriers they are separated into three main sections and many smaller ones. Each of these sections is divided by social barriers almost as rigid as the mountain ranges which divide the country. The result of this has been that for generations a few families have married and intermarried until everyone is related to everyone else. This is a subject which Chilean aristocrats do not like to discuss but among themselves they admit that there are some alarming symptoms of racial decline.

The development of trade between the different countries in which each would share the prosperity of the others might have done a great deal to make them forget old differences but this has not been the result. There is surprisingly little trade between the countries. We buy more from every South American country than it buys from all its nine neighbors: sell more than it sells to all its nine neighbors. For example we ordinarily buy from Brazil five times as much as is bought by all the South American states. The free development of both trade and travel are in many cases hampered by mountain ranges which make communication difficult and these national barriers have been added to and strengthened by selfish local interests. The countries have, in fact, missed few opportunities to raise tariff barriers against each other. Factories which have been started with the idea of catering to the needs of one or more adjacent countries have never done the volume of business their promoters had a right to expect because competing factories were almost invariably established in the other countries and the umbrella of a protective tariff raised over them. Each has copied the enterprises of the others.

Matches provide a good example of the way this works out. Some country—I have forgotten which one—started a match factory some years ago and the government established a match monopoly which would not only protect the manufacturer but also provide revenue for the government. That was the signal for similar action and now every country has one or more match factories and a monopoly. That will explain to the visitor at Montevideo the reason for the atrociously bad matches he is compelled to use. They are actually worse than Chinese matches which means that they are just about as bad as they could possibly be. But if they were manufactured for the purpose of creating a large match consumption they are ideal. The

visitor soon finds that it is sheer folly to attempt to light
a cigarette with a single match. The only sensible procedure is to hold four or five of them like a bunch of fagots
and strike them all together in the hope that one of the lot
will ignite and that one or more will be inflammable
enough to hold the flame.

Peru goes farther than any other country in making the
match monopoly an airtight affair. Federal laws provide
for a heavy fine as punishment to anyone caught using a
match other than that of the monopoly. This law is made
all the more effective because the informant who drags the
miscreant into court gets half of the fine. Then many
readers of John Gunther's books will doubtless feel a
certain gratitude to me when I say that on one occasion in
the Hotel Maury in Lima I could very easily have earned
twenty-five soles by informing the police that he had used
a Colombian match to light a cigarette. Instead I merely
warned him of his misdemeanor and destroyed the evidence.

That is not quite so silly as it may sound. A great many
people have been fined for using bootleg matches and
people who live in Peru or visit the country regularly are
very careful to avoid running foul of the law. Long before
a Grace Line boat touches Peruvian waters the stewards
carefully gather up and hide all matches and passengers are
warned to empty their pockets because mere possession of
a match made outside Peru is regarded as prima-facie evidence of crime. As to cigarette lighters, they are absolutely
prohibited. If there is one in all Peru it has been smuggled
in by some daring rascal who keeps it at his own peril. It
must be said for the Peruvians, that while their match
monopoly is the tightest, the matches offered for sale are
the best in South America.

If each of the countries was large enough to support a match industry there could be little criticism of the policy which has been followed. But this is not the case. Ecuador is not the smallest or the poorest of the countries. Yet its demand for matches is so small that a single modern match-making machine with four operatives could make a year's supply of matches in three eight-hour working days.

At his first meal in Brazil the traveler will come into direct and unpleasant contact with one of these regulations which has been made to stop the natural flow of trade with another country. The first taste of the bread in any restaurant will indicate that there is something wrong with it and if he makes an investigation he will find that the bread is vile because Brazilian economists have been monkeying with the cookbook in an attempt to hinder the sale of Argentine wheat and increase the consumption of Brazilian products.

While every country has experienced difficulties with its neighbors and none has ever shown much of a spirit of friendly helpfulness, the differences which have kept Argentina and Brazil sparring and feinting at each other for generations are probably more important than those which irritate any other two countries. Each would like to be lead dog in the South American pack and either would undoubtedly hold that position were it not for the other. Brazil has the greatest area and population, Argentina the greatest wealth. Each looks with a jealous eye on the progress of the other. In some things they are direct competitors. Each produces more beef and hides than can be absorbed by local consumption and with Uruguay they compete for the sale of these products in the foreign markets. On the other hand Brazil has to buy wheat from

Argentina and Argentina has to buy coffee from Brazil. Instead of encouraging a free exchange of these and other commodities which would increase the trade of each, the policy of each country has been just the opposite.

Brazilian economists noted the large purchases of wheat from Argentina and also noted that Brazil produced more mandioca than was needed to supply the demand. (Mandioca is a tuberous root from which tapioca and cassava are produced and is one of the cheapest of many cheap food products of Brazil.) Having failed in attempts to get the people to consume more mandioca the economists then hit on the idea of curtailing the purchases of Argentine wheat and increasing the consumption of mandioca by the simple process of compelling the millers to mix the two in a proportion set out in the mandate. Actually this resulted in decreasing the purchase of wheat by a greater quantity than was anticipated for the readily understandable reason that the bread was not tempting and people ate less of it. The best that can be said for it is that it is not quite so bad as the potato adulterated bread which Mussolini forced on his own countrymen and unfortunate travelers.

In fact attempts like these to legislate about matters that should be left to cooks have some curious kickbacks. Among the distinctive food products of Brazil are some very fine jellies, jams and marmalades and the government has done a great deal to promote their use. But jellies and jams and marmalades can only be used on bread and when the bread is poor the consumption of its allied foods must decrease. I know that was the case so far as I was concerned. I ate only as much bread as I had to eat with the result that my marmalade consumption was practically nil.

This is only one example of many impediments to trade

which various governments have set up in Brazil. In no
place does one find that exchange of products that might
be reasonably expected. Chile produces a very good light
wine of the Rhine type. Possibly it is sold in Argentina
and Brazil but I was never able to find it listed on any
wine card. Argentina produces a very good table claret
but again it could not be found on the wine cards in
Brazil and Chile. On the other hand every restaurant in
Brazil stocks quantities of Portuguese wine. These three
countries as well as Uruguay all produce wines and each
has great hopes of capturing some of the markets which
have been lost to Europe because of the war. In Montevideo I saw a very beautiful poster designed solely to encourage the use of wine. But each of these countries is
planning only for its own market and no one of them
produces wine in sufficient quantity seriously to interest
a wine importer.

With the growth of their own manufacturing industries
the South American countries have been bitten hard by
the bug of self-sufficiency, which in the opinion of many,
has led to the unnecessary duplication of factories and
halted what would have been a normal growth of trade between the countries.

"We are all to blame," a Chilean business man told me.
"If a Peruvian puts up a factory in his own country to do
most anything from weaving silk to the production of
enamelware, he has no difficulty about getting his government to protect him with a tariff. Under that protection
the Peruvian is fairly certain to prosper and if he is a successful manufacturer there is no reason why he shouldn't
build up a market in Chile and Bolivia and Ecuador and
other countries. But that never happens. If we see a lot of
Peruvian enamelware or silk handkerchiefs trickling into

Chile it is certain to inspire someone to put up similar factories in our country. Our government is just as obliging as any other in the matter of protective tariffs for the benefit of the manufacturer. The result is that every country tends to surround itself by a wall. Inefficient manufacturers continue in existence because no outsider is allowed to compete with them. A great many of them exist solely on what might be called economic blood transfusions. On the other hand there is a decided limitation to the incentive offered progressive manufacturers to expand or to improve the quality of their products. On every boundary there are tariff barriers with the red traffic light turned on. If some manufacturer improves his processes so that he can compete in spite of high tariffs, he can be certain that he will not hold the new market any longer than the time it will take to raise the tariffs still higher.

"The Import-Export Bank is planning to make a number of loans to encourage the development of South American industries. I hope that in making these loans the Import-Export Bank will give careful consideration to the fact that some countries are better fitted than others for certain types of manufacturing and will make the loans accordingly. If the Peruvians are better equipped than we are for the manufacture of soap, let us say, and we are better equipped for the manufacture of glassware, there is no reason why we shouldn't buy our soap from them and they buy their glassware from us. If the United States government through its help in developing these new industries will see that they are developed along rational rather than political lines it may set us on the right path."

There is a good deal of reason to believe that they have already started to develop a new policy toward each other. President Roosevelt's announcement of the good neighbor policy, followed by some genuine good neighborly acts brought into sharp relief the conduct of the South American countries toward each other.[1] At the same time the reverberation of the war in Europe, though faintly heard, brought a distant but insistent warning that small and defenseless countries faced dangers much more dreadful than those inherent in border disputes or economic rivalry with a neighbor. They would be false to their Latin temperament if their enthusiasm for an ideal were not tempered by a certain amount of cynicism and if they did not, with each forward step, make a careful calculation of the expense at which gains had been secured. But the loss of Europe's markets has turned thoughts toward their neighbors. Every country faces economic problems which are now serious and may grow dangerous. Instead of making ambitious plans for economic expansion at the expense of each other the statesmen of South America find it necessary to study methods by which they can preserve the gains of the past.

"I never really got acquainted with my neighbors," a Colombian landowner told me, "until we all faced the same problems of an overproduction of coffee. So long as we were all prosperous there was no need for us to work together but when we faced hard times we had to cooperate and now that we have learned how to do it we will probably keep it up after and if the wars are ended and we

[1] The first attempt to bring about unity was made in 1826 at the initiative of Bolivar. A treaty was drawn up pledging the countries to "union, league and perpetual confederation." The high purpose of Bolivar might have been realized but for the fact that Peru and Mexico refused to sign the treaty. It is significant that these were the strongest countries in the north and the south at that time and they declined to place themselves on anything like an equality with their weaker neighbors. While there may be some sympathy for the underdog in South America it is never strong enough to motivate any move to help him. On the other hand there is a very great respect for strength no matter how it is manifested.

again know what it is to feel secure. Maybe that is what the Latin-American countries will do."

There was an impressive display of gold lace and ceremonial clothing at the Copacabana Hotel in Rio only a few days after my discovery of the iniquity of the bread served in the hotel. The occasion was a banquet in honor of the Argentine delegates to a trade convention in which an attempt was to be made to iron out differences, reduce tariff barriers and promote an exchange of commodities. A few days later in Montevideo I visited a very interesting display of Argentine manufactured products. At the same time I read that the conference in Rio had met with great success. It has been followed by a number of others, participated in by all of the most important countries. Not all of these conferences have been entirely successful. Our own experiences in attempts at tariff reform show that once trade barriers are erected it is a very difficult thing to tear them down. But all have made progress in the right direction.

The initial conference at Rio opened the way for the exchange of a number of commodities and manufactures on a more liberal basis than before. For one thing it was agreed that over a three-year period the proportion of mandioca mixed with Argentine wheat is to be gradually reduced so that at the end of that period none will be used and the Brazilian mills will produce real flour. If this agreement is faithfully carried out it will mean that some time in November, 1943 the Brazilians will be able, for the first time in years, to enjoy a good piece of bread on which to spread their marmalade. Perhaps the Brazilian government will in the meantime abolish the regulation requiring the admixture of a certain amount of vegetable oils with butter. At the present rate of progress most of the other

South American countries will at that time be enjoying a greater degree of prosperity through increased trade with each other.

It might be made the occasion for the celebration of a new thanksgiving day, marking the beginning of a new era of friendship between the ten South American republics which have been such bad neighbors in the past. A loaf of good Brazilian bread would be as significant as a roast turkey is to us.

CHAPTER V

## *The City of the Cariocas*[1]

THERE is an old Chinese story about a famous portrait painter who at the height of his career was asked to paint a woman so resplendently beautiful that he found his skill completely baffled. After weeks of vain attempts to portray her he threw away his brushes, abandoned his profession and spent the remainder of his life looking after the welfare of the herd of water buffalo on his ancestral estate. This story, which I had not thought of for years, came to my mind as I wrote the heading to this chapter and paused to ponder on the vanity of any attempt I might make to paint a word picture of Rio de Janeiro, most beautiful of cities. No hackneyed phrases or trite expressions will do it justice; and in floundering for a suitable phrase I almost fell into the tritest of them all, for I was about to write that one must see Rio to appreciate its beauty. Since I can think of nothing better to say I

[1] The word Carioca means a person or a thing from Rio de Janeiro, especially a member of the white population.

will let that stand. And that led me to speculate on what might have happened to the English language if this city had been located on our own west coast, say in the state of California, where people are adept at painting word pictures and honeyed phrases drip from the silver tongues of the real-estate salesmen. I am afraid that if the Californians had Rio to write about and talk about a lot of words which now occupy useful places in the dictionary would in a short time become worn out and valueless.

There is nothing of the antique about the beauty of Rio as about London or Paris or Rome or other famous cities. The place has an appearance as fresh and clean as the flowers which bloom in its gardens all the year round or the neatly clipped hedges bordering the numerous parks. It is well groomed. One half of the city looks as if the last bit of plaster was put on day before yesterday and the other half looks as if the painters had just completed a job of repairs and repainting week before last. One thinks of a beautiful lady on her way to the opera, a lady whose beauty makes one unconscious of powder and rouge and perfumes. And the Cariocas, the people who were fortunate enough to have been born within sight of the Sugar Loaf, look on their city with the calm assurance of the lady who knows that she is beautiful. They do little boasting. It is just taken for granted that if they wished to talk about their city they have a monopoly of all the superlatives and there is no need to repeat them. They can afford to be indifferent to the opinions of others. Is there any significance to the fact that while the residents of San Francisco resent the abbreviation of "Frisco" the Cariocas revel in the affectionate nickname of Rio? The complete name is actually São Sebastio do Rio de Janeiro.[2]

---

[2] The name means River of January. It was given that name because the harbor was discovered on January 1, 1521 and the Portuguese explorers mistakenly thought the harbor was the mouth of a river.

Enjoyment of the beauty of the city is so intense that it has the suggestion of a religious cult. It is no enthusiasm promoted with an eye to the enhancement of realty values but a reverence for beauty similar to that the Japanese have for the majestic sweep of the snow-clad slopes of Fujiyama. If the Portuguese explorers who blindly stumbled into this bay had not been followed by priests the Cariocas might possibly have become a tribe of pagans who would worship beauty and burn incense to their city. Instead of a pagan shrine a huge statue of Christ located on top of a hill stands sentinel over the city and can be seen from any point in the harbor. As it is, there is something of the carefree pagan about them—a detachment from the sordid and serious things of life. With so much beauty on which to feast the eyes, such wonderful beaches and such gay little cafés where one may sip coffee and gossip with friends, the opportunities to let life slip by in idle enjoyment are found to a degree not to be duplicated in any other large city. The business of making a living becomes a necessary evil, to be attended to with the least possible interference with the more important matter of enjoying life. With all the temptation to have a wholesome good time it is a wonder to me that so much work is done.

The Cariocas have done so many things to add to the natural beauty of their city that it is difficult to determine which one should be mentioned first. But the famous pavements are doubtless the most distinctive. This is the one place where the work of beautification has not been confined to the architects and landscape gardeners, where the pavement builders have been given a chance and have made beautiful the surface on which you walk. When one stops to think that nothing strikes the eye so persistently as the pavement it does seem strange that there have been such few and futile attempts to relieve it of its drab ugliness. Even in parks in other cities they are ugly. That is the reason the highly decorated pavements of Rio strike one so forcibly and appear so unreal. I imagine that if one saw them for the first time in the dawn following a hearty birthday party or an extended celebration of New Year's Eve, they would prove very disconcerting for they suggest something out of dreams of fairyland rather than real life. Instead of an expanse of unattractive cement the pavement is composed of intricate patterns made of irregularly shaped blocks of black and white marble. It is the biggest mosaic in the world for it embraces in its decorative scheme an entire city of a million and a half population.

The designs are of infinite variety. There are dozens of different borders, fleur de lis, circles, elaborate floral attempts, triangles, squares—in fact every conventional design I can think of except the swastika. The most common design is suggestive of the conventional wave to be seen in old Chinese sculpture and more modern Japanese prints. Thus the very pavements suggest a continuation of the waves which pound ceaselessly on the miles of gleaming sandy beach.

The idea of mosaic pavements was brought to Brazil by the colonists from Portugal and in the early days all of the black and white marble blocks were imported from that country. It was one way by which the lonely colonists in this strange place could provide themselves with a constant reminder of their beloved homeland for the most famous square in Lisbon is paved in the same way. There, as in Rio, the predominant pattern is the wave design and it is know as "the Rolling Plaza." At about the same period other lonely exiles were building their villages in New England about squares of green turf to remind themselves of the homes they had left in England. The cost of the ornate pavements was so great in the early days that only the wealthy could afford them though it is said that many went into debt in order to show that if the Figuerados could afford pavements the Alamadas also could. Then marble quarries were developed in the neighborhood and this brought the cost down to a point where almost anyone could afford them and distinction was gained only by the intricacy of the designs and the space given over to them. Any walk along the residential streets will show that property owners have in some cases sacrificed valuable building space in order to provide wide pavements. The uniform black and white patterns give no hint of the riches of the Brazilian quarries. With so many beautiful marbles of different colors available there must have come to many a temptation to depart from the conventional arrangement of black and white, but no one has done it. Brazilian ladies of high degree dress in harmony, that is in black and white. A few rival cities such as São Paulo and Buenos Aires have made halfhearted attempts to copy these mosaics but in no place were more than a few blocks built.

In Rio these pavements are found from one end to the other of the great Avenida Rio Branco and on any street or avenue that has any pretentions. I suppose people who live on streets without them must feel very apologetic about it just like living on an unpaved street. In this as in all things there are frauds and imitations. A Brazilian friend told me of a skinflint in his neighborhood who put down an ordinary concrete pavement and painted black and white curlicues all over it to imitate the real thing. This was considered a disgrace to the neighborhood —something likely to effect realty values in the block. But possibly if some really satisfactory substitute for the black and white blocks could be found, it might mean the development of a new industry. It not only costs a great deal to lay these pavements but constant work is needed to maintain them. With the daily pounding of feet the blocks come loose and fall out and have to be replaced. Some workmen are always busy on Rio Branco. Every now and then, when there are high winds, huge waves climb past the beaches and wash out whole blocks and thousands of workmen are put to work on repairs. A fortune, of course, is waiting for the man who invents a process for mosaic streets which will withstand the wear and tear of motorcar traffic. I feel sure that regardless of the expense the Cariocas would see to it that the streets of Rio were paved in that way.

The expense of laying and maintaining these many square miles of mosaics does not comprise the total price the Carioca contributes to the beauty of his city. The bits of marble when laid in attractive patterns are beautiful to look at but as hard as the split flints of Norwich to walk on. The cobbled surfaces reach up through the leather and plant little hammer blows on the soles of your feet with every step. I wonder if they will be more comfortable a hundred years from now, after a few generations of feet have worn them to something like an even surface? In the meantime one does not walk very far before finding a convenient table and chair and if he sits down some one is sure to bring him a cup of coffee.

To speculate on whether the architecture of Rio conforms to the pavements or the pavements conform to the architecture is as futile as to argue about the priority of the chicken and the egg. But there can be little doubt that the two found inspiration in the same source. It was the majestic sweep of the beaches against which the surf is ever breaking, the pinnacled Sugar Loaf which the mists are always trying to hide, and riotous beauty of tropical vegetation which challenged the Cariocas to build a city worthy of its setting—a challenge which they have met boldly and successfully. While the surroundings provide a challenge to the architect, the wealth of material in the form of marbles and hardwoods tempt him to extravagance of design and ornamentation. The result might easily have been disastrous but it has not been.

One sees buildings, especially private residences, which provide constant reminders of structures seen in other parts of the world, but few that have not a distinctive touch. There are many colorful little homes so spick and span and shiny new that they look as if they might have just been brought home from a giant's toy shop. There are other large residences of two or three stories with turrets and towers and flying buttresses and other architectural fantasies. One would not be surprised to see a fairy princess leaning from a balcony or see a handsome young man leave his horse in the charge of the amiable Brazilian policeman while he went inside in search of the sleeping beauty. Gargoyles leer at one from the eaves of private residences and many are ornamented with statues. Such architecture would be out of place in the austere beauty of a New England landscape. But here with the rolling surf, the disdainful fringes of palms, the unbelievable hills and mountains, it all seems to be quite natural. In some buildings you see bold and effective adaptations of large designs on a small scale—private residences which somehow remind you of Notre Dame, small plots of ground and buildings that suggest Versailles. The newer buildings, both apartment houses and office buildings, are equally striking. Obviously the Brazilian architect does not bow to the limitations of any conventions. The recently completed Press Club is not only the largest and finest building of its kind in the world but purely as a piece of architecture would be a show place if located in New York City. But recently there has been some very hasty building. I had not been in Rio a week before I shared with the local resident grief over the fact that some of the modern apartment houses were introducing a false note.

After I had noted in my diary that the Brazilian architecture was "daring and extravagant" I was talking about the matter with an American artist who said the terms I should have used were "courageous and fundamental," which are the words I should have thought of in the first place. The Brazilian architect has made a real contribution but he appears to be unappreciated by his own countrymen. The official publication referred to in a later chapter mentions a very large number of writers and painters whose works are unknown outside their own country and devotes a chapter to the entirely unimportant Brazilian drama but the subject of architecture is not even mentioned.

Nowhere else have I seen such beautiful hardwoods as those which are used so lavishly in Rio. In the fine new Standard Oil Building the paneled walls and even the floors gleam with the beauty of the finest furniture. In fact I couldn't help thinking that a gang of good Chinese carpenters and cabinetmakers could dismember this building and from the salvaged material supply all the occupants at 26 Broadway with much finer furniture than is now in the directors' room. Even the wood in the floors could be utilized. I was told that the very wealth of Brazilian hardwood makes it a difficult product to market. A forest may be full of hardwood trees, but there will be dozens of varieties and in each variety a number of different shades of color. American manufacturers demand a reliable supply of wood of the same grade and color and this is very difficult to supply. New wood-working methods will probably have to be adopted before the woods can be made to fit into mass production for many of the Brazilian woods are so hard that hickory and maple appear soft by comparison.

While Brazilian architects have produced some beautiful as well as amazing buildings they have not been so happy in their engineering arrangements. Elevators have been neglected, which I am sure was not the fault of the representatives of the Otis Elevator Company which has a big manufacturing and assembly plant in Rio and practically no competition. The American Chamber of Commerce is housed near the top of A Noite, a twenty-story building, which is equipped with only four elevators. At any hour of the business day long queues of people will be seen lined up at all four of the elevator doors waiting to be transported to the upper floors. The capacity load is always exceeded and there are usually enough passengers left to make a respectable beginning for another queue and this building is better served than many others.

Not only are all the elevators in the Rio office buildings overcrowded but if a government official happens to be a tenant in the building or if officials make frequent visits to it, other tenants or visitors might as well get used to climbing the stairs or make up their minds to endure frequent and vexatious delays. I have known officials in the Far East to be so fussy about precedent that they would walk out on a dinner party if given the wrong seat but only in Rio have I seen them insist on precedence in the matter of elevator service. After waiting my turn in a queue I managed to get into an elevator in a big office building intending to go to the fourth floor. But as a high official was bound for the sixth floor the operator sailed past the fourth as if it did not exist. On the sixth floor another official got on for the eighth so we continued our upward journey. On the eighth a third official got in bound for the ground floor and down we went. Fortunately on this trip there were no official passengers and all the rest of us were decanted at the floors we intended to visit. The Cariocas who shuttled up and down with me didn't seem to mind. He is a devil-may-care fellow who is much more likely to smile than frown at petty annoyances such as this, who finds as much fun in life as it is possible to find. After we had purged ourselves of the official passengers everyone had something witty to say about them and we enjoyed a gay little party as a result.

The Carioca with his well-brushed suit, his well-barbered appearance, his Roy Howard mustache and his general air of jauntiness presents a convincing impression of prosperity and physical well being. If one wants to pry into what is a purely personal affair it is easy to discover that the material from which the suit is made is not of the best, that what appears to be a muscular shoulder could be amputated without spilling a drop of blood. These are trifles which do not humble the gay spirit. Spencer Tracy is his favorite actor because the roles in some of his earlier appearances presented what the Carioca thought to be a living mirror of himself. When Tracy later appeared in the role of Edison, his male following was even greater for the Carioca likes to think of himself as some day doing something that will bring distinction to himself and prosperity to his country.

Even if he is a government official the salary of the

Carioca is very small according to American standards. But in Rio one does not have to enjoy a large income in order to be a gay dog and quite a man about town. Just as in some American cities a large number of the local citizens make it a ritual to drop into the corner drug stores several times a day for a glass of Coca-Cola so Rio residents by the thousands drop into one of the many coffee shops from the time they open in the morning until they close at night. It is a habit the visitor soon acquires. No knowledge of Portuguese or any other language is needed in order to get service. The moment you sit down a waiter in a spotless white uniform puts a tiny cup in front of you and then returns to fill the cup with coffee, usually from a gleaming blue pot.

It is not the coffee to which you have been accustomed at home, for blending has had no part in its preparation. It is made from the Brazilian coffee bean alone with no mixtures from Colombia or any other rival producing centers. (I often wondered what would happen to me if I asked for Colombian or Peruvian coffee but never had courage enough to put the matter to a test.) There is always a full sugar bowl on the table and the patron can fill his cup with sugar if he likes. After you have consumed the cup of coffee you fish from your collection of coins a brass piece bearing the numerals 200, that is 200 reis, which is the equivalent of one cent in U. S. currency. That is the price of the coffee, a price regulated by government decree and applying all over the country from the smallest café in the interior to the most luxurious hotel. There is no tip for there is no coin even approximating the customary 10 per cent.

To the American this sounds like an outrageously cheap price for the coffee. The shipmate who told me about the price left me with the impression that it had been unjustly imposed by a government which in that way promoted the prosperity of the coffee growers at the expense of the poor restaurant and hotel keepers. Actually the price is a fair one—that is it gives the proprietor of the shop a very handsome profit if he gets a good turnover. I saw none that did not enjoy a thriving trade with tables always comfortably crowded.

The price of one cent for a cup of coffee is in line with other charges for food and drink. Feeling one afternoon that ten little cups of black coffee was enough for the day I ordered a cup of chocolate for a change, and the charge was two cents. This was not a cheap joint where you rub shoulders with others at a counter and the waiter faucets the stuff into a cup from a machine. It was in fact at a shop of the same class as Schrafft's in New York. The waiters wore dinner jackets and with the chocolate they served you a glass of water and a clean linen (part cotton) napkin. The service was, in fact, just what you would expect in a high-class restaurant. During the busy hours there was a small orchestra. It is experiences like this that lure one into the delusion that, with prices so cheap, he is saving money with every expenditure.

Even gilded vice is cheap in Rio. The Casino of the Copacabana Hotel is a large and luxurious place with all of the appointments one would expect to find at Monte Carlo. Yet one can play nickel roulette here and with no more than the ordinary bad luck a dollar will last a long time. And as I found from personal experience nickel roulette may be quite thrilling. A nickel is only five cents in the United States but it is 1,000 reis in Brazil. For those who scorn such cheap play there are more expensive tables but the nickel tables are most generously patronized. The evening I visited the casino there were more than 2,000 people at the roulette tables and only a half dozen waiters to serve from the one tiny bar. Most of them were engaged in serving small cups of black coffee. The Carioca at the roulette table does not refrain from the use of alcohol because he is a serious gambler and wants to keep his wits about him. He drinks very little. In fact he is so unaccustomed to the effects of alcohol that a very little of it usually goes a long way and often with disastrous results. The Brazilian government has very wisely decided that at carnival time one can be gay enough without the stimulus of hard liquor and sales in cafés are restricted to light wines and beer.

There are no gangsters in Rio. Everyone complains that there is a lot of petty thieving but such major crimes as burglary are very rare. Most of the crimes of violence are what the French call *crimes passionnel*. These are not uncommon but the sequel is never so tragic as in our less romantic land for there is no death penalty in Brazil. This leniency in the matter of punishment for a major crime was explained to me by a Brazilian bachelor now past middle age who entertained me with many stories about the romantic exploits of his youth. He didn't know whether the abolition of capital punishment was a good thing or not and remarked with reminiscent sadness:

"You would be surprised what trivial things will provoke a Brazilian husband to attempts at homicide."

With lottery tickets on sale in every block and a number of places where one can play roulette in comfortable and luxurious surroundings one would think that the needs of the gamblers had been adequately cared for. But the biggest gambling organization in the country, an illegal enterprise which makes more money than the government lottery itself, presents no visible evidence of its existence. It is a form of the numbers game and flourishes to an extent that would make our American racketeers appear like small-town pikers. The sole owner of the enterprise is a Spaniard whose name is known to everyone. I have visited the small retail shop which he runs as a blind and have been given verbal lists of the great apartment houses and other properties that he owns. Some say that he is the richest man in Brazil.

It is possible that this was the original numbers game—the great-granddaddy of them all and, if that is true, the game which has fallen into such lowly hands had a highly respectable origin and was in fact started under royal patronage. One of the many pet projects of Dom Pedro, the emperor of Brazil, was the establishment of a zoo in Rio. When it was opened it was a great success with throngs of visitors surrounding the cages daily. But after a time when everyone had seen all of the animals and no more were imported the attendance fell off. Then someone thought of a scheme to put new life into ticket sales. On each ticket was printed the picture of one of the animals in the zoo and once a week a drawing selected one of them as the winner in a fanciful contest for supremacy in the animal kingdom. The holders of ticket stubs bearing the picture of the winning animal were rewarded with cash prizes amounting to many times the cost of the ticket. They say that the Cariocas did not accept this as a purely gambling enterprise, buy their tickets and wait for the result of the drawing. Each would go out to see the animal he had drawn and speculate on his chances of success.

Eventually the new gambling game which is known as *bicho*, or animals, was taken over by an enterprising Spaniard who still runs it. The game is played by everyone from the highest to lowest. It is operated much like the numbers game in cities in America and has a high reputation for honesty. You pick a number—any number from one to one hundred—give it to anyone of the dozens of *bicho* agents to be found in any block with any coin or specimen of folding money you like. According to all the stories I have heard the agent who took your bet will surely hunt you up and pay you if your number should be drawn. But the Brazilian would not feel that he was getting his money's worth if this were only the simple numbers racket which could be devised by the dull brain of Dutch Schultz. *Bicho* is a little more complicated. The numbers from one to one hundred are divided into twenty-five sets of four and each of the sets is given the name of some animal. Thus the first series of one to four is known as the Eagle and so on down the line. You may play any number or a series and if your number should happen to fall in one of the winning series you will still win but of course with different odds.

The *bicho* game is not only conducted in violation of the law but is in direct competition with the legitimate lotteries and roulette wheels which share their profits with the government. Every now and then there is talk about suppressing it, which should not be a difficult matter since any tourist can with no difficulty learn the name of the man who runs the racket and see the fine new apartment houses he has built from the profits. But nothing ever comes of it. Public sentiment doesn't get stirred up and there have been hints that a part of the profits are divided among officials who provide protection. While I was in Brazil one of the perennial threats to close the game was made. This must have been taken seriously in some quarters for a petition was presented to the government stating that if *bicho* was closed down it would mean that 50,000 people would be thrown out of employment. If that figure is not exaggerated it would mean that *bicho* is one of the biggest businesses in Brazil.

It is because of the universal habit of playing *bicho* that the sales girls in Jim Marshall's big chain of five-and-ten-cent stores do not wear any numbered buttons on their blouses. He told me the story himself. He received a number of complaints that some of his sales girls were saucy and lazy but the person who made the complaint was rarely certain which girl had been offensive or was naturally reluctant to point out the girl in person. Jim conceived the idea of getting some neat numbered buttons which each girl was to wear, so that if a complaint was made the girl could be identified. He had recently come to Brazil and had never heard of *bicho*. The day the buttons were first put on was a hectic one. Several of the girls suddenly developed violent headaches and had to go home. Others were found red-eyed and weeping in the rest rooms. Students who flocked into the store were having a hilarious time. Seeing the number on a girl's blouse they would greet her as "Señorita Eagle," or "Horse" or "Peacock," or whatever animal classification her number fell into. The girls who had drawn numbers in the cow series were the ones who had developed headaches or wept in the rest rooms. No lady likes to be called a cow in the Portuguese or any other language. The buttons were in use for a few days and then they went into the discard.

Because these steady streams of coffee drinkers help to keep the fazenda proprietor from bankruptcy, the Brazilian government has never allowed Coca-Cola to be sold in the country and I doubt if it ever will. It is also barred from Chile and Argentina although neither of these countries produces coffee. The fame of the Coca-Cola Company for an ability to produce consumers in every country where they operate gives a Brazilian official and coffee grower the cold shivers. The coffee industry is in a bad way as it is and the government buys up and burns many tons every year. If the people who drop in ten to twenty times a day for a cup of coffee should instead go to the corner drugstore for a bottle of coke the coffee industry would be sunk. At any rate that is the way the Brazilians look at it. When one of them makes a visit to Peru it worries him to see Coca-Cola signs all over the country and the drink being sold for three cents a bottle.

The Brazilians feel that if the Coca-Cola habit were not so securely fastened on the American people we would spend for coffee the millions we spend for Coca-Cola and other soft drinks and the prosperity of the coffee industry would be secure. What they would like to see is the universal adoption in the United States of the oversized coffee cups used in the Harvard Club of New York. That would increase our consumption of coffee by 20 per cent and give the Brazilians and the nationals of other coffee-producing countries a good many more millions to spend for American motorcars. In the meantime the ban on Coca-Cola adds to the spice of life. Exiled Americans occasionally go to the incoming American boats and are able to get a bottle of coke, and at the same time enjoy the thrills that came with a clandestine drink in the good old days of prohibition. Some daring ones smuggle a bottle or two past the customs examiners.

The Carioca seldom gets away from the sight of a mountain after which he has taken his name. He is lonely without a daily view of the Sugar Loaf and a stroll along the beautiful but uncomfortable mosaic pavements of the Rio Branco. In spite of the fact that the endless procession of busses makes this one of the noisiest streets in the world it is his favorite loafing place, the location of the sidewalk coffee shop where he is sure to meet his cronies. And he has only to sit at the table to see all the ladies of the city go by on their never-ending shopping expeditions. They say that if you want to see anyone in Rio all you have to do is to find a seat at one of the sidewalk cafés and wait. Perhaps one reason why the local newspapers carry such a small amount of retail advertising is that everyone goes shopping on Rio Branco every day as a matter of routine and no bargain sale offers are needed to bring them out.

Sitting at the sidewalk cafés and watching his very satisfactory world go by, the Carioca provides all of South America with its most dependable supply of humor. Quips and wisecracks first heard here soon cross the Andes and are heard in Lima and Caracas while many are picked up and adapted by the Hollywood gag writers. It was a Brazilian wit who conceived the whimsical idea of winning a motorcar race by fitting a car with Italian tires in front and Greek tires in the rear. He said it means a great saving in gas because the front tires just ran away in fright.

Most of the Cariocas are descendants of Portuguese ancestors and they are linked to their ancestral homeland by strong sentimental ties in which politics plays no part. But that does not deter them from poking fun at what they pretend to be the excessive stupidity of the Portuguese, a mental trait which they have obviously not inherited. A Brazilian whose grandfather was born in Lisbon told me quite seriously that the Portuguese were the most honest businessmen in the world, and then he hastened to explain that they deserved little credit for their honesty because they were too dumb to be anything else.

The Carioca has a whimsical nickname for almost everything, providing an *argot* almost as rich as that of the Parisian. When the first of the water-beetle type of motorcar, with the front and rear looking very much alike, appeared on the streets of Rio everyone professed to be puzzled as to which was the front and which the back of the car. Within a few days someone had given it a nickname which stuck until the model was outmoded. The model was called "the Portuguese killers," the theory being a Portuguese is so dumb that he couldn't tell which way the car was traveling and would step in front of one which was going at full speed. The first hoodless snub-nosed busses appeared on the streets at a time when either the opera or the movie *Unfinished Symphony* was appearing and that is the name given the busses. A few years ago Rio was provided with its first double-deck busses, almost identical with those on Fifth Avenue, and when they appeared there seemed to be but one thing to call them: "papa and mama."

*Careta* is the name of a very lively little weekly published in Rio which is very much like *Puck* was at its best. It pokes gentle fun at everyone and everything and is widely read. Unlike other humorous periodicals published in Latin-America most of the jokes recounted in *Careta* could be told in a girl's boarding school. One of its regular features is a comic strip depicting the adventures of an energetic but impractical inventor who spends all of his time devising intricate gadgets that do not work. The one issue I bought and read (with the aid of a dictionary) showed the inventor busy testing out a machine which would automatically increase the calories in a plate of rice and beans, the staple dish of the common people. But while he was at work at this, a stray dog had eaten all the rice and beans on his plate. Every week there is a new version of the same theme of frustration and the Cariocas never tire of it, because it enables them to laugh at themselves.

The issue on which I employed my Portuguese dictionary happened to have a well-balanced selection of international jokes. This was in the period before the war had entered its serious stage. Two comic characters were standing under a palm tree discussing world affairs. One of them said:

"I haven't seen anything of this German blitzkrieg we have heard so much about."

"Of course not," said the other, "the blitzkrieg moves so fast that no one ever sees it."

On the next page two other characters were also discussing world affairs.

"Italy says she needs a place in the sun," remarked one.

"That's easy," replied the other wisecracker. "Ship all the Italians out to the Sahara Desert and keep them there. They will find all the sun they want."

Just to round off the issue Uncle Sam came in for attention, was in fact on the front cover in colors. With bulbous nose but frowning countenance he confronted a languishing blonde and a young man with bulging muscles.

"What's this," he said. "We are preparing for war and need soldiers. This is no time to think of getting married."

"But my dear Tio Samuel," says the languishing blonde, "we want to be ready for the next war."

The fact that President Vargas of Brazil has a lively sense of humor and enjoys a joke even if it is at his expense endears him to a great number of the people and makes it something of an anomaly to refer to him as a dictator. Almost everyone tells some story about him. The favorite is about his attempt to play golf which he made soon after he had dispensed with the formality of working with

Congress and began governing the country by the simpler and more direct method of issuing decrees which were backed only by his own authority.

Everyone in Brazil knew that the president had become a golf enthusiast and had been taking secret lessons from a professional. So when it was learned that he would make his first appearance in the links there was a big crowd of spectators. Accompanied by a squad of armed and uniformed guards the president arrived and took possession of the first tee. The spectators saw him address the ball and take a practice swing which indicated that he had received good instructions. Then he took a crack at the ball, topped it and it rolled about ten feet. The armed guards appeared not to notice and for a moment the spectators were silent. Then someone jumped to his feet and yelled:

"Mr. President! You can't play golf by decree!"

The crowd roared with laughter and the president joined them. That is not the way of a dictator and yet President Vargas has proven that he can be quite ruthless when carrying out his policies.

CHAPTER VI

## Brazilian Bouillabaisse

FOR more than a week I had been enjoying the attractions of Rio and the night before I left I gathered a new and striking bit of evidence of the Carioca's love for his city and pride in its matchless beauty. The evidence was brought to my attention by a man from Pittsburgh who is interested in selling electrical appliances and therefore keeps in close touch with everything that has anything to do with his business. He said that while the cost of electric power in Rio is not excessive as compared to rates paid in the United States, the rates do appear high when the bills have to be paid by people with generally low incomes. The result is that electrical appliances of all sorts are not used so generally as the manufacturers of such appliances think they should be. At any rate that was the opinion of my informant. He did not overlook the opportunity to point out that as artificial heat is never needed in Rio the universal use of electricity for cooking and hot water heating would make chimneys in private residences entirely unnecessary.

But, he said, the high cost of current did not in any way discourage the municipal authorities from spending a sum that must run into millions of milreis annually in what can only be described as a very extravagant system of illumination. The many miles of beaches are lined with ornamented electric lampposts and every evening at dusk the current is turned on. From any eminence one may see the glowing bulbs extend for miles in every direction providing still another scene of beauty which no other city can duplicate. Many people make trips to the Sugar Loaf or some other vantage point just to see the reckless display of lights spring into existence. It is a sight one will not soon forget.

The utility of this widespread illumination begins to wane about midnight and disappears soon afterward when the cafés close and people go to bed. But the lights are not extinguished until dawn. The only people who could possibly get full enjoyment from this spectacular display would be passengers on an incoming ship. As the port and harbor offices are closed except in daylight hours it would be most unusual for a ship to arrive late at night and I don't know that one ever has, but the Rio harbor is illuminated just in case some ship should come in. The electric appliance dealer who told me about this quoted a lot of figures which added up to the fact that the electric current wasted in this way was sufficient to operate an electric toaster and coffee percolator in every home in Rio.

The city could spend the money in a lot of more useful ways or could turn the lights off during the night and save money and reduce taxes but no one ever proposed an economy of this kind.

While on my way to the station I was speculating on this supreme manifestation of city pride when the taxi turned a corner and I saw the most outrageous abuse of outdoor advertising I could possibly imagine. A long double line of majestic palm trees came into view and as my eyes dropped from the graceful fronds I noticed an advertising poster pasted on the trunk of the first tree in just the place where it would have the greatest advertising value and at the same time and for the same reason spoil the beauty of the palm. It was as shocking as a poster would be on a Fifth Avenue elm. My natural conclusion was that this was the work of some prankster but as the car sauntered onward I saw there was a poster on every palm, each one showing marks of having been placed there by a professional. This is the same line of palms bordering an old canal that is seen pictured in illustrations of booklets advertising the beauties of Rio to prospective tourists, but without the disfiguring posters.

After seeing these posters I had to make an uncomfortable rearrangement of my ideas about the Brazilian's love of beauty. How could people of the same city spend millions in illuminating vacant beaches and then allow the beauty of a line of palms like this to be disfigured? After all I suppose this irritating little incident doesn't do anything more than prove that the Brazilians like a great many other people, keep their front yards neat and tidy and do not worry themselves sick about the tin cans that may litter the back yard. That was what I was to find later in many South American cities. The approach is always attractive. How surprising it must be to them when they arrive in New York, travel through the sordid districts surrounding the wharves and finally reach Fifth Avenue!

As soon as I reached the station and found a seat in the waiting shed I began to regret my limited knowledge of Portuguese for I was afraid that I had come to the wrong station and might get on the wrong train. That was something I had once done in Japan and I didn't want to repeat the experience. Everyone had told me that the train to São Paulo consisted of a single large car, a kind of passenger bus on wheels, which would accommodate just sixty passengers and no more. They said that if I delayed too long about my reservations the seats would all be taken and I would just have to stay over another day. Just sixty seats would be sold, no more and no less, for there was always a big demand for them. The hotel porter had done a lot of telephoning and with the air of having pulled off an important coup told me that he had secured for me the sole and undivided occupancy of Seat No. 17. That left seats for only fifty-nine others.

Yet there were more than two hundred people waiting for the train and more arriving every minute. Why so many people if the train could carry only sixty? Just to make sure that I was at least headed in the right direction I showed my ticket to the gateman and though his rapid flow of Portuguese was not entirely intelligible the tone was reassuring. I went about the business of checking my bags, a procedure so simple that it would send any American baggage clerk to sleep. With a big blue marking pencil the railway official wrote numbers on squares of plain white paper which he cut from a sheet and pasted them on the bags and gave me a list of the numbers also written on a plain piece of paper. That was all there was to it. No printed forms with long legalistic regulations limiting the responsibility of the carrier in the event the baggage was lost or damaged, no precautions against a fellow passenger who might feloniously claim my portable typewriter as his own. It was as casual as the handling of luggage on a British railway and just as efficient.

The one-car train finally pulled into the station and as the seats filled up it became apparent that the overflow which had worried me consisted of friends and relatives who had come down to see the travelers off on their journey, an average of five or more visitors for every traveler. Of the sixty passengers I was the only one who went to his seat without the cheerful banter of friends and wishes for a safe and pleasant journey. The trip from Rio to São Paulo takes only eight hours but the Brazilians surround it with all the forms and ceremonies of a departure for a long ocean voyage. It was obvious that to many the journey was an unusual event, attended by a good many misgivings. The Brazilians, like all other South Americans, travel very little. They have not, like most of us, relatives scattered all over the country so there is no occasion for the constant visiting back and forth which is a part of our national life. It appeared that a couple of elderly people had never been on a train before. There was excited conversation, kisses by the women and bear hugs by the men who saluted each other in Brazilian fashion. A few little girls whimpered in the excitement. Then the Diesel engine made a vulgar noise and we were off from the sea level of Rio to the cool 2500-feet elevation of São Paulo where the climate is anything but tropical. The few experienced travelers in the car looked approvingly at their overcoats. They are not needed in Rio but it would be comfortable to slip into them at the end of the journey.

The suburbs through which we sped offered no hint of kinship with the gorgeous city we were leaving and the country villages whch succeeded them were poor and mean. This is typical of all South America where wealth is produced in the country and is spent in the city. Perhaps it is one manifestation of the instinct of self-preservation which goes back to the rough periods of European history when life and movable property were unsafe in the country and the only secure residence for the wealthy was inside the walls of the city. Whatever the cause may be there is no country in South America where the poverty of the rural districts does not stand out in sharp contrast with the ostentatious wealth of the cities.

The many negroes along the line provided constant reminder that slave labor was once as important in Brazil as in our own Southern states.[1] No negro home in the South would appear complete without one or more mongrel dogs around the doorstep and here the negroes had the same ill-bred pets. The train was no novelty to them but we were barely out of the suburbs when one of them chased us. By the time he was out of breath from barking and running another one had taken up the chase and so with a few lapses we had a canine escort all the way from Rio to São Paulo.

Negro slavery existed in Brazil for generations without the drawing of sharp color lines or the development of racial prejudices. No one who spends a few days in the country needs to look up figures in the census returns to see that there has been a great deal of intermarriage between the different races, European whites, African blacks and native Indians or, at any rate, a great many children

---

[1] Slavery was gradually abolished in Brazil by granting freedom to children of slave parents. No compensation was paid to slaveowners.

have been born of mixed parentages. Many among the poorer classes never bothered about going through with the troublesome ceremony of marriage, which was looked on as an expensive form of social ostentation reserved for the wealthy upper classes. The percentage of technically illegitimate births is decreasing, however, for in many places the police have taken matters into their own hands. When they find a couple living together without benefit of clergy they simply haul them off to the police station where they are married whether they like it or not. And thereby hangs many a merry tale.

There has been so much mixture of blood in Brazil that the divisions of color are no more sharply marked than they are in a rainbow. There are many negroes as black as any that ever came out of Africa. Others have white skins with blue eyes and startling yellow hair. In between every conceivable shade will be found. Since coffee is always on the minds of most Brazilians it follows naturally that the blood mixtures should be given coffee classification and that the ordinary mulatto should be called "café au lait." More than a third of the population consists of mixtures. Brazilians refer to this as indicating their broad-minded tolerance and affect to be proud of the fact that they have assimilated different races much more thoroughly than we have. The Argentines who are proud of their unmixed white blood are vocally contemptuous about it.

Aside from these mixtures of the lower classes in which there are definite and unmistakable strains of colored or Indian blood there is an even more varied mixture of white blood among the upper classes. I do not recall a single conversation with a Brazilian that had progressed very far before he told me with a certain amount of pride about his mixed ancestry, usually of an amazing assortment of grandparents who were born in different parts of the world. It often seemed to me that in the recounting of these exciting genealogies the Brazilians were presenting a point of view directly contrary to that of Hitler—or the Daughters of the American Revolution. Their family trees do not contain a dull list of names of ancestors all of whom were very much alike but of many strains from different parts of the world which makes the fact that one was born at all appear to the Brazilian to have been something of a biological adventure. He is proud of his mixed ancestry and takes still greater pride in the fact that out of this mixture the Brazilian race has been produced. Anyone who talks to him about racial superiority is treading on dangerous ground.

Their obvious poverty does not weigh heavily on the Brazilian negroes nor on their white neighbors who exist under the mild climate along the coast. They do not know what it is to suffer from the cold. The problems of clothing and shelter are simple ones. There is no need for anyone to go hungry for there is food in abundance all about. But having easily satisfied his most primitive needs there are no further opportunities. The wage scale, if it may be called that, is so low that it provides little more than enough to pay for the absolute necessities. A hard-working family could not in a lifetime save enough money to buy a second-hand motorcar and even if they owned one the purchase of a gallon of gas once a week would present a serious problem. The Chinese farmer who lives in a house with a pounded dirt floor and works his tiny patch of ground is a prosperous individual by comparison—not only more prosperous in a material way but enjoys greater prosperity of the soul.

A pleasing panorama of Brazil sped past us. It was Sunday morning and at every stop we heard the bells calling people to church—the most colorful experience in their drab lives. But there are other Sunday diversions. As a negro family approached the entrance they left their fishing poles against the wall of the church. It was October and the little vegetable gardens were beginning to show patches of green. Somehow it is very difficult for one who has lived all of his life north of the equator to get accustomed to this reversal of seasons—to see Christmas cards and straw hats put on sale at the same time, to drink mint juleps at Christmas and in the higher elevations hot buttered rum on the Fourth of July. The Christmas season was approaching but, as a husband in Rio had observed to me, no one had to think about Christmas and fur coats in the same connection. In these strange surroundings we paused for a moment at Santa Rosa and I couldn't avoid a little thrill when I noted that its elevation was the same as that of the home in Ashley Falls which I had just left. There the crops would be harvested, the trees bare of leaves. Here the corn was only a few inches high and all the shrubs were in bloom.

The valley through which we traveled spread at times for miles on either side, with unpretentious little houses for the workmen on the big estates but no big residence for the owner of these fertile fields. He was probably living in one of those beautiful residences I had seen in Rio. Following the bank of a shallow little stream we skirted low softly rounded hills which were in striking contrast to the high rugged mountains with jagged peaks which one could always see in the distance. At every village children who were black and children who were white and children who were neither black nor white waved to us. I have always wondered why it is that more little girls than little boys wave at trains.

We passed mile after mile of orange groves and saw many happy little black pigs roaming about in search of windfalls. I wondered what orange-fattened pork would taste like and I thought about it so intently that it made me very hungry. A stop at a large station brought a diversion for a much larger train with many cars stopped alongside ours. Smart little boys offered oranges, bananas and chocolate for sale. A basket of oranges or a generous sprig of bananas for five cents, a chocolate bar for one cent. That was the sum of most of the purchases made for few plunged to the extent of spending an entire nickel. A man with a big and hungry family could buy fruit or chocolate for all of them for that amount. There was a new type of Brazilian on the other train, a type I had not seen in Rio. They were the provincials whose individual characteristics had not been rounded off and smoothed down by contact with metropolitan life. There were no dapper young men with neatly pressed clothing and freshly shined shoes but grizzled old-timers with patched and faded shirts, felt hats so burned by the sun that one could only guess what the original color may have been. The young men in their ill-fitting clothes were just plain hicks, their eyes wide, their mouths gaping at the strange sights of an unaccustomed journey.

Newsboys appeared with the São Paulo papers and I was one of the few who bought them in spite of the fact that most of the other passengers could read them and all I could do was to puzzle out the headlines and enough of the text to get an idea of what was happening in the world. In Rio the people bought the newspapers as fast as they were published but up here in the country they had no such curiosity about world affairs.

To one who has only a rudimentary knowledge of Portuguese or of any other language than English, the São Paulo papers were much more satisfactory than those published in Rio. The headline writers of the metropolis follow a technique that makes them brethren of the men who write the titles for the Hollywood films. Headlines are not written to inform the reader but to intrigue him into reading the story. A glance at the headlines will show that something interesting has happened but only by buying and reading a paper can one learn what it was. After the war got well under way the favorite headlines, which lent themselves to very large type were:

CITY IN FLAMES
NIGHT OF TERROR
SHIP SUNK
LIVES LOST

After several months of this during which time a great many cities had been in flames, ships had been sunk and lives lost and nights of terror had become a matter of routine for millions it was found that the old headlines had lost their appeal. Editors of the Rio newspapers telephoned the managers of the American news agencies and said their readers were getting very tired of a war in which the Germans and the British were simply seesawing back and forth and they would like to get some different kind of news.

A very strict code of journalistic conduct is enforced in Brazil and newspapers which violate it may be suspended or suppressed. Within certain limitations the editor has perfect freedom but there are some things he cannot do. Among other things he cannot insult the officials of a friendly government. A few days after I arrived in Rio, Sumner Welles made one of his characteristically incisive statements about foreign affairs with special reference to Nazi activities. A propaganda organ subsidized and directed by the German embassy published an editorial calling the Under Secretary of State some uncomplimentary names. The paper was promptly suspended for five days but the order for suspension was worded so that the punishment would fall only on the proprietors. It provided that all employees be paid full wages so they enjoyed a holiday at the expense of the German embassy.

At the same time this happened local American residents were boiling about a story written by a young newspaperman from one of the Southern States. It appears that he was an honor graduate of the journalism department of his university or had won an award of some kind which gave him a free trip to South America. This was one good-will gesture which went sour. In one of his stories which consisted of a casual and not very well-informed discussion of Brazilian politics he said that anyone with a lot of money to spend bribing army officials could start a revolution against the present government. That is the kind of nonsense one can hear talked by irresponsible people in any Latin-American country. The school of journalism from which the young fellow graduated had evidently failed to teach him the elements of good taste or accuracy in reporting. A big Georgia newspaper published the story and of course it found its way back to Brazil. Its publication was an open insult to the Brazilian army whose officers are proud of their traditions and if the young newspaperman had still been in Rio when the clipping got back there he would probably have had some interviews—

painful ones. The Brazilians don't understand our lack of legal machinery to take care of such matters. Their government swiftly punishes a newspaper which insults or libels a single official. An American newspaper can insult and libel the whole Brazilian army and our government is powerless to do anything about it.

People had told me that unless I took a lunch with me on the Diesel I would probably arrive in São Paulo very hungry as all I could get en route would be fruit at the stations and a cold box lunch supplied by the train porter. Why do people always exaggerate the bad reputations of hotels, restaurants and women? My advisers told me so many stories that it was interesting. I wondered if it could be as bad as meals I had eaten or tried to eat in the Shan States or a breakfast on the edge of Persia.

Without asking me whether or not I wanted it the porter brought me the box prepared by a firm of Rio caterers. Rolls, fried chicken, fried fish, boiled ham, cheese, butter, fruit—enough for a family—at a cost of thirty cents. The ham was about what I had been thinking would be produced by orange-fattened pigs. There was so much of it that I had only an academic interest in the fish and the chicken. The latter brought back memories of China. Poor little chicken! I couldn't help reflecting on what a hard life it must have led to get so tough at an early age.

CHAPTER VII

## São Paulo—City in a Hurry

IF YOU try to talk to a Paulista, that is, a resident of São
Paulo[1] about the beauties of Rio, his country's capital,
he will be attentively polite for a little time and then
grow restive unless the conversation turns in another geographical direction and he gets an opportunity to say
something about his own city. São Paulo, unlike many
other South American cities, does not live in contemplation of fortunes accumulated by past generations. It does
not find its wealthy residents largely in the ranks of absentee landlords who own distant plantations. Its prominent citizens include a great many men who have created
the wealth that they now enjoy—certainly a greater proportion than is to be found in any other city south of the

[1] The independence of Brazil was proclaimed in São Paulo in 1822 by the
Portuguese ruler, Prince Dom Pedro and was attained without loss of life.
The republic was established in 1889 by a bloodless revolution.

[ 99 ]

Rio Grande. It is an industrial city more interested in machines than in family trees.

There will undoubtedly be many other industrial cities in South America in the future for the trend of development is all in that direction. São Paulo will always have the distinction of being the first. At present it is the only one. Cotton and coffee are both grown in the immediate neighborhood but the existence of these important crops is almost forgotten by people who are watching the erection of new factory buildings and new skyscrapers. To the Paulistas the capital and metropolis of Rio is just a quiet old-fashioned city. It has nice beaches, of course, and they certainly need them there in the hot weather. It is pleasantly cool here on this upland plateau and if one wants surf bathing he can find it at Santos only fifty miles away. The Paulistas are too busy to bother much about beaches or any other time-wasting amusements. They are building a city by their own efforts instead of just watching one grow. It is one of those cities whose residents never know just what the population figure is but are sure that it is much larger than the last published figure because it is constantly growing. The population now is well over a million and a quarter. At the present rate of increase it will soon surpass Rio in size and be the largest city in Brazil. It is almost inconceivable that in any other country in South America any purely commercial city would be able to outstrip the national capital in population.

São Paulo long ago lost the sleepy characteristics of an agricultural town—a town whose trade depended on the prosperity of the coffee fazendas in the neighborhood. It is the most important coffee-producing center in the world and several generations were content with their easily earned incomes. Then almost before they knew it factories sprang up and leadership in public affairs shifted from agriculturalists to industrialists. The coffee trees are still there and still productive as are the fields of cotton but the great dreams for the future are based on the increase in the number of factories rather than increase in the production of coffee or cotton. In talking about the factories of the future the Paulistas point out that they have an abundant supply of cheap hydroelectric power. When I ignorantly inquired whether or not there was coal in the neighborhood a Rotarian snapped at me.

"No," he said, "and we don't need it. We have wood and water. Wood grows which is more than coal does. And water will always run downhill and supply power. Coal is old fashioned."

Several people who should know what they are talking about assured me the power was the cheapest in the world and gave me the rate. But when I tried to convert milreis and dollars and kilowatts into one common denominator I found myself in a hopeless confusion of figures and gave up. In any event the supply of power must be both dependable and cheap for more and more money is being invested in enterprises which depend on cheap and dependable power for their existence. A failure of the supply or a sharp increase in rates would bankrupt enterprises in which many hundreds of billions of milreis have been invested. In addition to cheap power they have cheap labor for low wages are justified by the fact that the cost of living is low. The one-cent cup of coffee sets the scale for food prices and other things are in about the same proportion. There is a cheap supply of many basic raw materials; animal, mineral and vegetable. In addition to those whose uses are already well known there are dozens if not hundreds of Brazilian products waiting for the ingenuity of

man to develop some process by which they can be turned
into useful merchandise. There is a big home market for
everything that can at present be produced—a market in
Brazil itself which cannot be disturbed by tariffs or trade
agreements. Having established the fact that they have
cheap power, labor and raw materials and a dependable
market it would appear that the Paulistas had said about all
that could be said about the advantages of a city that is
already an important industrial center and hopes to become of much greater importance.

There is one thing more, and that is climate. Santiago
and Valparaiso talk about the climate they enjoy as a
means of attracting tourists. There is surf bathing all the
year round at Rio. Montevideo has beaches and a glamorous casino where one may enjoy the greatest comforts
while losing at roulette. But in its boasting about climate
São Paulo throws out no lures to catch the fickle tourist
dollar. They talk of climate as an aid to industry. They
point out that as the city lies in the tropics but is at an
altitude of about 2500 feet the struggle between heat and
cold is always happily compromised. Altitude mitigates the
heat of summer, proximity to the equator takes the chill
off winter. It is, they insist, never very hot and never
very cold. This simplifies the construction of factories as
well as residences and makes many economies possible because the whole elevated plateau on which São Paulo
stands is, in effect, air-conditioned by nature. Since Paulistas are industrial-minded they point out that this kindly
but invigorating climate enables the factory hands and
other laborers to work with the highest degree of efficiency and hence there is more assurance that São Paulo
will be a great industrial city. No matter how a conversation starts that is the note on which it always ends.

Actually the climate at São Paulo is not quite so ideal as it is represented to be though I do not know of any other industrial city that has a better one. The comforting theory that artificial heat is never needed is given visible evidence of authenticity by the fact that in São Paulo as in Rio there are no fireplaces and no steam heat. The local residents admit that it does at times get a little chilly. As a matter of fact, after an especially cold August night, they sometimes wake to find that exposed pools are covered with a thin layer of ice. Such conduct on the part of the elements meets with stern disapproval of the local Rotary Club, the Chamber of Commerce and similar organizations who look on it as a treasonable betrayal of trust. No matter how often this happens it is considered, as in Los Angeles, as being a most unusual freak of nature which has never happened before and will most probably never happen again. Nevertheless, in spite of these observations the climate of São Paulo is all that an industrial city could desire.

There is no suggestion of tropical languor about this hustling city. The air is cool and bracing and people walk briskly, as if they were going some place and in a hurry to get there. It is the only place I have ever visited where pedestrian traffic is subject to the same rules as motorcar traffic. The Paulistas have no time for interruptions. The first time I left the hotel a policeman gently chided me because I was walking on the wrong side of the pavement. It was early in the morning and very few people were afoot but the policeman rightly thought that I might as well learn how to conduct myself in a bustling city. Police regulations of pedestrians go even further than that. At the various bus stops people line up in orderly queues while waiting for the bus to arrive, instead of collecting in jostling and competitive groups as on Fifth Avenue, or any other place in the United States. When the bus halts the seats are occupied with the least possible waste of time. This time- and temper-saving arrangment is no longer a matter to which the police have to pay any particular attention for it is now a routine habit just as we queue up for theater tickets. Visitors from São Paulo to New York must be struck by our uncouth ways in the matter of traffic just as they are struck by the prodigality with which the tobacco shops give away matches and the hotels keep the bathrooms well supplied with soap. Then soak you for a cup of coffee!

Any list of the products of the São Paulo factories would be out of date before it could be published for new lines are being added all the time. Only a few years ago they were making shoes and hats and silk stockings but there was not a doll factory in all of Brazil or in all South America for that matter. The demand for dolls by the little girls of South America was met by importations especially from Germany. The first factory of many that I saw made nothing but dolls and is making them so well and so cheaply that the market for German-made dolls in Brazil will in the future be very small if not completely nonexistent. There is an element of poetic justice in this for the competition was brought about by Hitler himself through his persecution of the Jews. The young Jew who owns this fast-growing São Paulo factory was in the same business in Bavaria. When persecution of his people began he managed to get to Brazil with a fragment of his savings and started a factory with two sewing machines and less than a dozen women operators. For some months he designed and superintended the making of the dolls and then sold and delivered them to the local shops himself.

The dolls were just as good as the ones he had made in Germany and were sold at a cheaper price. From the time he turned out the first order the growth of his business has depended entirely on the rapidity with which he could plow back his profits into additional equipment. The pace has not been slow. He now has several hundred employees crowded into three isolated buildings and is looking for larger quarters—something that is difficult to find in a city that outgrows its pants every year. He now sells dolls to all parts of Brazil and neighboring countries and has made shipments to South Africa and Mexico. A few days before I visited the factory a New York wholesaler bought a sample order amounting to five hundred dollars. A sample order, by the way, consisted of no less than two hundred different kinds of dolls, ranging in price from five cents to about ten dollars. Some of those in the higher price range are beautifully gowned in miniature adaptations of Paris creations. Others represent Brazilian types and costumes.

The mechanical equipment of this factory consists almost entirely of sewing machines and all have the familiar Singer trade-mark. The proprietor said he could get German machines very much cheaper so far as the initial cost was concerned but in the long run they were more expensive because they soon wore out and always required replacements and repairs. This was the story I heard on every hand not only about sewing machines but about all kinds of factory equipment. No one preferred German machines of any kind and when they were installed in a factory it was only because nothing better could be afforded. The doll manufacturer also said that he did not use Japanese cloth because the irregularity of the texture causes damage to sewing machines. But cloth produced in

São Paulo was satisfactory. He imports from the United States large quantities of those odds and ends known to the dress trade as "findings" and also the mechanical gadget that makes the dolls say "mama." These came at varying prices and the ones which draw the name out long and affectionately cost the most. It appears that even in supplying voices for dolls our manufacturers excel in the quality market for the "mama" of the German-made dolls is short and stingy, a trifle like a baby with a wet diaper, but the São Paulo dolls with Yankee voices speak the word as soothingly as a radio singer doing a commercial broadcast.

This refugee from Hitler's persecutions bears little personal resentment against the Nazi dictator because his exile has brought him a more secure prosperity than he enjoyed in his homeland. He has not yet regained the modest fortune he formerly had but is well on his way toward that goal. He sees in Brazil greater opportunities than ever existed in Germany—greater opportunities not only in the market in his newly adopted country but in the possibilities of building up an export business which will be able to compete successfully with the German factories. He was only one of a number of Jewish exiles I met who have either established factories themselves or are helping other factories to produce in South America the kind of goods Germany has sold to these countries in the past and will want to sell them in the future. A very large number of Jews in Europe saw the approach of the Nazi menace and managed to get away or to transfer their valuables before it was too late. South America was the goal of many of them and in one way or another they brought to various countries millions of dollars. This "refugee money" about which very little is known is helping to establish factories in many countries and most of them are in direct competition with similar establishments in Germany.

Of perhaps equal importance is the fact that thousands of technical experts, ranging from well-known scientists to factory foremen have fled from Europe for political reasons and settled in South America. At the next factory I visited, a textile mill, the only employee who could speak English was an Austrian lady who had been a clothing designer in Vienna. Here in São Paulo she was enabling her employer to produce a line of goods which had formerly been imported. When the war is ended and the German manufacturers are able to resume business in South America they will find a lot of new competition they never had to face before and an important part of that will have been created by Hitler's denial of the right of Jews to live.

There are many other São Paulo factories which are veteran establishments compared to the new doll factory. One suburban group of very fine residences is known as "the Syrian settlement" for these are the homes of the Syrian textile manufacturers who enjoy a peace and prosperity here that is unknown in their homeland. The factory that I visited was more than ordinarily interesting for here one could follow the raw cotton through all the processes of manufacture until the bale emerges in the form of finished products—shirts, underclothing, sport suits—in fact almost everything in the way of ready-to-wear garments that can be produced from cotton. There was only one of 510 textile mills and factories in the São Paulo district employing more than 75,000 operatives.[2]

[2] Almost all statistics regarding the industries of South America are mildly exaggerated, probably through the desire of each country or community to make the best possible showing. For example a tailor shop or a dressmaking establishment will be included among the textile factories or a garage which does repair work will be listed as a metal-working establishment. A very large number of the so-called factories consist of nothing more than shops employing less than a dozen workmen.

The well-known American firm of Anderson, Clayton & Co. which has branches in all places where cotton is grown or used, does its part in the development of the growing Brazilian textile industry. The company finances the cotton grower, buys his crop and spins the cotton. The cotton seed is crushed and provides salad or cooking oil for which there is a large local demand.

After neglecting the crop for years Brazil is now devoting an increasing acreage to cotton. The increased production has thrown a scare into our own Southern growers for it is in direct competition with them and Brazil actually has more available cotton land than we have. The idea that Brazilian cotton was inferior and suitable only for the coarse weaves produced by the Japanese and German mills was probably the result of wishful and malicious thinking on the part of our cotton growers for it had no foundation in fact. Actually there is no difference between the cotton grown in the neighborhood of São Paulo and that grown in our Southern States. It was just a new product on the world market and the mills were slow to take it up. The whole process of textile manufacture is so delicate that a difference of one sixteenth of an inch in the length of the staple will seriously upset it. Now that Brazilian cotton has stood the test in mills of many countries it is recognized as a standard product.

Less than ten years ago Brazil produced no cotton for export but in 1938 the export sales amounted to several million dollars. There is little doubt but that Brazil will be an increasingly important factor in world cotton trade and as a manufacturer of textiles as well as a producer of raw cotton. It appears more than probable that the mills of Osaka and Hamburg will be hit more directly than our own growers. The Brazilian mills have been running only a short time and complete efficiency in operation has not yet been attained. But it has been convincingly demonstrated that they can produce cotton cloth as cheaply as any mill in the world, including those of Japan. At the present time the mills use only about 250,000 bales a year, or one sixth of the total Brazilians production.

North American experts who have watched the development of textile manufacturing in São Paulo believe that the rate of consumption will be increased very rapidly and will absorb an increasing proportion of the national cotton crop. Millions of customers are waiting for cheaper shirts, just as millions are waiting for shoes they can afford to buy. There will always be a demand for special imported products just as there is even in Japan a restricted but steady sale of calicos produced in Manchester. But there is no reason why mills of São Paulo, and others which are certain to follow them should not supply all of South America with the cheap textiles they have formerly imported. They have one advantage which the German and Japanese mills can never overcome—that of a favorable position enjoyed not only by the São Paulo cotton mills but by many other South American factories. Raw materials, factories and consumers are all in the same neighborhood.

One of the lightest, airiest and cleanest factories I have ever seen is devoted to lithographed tin products, one representative of the metal-working industries which give employment to about 30,000 São Paulo workmen. In the sales room there was a representative collection of toys ranging from the tin railway trains which have been standard for a generation or more to the latest creations of toyland. There were Snow Whites, Mickey Mice, Donald Ducks, etc. As we had just come from the doll factory I remarked to my Brazilian guide that São Paulo appeared to be specializing in the toy business. He said that in a way it was about the soundest business in which any manufacturer could engage because there was no saturation point to be feared. No matter how many or what toys were produced there would always be a demand for them by children. In fact, he said, if parents bought all the toys children wanted it would never be possible to meet the demand. As was the case with the doll factory these toys do not compete with our products but do compete directly with the German and Japanese factories. Our manufacturers supply the voices for the dolls and the springs that make the toy locomotives run.

The gaily colored toy patterns going through the giant printing presses added a kind of Santa Claus touch to the place but the principal business of the factory is the making of cans. One machine at the time of my visit was busy turning out cans for Royal Baking Powder which has a factory in São Paulo. Another unit was making five-gallon oil cans at the rate of one thousand an hour, but by far the busiest of the many busy machines were those turning out round and square corned beef tins at an even speedier rate. All of these machines were American; the thermometers in the huge drying ovens for the lithographed tin plate were made in U.S.A., so was the time clock, or the several time clocks near the workmen's entrance, so were the typewriters and the adding machines. In fact I looked all over the place for some equipment not made in the U.S.A. and failed to find any. But there was not a penny of American capital invested in the enterprise. Some might refer to this factory as being Italian since it is the outgrowth of an enterprise started by an Italian more than fifty years ago. Everyone connected with it now is

Brazilian though many of them are of Italian descent. There would really be no more reason for giving it that national classification than there would be to refer to the great Du Pont interests as French.

There were huge stocks of tin plate in the warehouse and every case was marked "made in U.S.A." In the many stories I had heard about the refusal of our manufacturers to grant reasonable credit terms to South American business the United States Steel Corporation was said to be the most uncompromising of all,—demanding, I was told, cash on the barrel head before a pound of its products would be shipped. Hoping to get the other fellow's point of view I said to the manager:

"I suppose you have to pay cash for all that tin."

"Oh, no," he said, "we get it on reasonable credit terms."

It seemed to me that this factory provided a fine example of the way in which American enterprise, no matter where it makes itself felt, benefits our trade in many direct and indirect ways. The executives of great packing houses years ago saw the opportunities offered by the cheap and abundant food supplies of the east coast of South America and established plants in Brazil, Uruguay and Argentina. Meats packed here could be sold much cheaper than the products of the Chicago packing houses and though little of it was ever sold in the United States the companies built up a big business in Europe—which some one else would have gotten if they hadn't been the first to see the opportunities. Corned beef from these South American plants competes so successfully with ours that it is no longer produced in Chicago—except to fill orders for the U. S. Navy. As a result our packing houses operating in South America have come in for some criticism and abuse which they do not deserve.

We can't compete with any of these countries in meat products and never will be able to. It was inevitable that they instead of us should supply the world's markets and very much to our advantage that such a large part of the machinery of distribution should be in our hands. A great many people share the benefits. The tin lithographing establishment not only buys machines from us but also sheet tin, lithographing inks, lubricating oil and all the hundred and one odds and ends of supplies that a busy factory uses. The interchange is too complicated to be set down in a balance sheet but if that were possible it would probably be found that these gains alone would more than offset any loss through the sale at home of competitive food products. The indirect benefits to our trade are much greater. The packing houses not only provide a market for the products of Brazil, Argentina and Uruguay but their payrolls put into circulation a great deal of money which supports retail shops and so creates more customers for an infinite variety of products of American factories.

It is in this indirect way, by sharing in the prosperity that we help to create, that the building of the Brazilian steel mill will help to keep our own factory wheels turning. The construction of the mill will be made possible through a loan agreement with the Import-Export Bank providing for aggregate credits of $20,000,000, a larger amount to be invested by Brazil. A large part, if not all of the $20,000,000 will go for the purchase of equipment made in the United States and for the employment of American technicians. The success of the mill appears to be assured. The field of iron ore to be converted into useful products would make any steel mill smack its metallic lips. There are millions of tons of it lying on the ground and 80 per cent pure. The experts who have investigated the matter say that, like the cotton textiles of São Paulo, the products of the steel mill will be as cheap as any in the world.

The mill will produce the cheap grades of iron and steel in which we cannot or do not compete, which have formerly been bought in Germany and Belgium. Cheap rails will help railway development in all the South American countries. Bars and plates will provide the material for hundreds of light metal industries which will need our machines, tools and lubricating oils and belts and electric motors and hundreds of other items. The pay roll of the steel mill, the prosperity of the many subsidiary and affiliated interests will so add to the purchasing power of thousands of South Americans that the effect will be felt throughout our own country. If it were not in violation of all the old-fashioned economic ideas one would be tempted to say that this promises to be an investment that will be profitable even if no interest is ever paid and the debt is never liquidated.

In the development of factories and industries in São Paulo and in other parts of the continent the South Americans are starting on a sounder social foundation than we had during the period that we were going through the same experience. Our pioneer factories and other industrial establishments were started and grew to great size when we had no legislation or totally inadequate legislation concerning such vitally important matters as wages, hours and conditions of labor. The result was that when labor legislation was finally enacted it necessarily disturbed conditions which had existed for many years and created unnecessary ill will between capital and labor. That need not occur in any part of South America. Labor legislation which has already been enacted will prevent the growth of abuses because they will have no opportunity to start. What is even more important than the purely legalistic point of view is the fact that employee and employer are developing new industries together with a clear understanding of their mutual responsibilities. That is something we are just beginning to learn.

São Paulo is one city where there is no casino with tables for roulette and other gambling. The Paulistas are too busy to waste time on such things, though lottery tickets are sold as they are in every South American city. But they have not forgotten that the city bears the name of a saint. At almost all hours of the day church bells can be heard over the tooting of the motorcar horns and the shouts of the newsboys. In the center of the city a fine new cathedral is half finished, enough to show that it will be a remarkably fine and imposing building. I was told that it had been under construction for twenty years and that it would not be completed for another twenty, not because of lack of funds but because of the time it would take to prepare the elaborately carved stonework. This was the only church building I saw under construction. Most of the cities and especially Lima and Bogotá, have so many old and decaying churches and cathedrals that it must be a constant strain on the parishioners just to keep them in repair.

São Paulo is a symbol of the future of South America— a city which thrived on agricultural feudalism and might have lived comfortably through many generations on the cotton and coffee crops. But a modern São Paulo has justified its existence by its own efforts and is not just a magnified county seat, provincial or national capital.

CHAPTER VIII

## *Drake, Windsor and Pat Mulcahy*

A FEW years ago some writer referred to the fact that
Santos is the greatest coffee port of the world and
in order to give color to his statistics and make
them more convincing he made a statement that has since
been widely quoted. He said that when a ship far out at sea
was approaching Santos the odor of coffee was plainly dis-
tinguishable if the wind was in the right direction. One
would infer from this story that Santos offered a novel
aid to navigation by which skippers could set their course
by the sense of smell without the aid of lighthouses or
landmarks. Generations before this another writer said the
same thing about what were then called the Spice Islands.
Navigators were supposed to sniff the breeze and when
they smelled cinnamon or cloves or nutmegs they would
head their ships in the right direction.

Unfortunately for those who love the picturesque and the improbable these stories are not true. It really doesn't matter very much but the people of Santos were all wrought up about it and my friends there urged me not to make the same exaggerated statement. They said I would probably want to come back to Santos sometime and it would be embarrassing all around if I had written something that would make club committees hesitate about extending me the usual privileges. To most of us coffee is just something to drink but to the people of Santos it is a commodity on which the prosperity of the port depends as well as the livelihood of most of the local residents. It is not anything to be flippant about. One friend insisted on taking me through an uncomfortably hot warehouse where there were thousands of bags of coffee waiting to be loaded into a steamer and triumphantly demanded to know whether or not I smelled any coffee which of course I did not for the coffee beans had not been roasted and so had no more odor than so many bags of rice.

If there is any spot in the world that should be redolent of the smell of coffee it is Santos and yet the pleasant odor is not so noticeable as at Rio or over in Buenos Aires. There are places where one can buy a cup of coffee for the equivalent of one cent, as in other places in Brazil, but they are not so numerous. One does not see the sight so common in other South American cities—groups of people at sidewalk cafés and waiters hurrying about with coffee pots in their hands. The reason is that for a great many Santos people the drinking of coffee—or at least the tasting of coffee—is a daily job, one at which they work from the time their offices open in the morning until they close in the afternoons. For them to drink coffee outside working hours would be like the London busman's proverbial holiday.

No coffee is grown near Santos for the coastal plain is only a few feet above the sea level. All the coffee in the world is grown at an elevation of a few thousand feet except the inferior coffee of Liberia which plays a very small part in world trade. The American advertiser who each year spends a great deal of money giving publicity to the fact that all the coffee beans used in his blend come from upland plantations is not indulging in any exaggeration for exactly the same thing could be said about every coffee blend in the world. It is about like advertising that bananas are grown in the tropics. The plateau on which the industrial city of São Paulo is located is at the right altitude for coffee growing, the climate is suitable and so this has become one of the most important centers for the production of coffee. Brazil is the principal coffee country in the world—the São Paulo district is the most important in Brazil. In fact there are around São Paulo enough coffee trees to provide one for every inhabitant of the globe with a few million left over. The development of the formerly sleepy and unimportant old port of Santos came as a result of this production of coffee. It has passed the proud city of Rio de Janeiro in the value of its exports and ships an average of more than 10 million bags of coffee annually.

Connecting the two cities of São Paulo and Santos is one of the most remarkable railways in the world, remarkable not only for its engineering but also for its uninterrupted record of earnings. In a distance of only forty-nine miles from São Paulo to Santos the road descends from an elevation of 2,500 feet to sea level. Much of this descent is made during the first six miles of the journey, the trains being lowered or hauled upward by means of an intricate system of cables which gives way to locomotives on the comparatively level stretch of banana-bordered road leading into Santos.

The railway was built by a British company under a concession which limits the amount of the dividends that can be paid to the stockholders. Year after year the enterprise has earned much more than enough to meet the dividends and the only thing that can be done is to spend the money on improvements. As there was no need to economize on these expenditures the best possible materials were used and this only added to the stability of the earnings because no replacements were necessary and efficiency in operation has constantly improved. There is a rainfall of a hundred inches a year here and every possible precaution has been taken against washouts and landslides. Rivulets far up the side of the mountain are confined by concrete gutters so that the heaviest rainfall is carried harmlessly past the roadbed to the lowlands. Even the rocks alongside the track are covered with tar to prevent erosion.

The fares are surprisingly cheap. A round trip of just under a hundred miles with Pullman accommodations costs approximately one dollar. It is the railway of railway men just as Spenser is the poet's poet. Many of them have made a trip over the road the high spot of a South American tour—to marvel at the engineering and think enviously of the earnings. The local residents of São Paulo and Santos always tell the story of a famous railway executive from New York who traveled up and down the road as the guest of its management and made a very thorough inspection. On the eve of his departure the British manager asked if he could make any suggestions for improvement.

"You appear to have overlooked one thing," said the visitor. "You might gold plate the spikes."

My final contact with the bustling life of São Paulo was provided in the railway station. There were no reserved seats on the train in which I was traveling and I did not learn the São Paulo technique of securing a seat until it was too late to be of any practical benefit to me. The next time I travel from São Paulo to Santos I will know how to do it. All the windows of the train were open as it halted beside the platform. Experienced travelers instead of piling into the train merely tossed hats, gloves or handbags through the windows onto the seats thereby staking out a claim which everyone respected.

The short trip provides an instructive sample of the topography of Brazil. Even before leaving the elevated plain on which São Paulo is built the train passes mile after mile of alternating swamp, jungle and forest. Were it not for the constant battle against the cruel vegetable growths of the jungle this very fine railway would soon be covered and disappear from view under the tropical growth of trees and creepers. Everywhere in the jungle you can see evidence of the constant struggle and the ever-recurring cycle of birth, life and death. Creeping vines surround a tree and thrive on its sap. Eventually the tree dies and so do the vines when deprived of their natural food. The whole mass of vegetation falls to the ground to rot and for a brief space of time there is a comparatively bare spot in the jungle. Then another three grows, the vines again strangle it and again all die together. This is the constantly recurring cycle in the jungle interrupted only when man clears and plants it. There is something rather terrifying about the wild life of a tropical jungle even when seen from the safe and detached quarters of a railway train. The cultivated areas which flashed on us with movie film suddenness brought welcome relief. Maybe the strong contrast gave the orchards an exaggerated appearance of tidiness. The fruit trees were in orderly rows, the lower parts of the trunks so neatly whitewashed that from the train window they looked as if they had been painted with white enamel.

During my stay in Santos Pat Mulcahy, the best-known Yankee in South America, was my host and taught me what I know about coffee as a business. Pat's environment and personal experience span the centuries of history in this part of the world. The rocks on the edge of his shorefront suburban home provided the landing place for the forces under Sir Francis Drake who sacked the city in the sixteenth century, robbing the church of all its silver plate and ornaments. It was on these same rocks, which now belong to Pat, that the wretched people of Santos stood to watch Drake's ships sail away and as they saw the hated craft disappear over the horizon they prayed that the approach to the harbor would silt up so that no ships could anchor at this landing place again. And sure enough this approach to the harbor did silt up so completely that no ships followed those of Drake. That is the reason that Pat has a beautiful country home on a secluded spot of seashore that might otherwise be crowded with shipping. There is another story to the effect that the Santos people also prayed that the black soul of Drake might be eternally damned and that to this day there are those who still lay curses on him. That may be just another story like the one about smelling the coffee of Santos far out at sea.

A little more than three hundred years after Drake's ships came to Santos the place was visited by another famous Englishman, the present Duke of Windsor, who was then the Prince of Wales. He made a hole in one on the Santos golf course which was the first time His Royal Highness had ever accomplished that feat and the first time anyone had ever made a hole in one on the Santos course—providing a double reason for celebration. Pat was at the time the acting president of the golf club and enjoyed the pleasant duty of presenting the appropriate prizes to the prince. All of these things Pat told me as we sat under a papaya tree on his orchid-bordered terrace and drank cool drinks and looked across the harbor as evening fell and the lights of Santos blinked on. It was with something of an air of proprietorship that my host pointed out the landmarks of the place for this has been his home for twenty-six years and he never expects to live in any other.

The following morning I began to learn about coffee. In the interim between the visit of Sir Francis Drake and the Prince of Wales a new approach to the harbor had been discovered and developed, an approach so torturous that every ship coming into the port must steer at various times toward every point of the compass. It is really a very beautiful as well as interesting harbor and much more would be said about it but for the fact that writers who have usually just seen the harbor of Rio first are all out of breath and are fresh out of adjectives. Pat Mulcahy, born in Ireland but an adopted son of New York City, was doing more than any other one man to keep the port of Santos busy, for as the representative of the American Coffee Corporation he buys more coffee than anyone else in the world.

He is one purchasing agent who never has to listen to the talk of a salesman, does not even have to see them. In the buying of coffee as in the drinking it is taste alone that counts. For several very interesting hours I watched the way in which the coffee which will be boiled or dripped or percolated into billions of cups is selected. The grower or dealer or jobber who has green coffee beans to sell sends to the coffee buyer a sample with a notation on a printed form as to the quantity he has for sale and the price he wants for it. Each morning the coffee buyer's staff start on their day's routine of roasting, grinding, brewing and tasting these samples. First a measured portion of the sample is spread out on a table and every bean is carefully examined. Even in the best samples submitted there are always some beans that are broken or not quite ripe, some in which small bits of the leaves and twigs of the coffee tree are mixed. Because of this there is no coffee that is known as first grade. That is just an ideal toward which few strive and one which none attains. What a contrast to the system of grading olives in which the smallest are rated as large and those of medium size are mammoth! The cleanest coffee comes from the few small growers who live on their own fazendas and manage them just as our farmers manage their own farms. But the coffee baron, just like the cattle barons are usually absentee landlords whose estates are managed by superintendents, and it is from their plantations that most of the coffee comes.

Having counted the unripe and defective beans the sample is then roasted and ground and next appears as a small pot of black coffee ready for the tasters. Housewives who guess at the amount of coffee or water in the pot should take a lesson from the way coffee is prepared for tasting. The amount of coffee is weighed as accurately as a druggist weighs the ingredients in a prescription and the water is measured just as carefully. If there is any difference in the taste of the coffee it must come from the quality of the bean and from no other cause. I had often seen teatasters at work in China but this was a better show. There dozens of small cups of tea are set out on a long table and the teataster walks about in a leisurely fashion sipping from each sample and writing down his comments. The coffee tasters work at a faster pace. The numbered coffee cups are ranged on a circular revolving table not unlike the Lazy Susan I have always wanted to have on my own breakfast table. Seated at the table the taster dips a long spoon into the cup nearest him and not only tastes but audibly sniffs the aroma through his nostrils so audibly in fact that the sniff becomes a kind of a snort. Then he spits the coffee into the largest cuspidor I have ever seen. The human stomach, the old physiology books used to say, is capable of great extension but none could possibly accommodate the great quantity of liquid the coffee taster takes into his mouth every day. Having passed judgment on one cup the taster, with a twist of his wrist brings another cup in front of him and the process is repeated—all with the mechanical precision and rapidity of an automatic bottle-filling machine.

The routine was interrupted when the taster struck a cup sharply with his spoon. That was the indication that the sample in cup no. 4 was not acceptable. A clerk who had been standing back of him all the time made a note on the score card he was keeping. Having made the round of the cups the taster went over them again and again his spoon rapped disapproval of cup no. 4. A second taster was called in from an outside room and repeated the performance. It was like a trial by jury in which the jurors had no opportunity to compare notes or discuss matters with each other. When he came to cup no. 4 he also smacked it with his spoon. A third taster went through the samples and his verdict was the same as that of his two colleagues. It began to look like one of those tricks in which the magician tells you what card you thought of. Then I tasted all the cups and couldn't see that there was anything wrong with the coffee in cup no. 4. To me it tasted like all the rest of them.

Pat told me that he once asked a visiting New York banker who looked on himself as a connoisseur of coffee to taste the samples and pick out the best one. The one he selected was the worst of the lot—one which no professional taster would pass. However tastes in coffee differ. Practically all that is bought for the New York market is no. 2 grade which is the best obtainable. The French and the Germans on the other hand, buy only third- and fourth-grade coffee which explains why a breakfast in Paris or Berlin was always such a completely disappointing affair. The reason the coffee growers of South and Central America have been hit so hard by the closing of their European markets is not only because of the volume taken there but because the Europeans bought grades for which there is no market elsewhere. They tell a story in Santos about a local jobber who had a contract with a firm in Paris to supply a certain number of bags of fourth-grade coffee. For some reason he couldn't get the quantity he wanted in time to meet his contract obligations and so at considerable loss to himself he filled out the shipment with coffee of a better grade. He thought his customers would be appreciative but after they had sampled this superior coffee they threatened to sue him for breach of contract.

After the samples have been tasted a note is made on the jobber's card accepting or rejecting the lot he has for sale or offering a lower price. During the day he drops in and has a look at the notation on his card and either closes a deal or offers his cargo elsewhere. Thus deals involving in the aggregate millions of dollars are closed with less conversation than a motorcar salesman would use in leading up to his selling talk.

It would be an easy matter for any grower or jobber to doctor up a sample of coffee before it was submitted to the buyer by picking out all of the immature and broken beans and bits of stem, leaves and hull. But if the experts found a sample that was too clean they would doubtless be suspicious. Coffee just doesn't come from the trees in that way. Even if a ruse like this did succeed in getting past the first tests there is little chance that any of the inferior coffee would ever get on the market. On the arrival of every shipment in New York it is turned over to another set of testers and tasters and the procedure which I found so interesting in Santos is repeated. In fact a test is made every time a lot of coffee changes hands. The case history of every lot is followed until after it has reached the roasting ovens at home. No matter where the coffee is roasted, if it turns out to be below what was expected of it a report goes back to Santos and the buyers can at once trace the origin of the lot. Very seldom does it occur that the tasters of New York disagree with those of Santos. After they get through the blenders start for there is a great deal of difference between the tastes of coffees coming from different countries.

American advertising succeeded so thoroughly in convincing me that freshness was the all-important thing in coffee that I somehow got the idea that the best coffee is the kind that is rushed from tree to roasting oven, to percolator and then to the consumer. That is done at one golf club in Colombia for the club house is surrounded by coffee trees and members can go out and pick their own coffee beans if they like. But the importance of freshness applies only to the period between roasting and drinking. The ripe coffee bean does not deteriorate with age but in the opinion of some connoisseurs improves in flavor. Here is an opportunity for a new line in coffee advertising which I will pass out for anyone to grab who likes.

"Don't drink harsh new coffees. Our coffee is aged in antiseptic gunny sacks and not a bean is roasted until it is seven years old."

If the coffee comes from Brazil the chances are that the statement about the seven-year period would be just a slight exaggeration. With year after year of overproduction the Brazilian government has been buying up surplus crops of coffee, storing some, selling some, burning some. It is possible that some of the coffee which is in American warehouses today was ripening on the trees when Hitler the non-coffee drinker was just a little man with a trick mustache.

Brazil is often referred to as being our best South American friend. While there are other reasons for the existence of this friendship, it could not exist on such a solid and permanent basis were it not for the fact that we are Brazil's best customer. The reason we are her best customer is because we like strong coffee and that is what Brazil produces. The English, with their traditional taste for tea, prefer the milder coffee of Colombia and the Central American states. We buy large quantities of these coffees to blend with the Brazilian. The French and other continentals, as has been noted, prefer anything so long as it is cheap. We are the only faithful consumers of Brazilian coffee and it goes far toward filling our national coffee cup. That old hash-house slang about "a cup of Java" was outmoded soon after it became hackneyed. We buy little from Java now and Java produces less than it did a hundred years ago. Venezuela is not looked on as an important producer of coffee but exports more than all the Dutch East Indies. The snappy young smart aleck should say to the waiter, "pass me a cup of Brazil."

We were not always coffee drinkers. In fact the coffee habit is comparatively new throughout the world and we were among the latest to adopt it. Perhaps coffee would never have become a favorite beverage but for the fact that pious Mohammedans discovered that it would serve to keep them awake during the long and tedious hours of religious ceremonies. And so its use spread to the rest of the world from Mohammedan Arabia at the same time that the use of tea spread from Buddhist China. It is curious that for centuries before any other countries knew of the existence of either drink Arabian traders were frequent visitors to China; yet the Arabians never learned to drink tea—and the Chinese never learned to drink coffee. At the time of the revolution we were tea drinkers and hence as soon as we got control of our own foreign trade our skippers and merchants turned their attention toward China. They evidently did not know that there was available in several countries in South America and especially in Paraguay an herb known as maté or "Paraguayan tea" which provides a very satisfactory substitute for tea. Our taste in tea was not in any way refined as we only got the poorer grades which the English did not want. It is very interesting to reflect what might have happened if the Yankee skippers and traders had known of the existence of this plant, which was plentiful and cheap and better suited to our thin purses than the more luxurious China tea. We might have become a nation of maté drinkers, our eyes would have been turned toward South America instead of the Far East and the history of the world would have been changed.

Though it would be impossible for me to prove the allegation and therefore I do not make it there were many occasions when I had reason to believe that in the preparation of breakfast coffee the cooks of South America followed the French tradition and used only third- or fourth-rate coffee. Even in Brazil the cup of breakfast coffee was seldom satisfactory. On the west coast where coffee is not such an important crop it was all but undrinkable. There is one school of thought among North American coffee drinkers—especially those living in Peru—that it is not coffee at all but a concoction made from the bark ordinarily used for tanning. The theory of the conservative school to which I belong, is that it consists of the coffee left over from the day before and heated again just enough to take off the chill. The sad truth of the matter is that South American cooks follow the French tradition and do not know how to make a good cup of coffee. They are also handicapped by the fact that in the coffee-producing countries only the native-grown beans are used so that blends are impossible. Perhaps with the increase in tourists from the United States the cooks will learn that breakfast coffee should be something more than just a liquid used to give a little flavor to hot milk. In the meantime what a joy it always was to get back on a Grace boat and enjoy a good cup of coffee with cream and sugar in it.

Santos is one of the many places that has been referred to as "the white man's grave." That was a phrase much more commonly used a few decades ago when people did not know that it was mosquitoes and rats and unsanitary surroundings instead of strange climates that caused disease and deaths. When Santos was cleaned up it was found to be just as healthy as any other place in the world as is true of other tropical places. The three miles of wharves have been ratproofed and the swampy places drained so that mosquitoes have been completely exterminated. I suppose I can claim credit for completing the work of extermination. Everyone told me that there wasn't a mosquito in the port so I presume it was the last survivor who bit me. But I killed her with a folded copy of the *New York Times*. This historic event occurred in the Parque Balneario Hotel at two o'clock on the morning of October 17, 1940.

I cannot say my last word about Santos without recording one little incident that was of great interest to me but otherwise of no special significance or importance except that it indicated the smallness of the world in which we live. After night had fallen and we could no longer see the rocks on which Drake's men had landed Mulcahy and I drove to Santos for dinner in his apartment, the only penthouse in the place. A middle-aged brindled Scottie—about eight or nine years old—came into the room and Pat commanded:

"Sandy, pray for the poor Chinese."

Sandy put his forepaws on the couch and his head between them in an attitude of supplication. When I asked why he had been taught to "pray for the poor Chinese" Pat said it was quite appropriate as Sandy had been born in Shanghai. We traced the history of Sandy's travels and found that he was a dog I had owned and given away in Shanghai about six or seven years before this. From Shanghai to Santos is a long migration for a dog but the explanation was absurdly simple. I had given Sandy to the captain of a ship on a run between Seattle and Shanghai. When the Japanese started their assaults on the coast of China, the skipper and his ship were sent on a new route, down the west coast of South America, around the Horn and back to the home port of Seattle by way of the Panama Canal. His wife found that by living in Santos she could not only cut living expenses in half but, by joining her husband in Buenos Aires and traveling north to Santos with him, they would on each voyage be united about twice as long as would have been possible if she had remained in Seattle.

And so she moved to Santos and brought Sandy with her. She was in Buenos Aires at the time of my visit to meet her seafaring husband and Pat was taking care of the dog. And so in this strange fashion I met an old friend in a distant part of the world. Of course he didn't recognize my odor. Maybe it changed after I left Shanghai. But, anyway, six or seven years is a long time in the life of a dog.

## CHAPTER IX

## *"I See a Mountain"*

ACCORDING to the story, which has been told over and over again, Magellan was cruising down the East Coast of South America on the first leg of what was to be the first circumnavigation of the globe when one of his lookouts shouted excitedly, "monte video" which is the Spanish for "I see a mountain." The lookout must have been one of those unfortunate people who always have to exaggerate their own achievements for what he saw was nothing more than a hill only a few hundred feet high. Or he may have been a wag who enjoyed a joke at the expense of his comrades and had a good laugh when they rushed to the rail to see a warty little eminence. Whatever the reason may have been his cry was remembered. He saw the little hill in 1520 but when a city was established here in 1726, more than two hundred years later, it was called Montevideo.

That circumstance gave me a new conception of the character of the men who made up Magellan's expedition. Maybe in spite of the hardships they suffered, the mutinies and the death of their leader, they were a jolly crew who overlooked no opportunity to break the tedium of a voyage with pranks and jokes and wisecracks. Montevideo was not the only place that was given a whimsical name. When they reached the southern tip of the continent and saw the natives living in that frozen forbidding area someone remarked about the unusual size of their feet. And so the region was nicknamed "big feet" or Patagonia. After the death of their leader in what is now the Philippines the survivors must have had some unpleasant experiences with the pirates who lived on the islands off the South Coast of China for they called them the Ladrones, or "thieves" islands, a name which is still appropriate.

Magellan's fleet of five vessels left Seville on August 10, 1519. Almost three years later a single vessel with thirty-one men returned to Seville, being the first men to circumnavigate the globe. They were half dead from illness and starvation. During the voyage they had eaten rats, sawdust and oxhides. But after they recovered they must have had many gay stories to tell about the braggart who cried "monte video" and then told entertaining lies themselves about the tremendous size of the feet of the natives they saw a few hundred miles farther south. And so when a settlement was founded which grew into a city they perpetuated the cry of the lookout by calling it Montevideo.

This capital and metropolis of the spunky little state of Uruguay is the greatest tourist center in South America, the only one where the tourist peso is really important. Very few North Americans spend more than a few hours there going ashore when the Moore-McCormack steamers dock and returning just before sailing time which is usually late at night. But each year many thousands residents of the capital of Argentina holiday in Montevideo or at some of the beach towns farther up the coast where they escape the muddy waters of the La Plata estuary. It is only an overnight journey by water between the two capitals and ferries run each way nightly. The traffic is constantly growing. When the construction of the Golden Gate bridge between Oakland and San Francisco made some of the ferry boats idle, one of them was sold to an Argentine company and placed on the run. American ladies living in Montevideo go to Buenos Aires to do their shopping and there is a good deal of visiting back and forth —much more than between any other two cities in different South American countries. A few months ago when the police authorities of Buenos Aires banned a showing of Chaplin's film *The Great Dictator* a Montevideo distributor who was showing the film promptly advertised in Buenos Aires papers offering a ticket to the show and a round trip by ferry at an inclusive price.

There was a little more than just business enterprise in this offer—a desire to do a little flaunting. Here was a chance for Montevideo to make a bold gesture and show the world its complete independence of Axis influence. The Uruguayans knew very well that the film was not banned in the big sister city because of any Argentine sympathy for the Axis cause but because with the large German and Italian populations the showing of such a provocative film would be certain to stir up more trouble than the police wanted to deal with. It was just a sensible police precaution which was adopted in Rio at the same time and for the same reason. The Montevideo police were not so cautious. There are Germans and Italians in Montevideo but the authorities felt quite capable of taking care of them if they started anything. Only a few months before that they had uncovered a reckless and stupid Nazi plot to make Uruguay a German colony and had thrown the Nazi ringleaders into jail.

Montevideo provides an interesting and illuminating example of trend of development of South American countries which is quite different from our own. The South American city is an enlargement of a baronial castle on a feudal estate. There the baron lives with his family and retainers; there the produce of the estate is stored and the money made from its operation spent. All that is asked of the estate is that it be productive. All effort is centered on attempts to enable the baron to enjoy a life of comfort and security with a show of opulence calculated to place him in the proper social perspective so far as his neighbors are concerned. And so in every South American country we find that while the countries are predominantly agricultural there is what appears to be an unnatural concentration of population and wealth in the big cities. For example one fifth of the people of Argentina live in Buenos Aires. An even greater proportion of Uruguayans live in Montevideo. The country has a population of about two million, the city with suburbs about three quarters of a million.

There is inevitable rivalry in city-building, each one striving for the widest thoroughfares, the most beautiful plazas, the finest statues and public buildings. With the two giants of Brazil and Argentina to the north and the south, little Uruguay was greatly handicapped in this rivalry but by no means defeated. Without doubt the finest and most impressive building in South America is the capital building at Montevideo toward which every guide will hurry you at the first opportunity. It cost no less than $12,000,000. That figure, however, gives an inadequate picture of the accomplishment it represents. Uruguay has one sixth of the population of the state of New York and the per capita wealth is probably one tenth.

Labor cost in Uruguay was but a fraction of what it would be in New York, and this was a building constructed with great expenditure of highly skilled labor. By any reasonable standard of comparison, the Empire State of New York could with less of a burden to the taxpayers spend about $600,000,000 on a state capital building.

One can imagine what an uproar would be caused if one expenditure of this size was ever proposed. Yet city after city in South America is constantly going ahead with improvements which mean expensive charges on the tax-payers. This is not an evidence of prosperity but of pride. We might say that we would spend less on beautiful buildings in the cities and make life in the country more comfortable and attractive. But a quibble like that would be quite beside the point. South Americans may live off the land but they are city dwellers. And in their attempts to beautify their cities they work much harder and spend relatively a great deal more money than we do.

The capital building is a good deal more than just a structure on which $12,000,000 has been spent. Unlike some other public buildings which I could mention it has the appearance of being worth all that it cost. With the lavish use of the beautiful Uruguayan marbles and granites, of genuine gold leaf on cornices, specially woven carpets—it is a building giving no hint that there is any poverty in the country. Rio spent a similar amount on an opera house which will seat only 1,700 people. The Argentine Hall of Congress at Buenos Aires may cost more by the time it is completed but Buenos Aires alone has a population greater than that of the republic of Uruguay.

After showing you the capital building the next sight on any list is the bronze statuary group "Spirit of the Pioneers." Of the thousands of statues to be seen in South

America this is one that the visitor will remember the longest. Other statues may be more famous or may be the work of greater artists but it would be difficult to find one more interesting. In the center of the group is a covered cart, something like our own covered wagons, with which the pioneer of South America pushed into the wilderness. Five oxen are hitched to the cart and two others are tethered to the back. A mounted horseman completes the group. The statue is not on a granite pedestal in a city park but on a grassy knoll in the suburbs giving the group a startling appearance of life and action. The cart has been halted because one of the wheels is hub deep in the mud and the lead oxen snatch this opportunity to browse on the grass—real grass. A clump of cactus in the foreground adds to the naturalness of the scene.

This is only one of many monuments in South America created in honor of the memory of their pioneers. Indeed it appeared to me that they have made much greater efforts than we have to acknowledge their debt of gratitude to the men and women who braved the hardships and dangers of frontier life. However, the erection of monuments is a South American custom. Every historical event of any great importance has been commemorated in this way and every national or provincial hero honored. There are probably more statues of Bolivar in South America than of both Lincoln and Washington in North America. In the big cities he is always shown on a horse. In smaller places where the budget is limited they leave out the horse.

Not only do they commemorate events and honor heroes with monuments but there are many which honor classes or occupations. On busy and crowded Rio Branco in Rio there is a statue in honor of the newsboys who are always so much in evidence on that noisy avenue. In Santiago I saw a statue in honor of the firemen of the city and I understand there are others. In a great many cities there are monuments dedicated to labor. There is a rather striking one in Buenos Aires showing a group of workmen pulling a huge block of stone and a rather unconvincing one in Lima for the oxen in the group appear to be doing all of the work.

The interesting circumstances about all of these statues in honor of labor is the fact that they were created before there was any general acceptance of the idea that labor deserved a better deal in the form of shorter hours and a living wage or decent housing. To some people that may look like a backward way of doing things but in the end it worked out very satisfactorily. The laborers may have been honored by statues first but now they also have shorter hours and better wages. Maybe the statues were intended to represent a hope for the future. That is the way the residents of one South American city look on a statue in one of their plazas. A decade or more ago a dictator who was ruling the country at the time promised the residents a water system of which they were greatly in need. There were many expressions of gratitude and some one went so far as to say that when the water system had been completed a monument should be erected to commemorate the event and honor the statesman who had thought of such a great public improvement. Full of pride and self-satisfaction, this suggestion struck a responsive chord in the heart of the dictator. So he built the monument at once and then as other matters came up for his pressing attention he forgot all about the water works. However he has been deposed and replaced by a legitimate government which is now installing the water system.

I suppose that if anything like this had happened in a New England town the citizenry would start by setting the record straight and justifying their own consciences. They would tear down the monument. But in this South American city they will probably leave it undisturbed. It is not an eyesore and gives them something to laugh about.

As a resident of Pelham with its many beautiful small homes I have often thought of suggesting that the village should at public expense maintain some kind of an eyesore just to give visitors a good standard of comparison. Montevideo has an eyesore of this kind, the Palacio Salvo, a building erected by an Italian resident. It has taken the form of the most conspicuous building in the city—a skyscraper of hideous aspect which is the first thing the visitor sees from an approaching steamer—the last to fade from view in a departing one. Photographs of the thing have been reproduced all over the world, giving South Americans generally and the residents of Montevideo in particular, a reputation for bad taste they do not deserve. The building made me think of a tall man suffering from several huge goiters and a middle-age spread. One marvels that a single architect could think of so many hideous and unnecessary things to do to a building. Beside it almost any kind of a structure would appear attractive. The many beautiful buildings do stand out in sharp contrast.

The older residential sections with solid rows of houses built flush with the street reminds one of the modest residential sections of Paris. In the suburbs and especially around the beaches there are many houses which would look at home in California though they have, as yet, escaped the soul-cramping bungalow type. Some of the finest houses are the summer homes of wealthy residents of Buenos Aires. In fact if a home has the quality known as "ostentatious" it is generally taken for granted that it belongs to an Argentine. The architects of Montevideo are not content to remain anonymous. When one of them designs a structure he is proud of, whether it be a big office building or a modest suburban home, he puts his name on it so that it can be seen and read from a passing taxi. This must be of great advantage to the man who is planning to build a home. Without putting himself under obligation to anyone he can have a look at all the houses in the place and pick the architect he thinks is best qualified to build the kind of a home he wants.

In spite of its metropolitan air Montevideo is a farm town. Above the odor of gasoline from motorcar fumes one gets the smell of horses and of sweaty men. There are horse-drawn carts on the streets and the sparrows have a more contented and prosperous appearance than in São Paulo. Because they are much more vocal one is accustomed to think of Argentina as being the one great livestock country of the South. Actually the industry is of relatively greater importance in Uruguay. If evenly divided every resident of Argentina would have three cows and four sheep; Uruguay four cows and eight sheep, Brazil one cow. Mutton is the food of the country. On the sheep ranches it is customary for the landlords to supply the workmen with food and a laborer and his family will eat from seventy to one hundred sheep a year.

In Uruguay as well as in all other agricultural sections farm machinery made in the United States will always have the advantage over competitive products. Farming conditions in the two Americas are much the same. Improvements made for the benefit of our farmers will be equally valuable to the farmers of Uruguay, Brazil, Argentina or any other country. The Germans have tried to compete in those lines but could only do so by making the machines with which they were unfamiliar and which were useless at home. They are quick to copy our improvements but will always be one jump behind us.

Montevideo is the Reno of the South, Uruguay the one country where divorces are easily granted. In fact it is, so far as I know the only South American country where divorces are granted at all as it is the only one in which the Catholic church has not had a strong influence in shaping social legislation. Certainly divorces are impossible in Argentina and it is from there that many of the divorce suits which are tried in Montevideo are initiated. Montevideo law firms use regular advertising space in the Buenos Aires papers to tell about how easy it is to get a divorce in Uruguay and offering their services to anyone who wants to get rid of the ball and chain. It is all very cheap and very easy and a client of either sex has the roulette wheels and the bathing beaches to help pass the time while waiting to establish a legal residence. There is just one catch in it: Argentina and the other South American countries do not recognize Montevideo divorce.

It would be natural to expect gaiety and a lightness of heart in a city with a whimsical name like "I See a Mountain." But cities rarely live up to their names. St. Paul is certainly no more pious or churchgoing than its rival city of Minneapolis. What Cheer is no more cheerful than any other town in Iowa. Cicero was the home of Al Capone and his gang. Zephyr was the name of a town in Texas until it was blown completely off the map by a cyclone.

But just as I was leaving Montevideo I found a bit of evidence that the local people retain the tradition of playful names. On the water front where the many bars are now deserted because of the lack of shipping there was a show window completely filled with bottles of cheap red wine which is commonly known as dago red. It was very appropriately labeled *El Pobre Marino*, "the poor sailor."

## CHAPTER X

## "We Are Superior"

BUSINESS men who have had long and varied experience in a number of South American countries generally agree that the Argentines are the ones they know least intimately, the ones with whom it is the most difficult to establish informal and cordial personal relations. While the Chilean, the Peruvian or the Brazilian will respond generously to any friendly advances, the Argentine is inclined to maintain a reserve and be unresponsive—something after the manner of the shy and diffident Englishman or the man of any nationality who wants to be sure that he associates only with the best people. There is nothing casual about the social contacts of the Argentine. His clubs are exclusive and membership is not easily secured.

A businessman whose home was in the Middle West told me he had lived in Buenos Aires for years before he felt that he had any real friends among the Argentine businessmen with whom he was in almost daily contact. They never met except in offices, never fell into the friendly habit of calling each other by their first names. The Middle Westerner worried about it. There wasn't any difficulty about language for he spoke Spanish fluently, as do most Yankees who do business in Argentina. But after a period of four or five years the reserve of some of the Argentines dissolved and eventually he was delighted to find that he had surrounded himself by a little group of friends with whom he could exchange pleasantries and confidences and who would invite him to their homes for dinner. After this had been going on for some time one of these men said to him:

"I wish you would tell me why we Argentines are so unpopular in South America. The Chileans don't like us. The Peruvians don't like us. The Brazilians don't like us. Of course they don't like each other any too well but they get along with each other a great deal better than they do with us. We are unpopular everywhere and I just can't understand why it is."

"Well," said the North American, "if you want me to be frank about it, I will be and since you have asked for my opinion you can't take offense at it. I think it is because of the air of superiority all of you appear to have. From the way you treat the Brazilians, Chileans, and Peruvians and almost everyone with whom you come in contact they get the impression that you think you are better than they are and people always resent that."

The Argentine listened attentively, studied a moment and then gave what must be considered the final answer to his own question.

"But," he said, "we are superior."

That is what a Bengali might say about his people in

comparison with the other people of India—what a New Englander might think but be too polite to say.

I have no doubt but that this incident did occur and that it does not present the self-appraisement of the Argentine with a great deal of exaggeration. While this smug assumption of superiority is naturally irritating to others it is only fair to acknowledge that the Argentine has a good deal of justification for it. Of all the people of South America he has the most reason to be satisfied with the achievements of his ancestors and to be complacent about the future. He cannot recount the history of his country without a glow of pride at the distance his people have traveled to reach their present goal. He would be unlike other people if he did not regard as national achievements many things that were due to fate and fortune.

Among the Spanish-American colonists south of the equator those who settled around the estuary of the Plate started near the bottom of the heap. Buenos Aires the first home of the Argentines was not founded, like Lima, with the prestige of royal approval but was for generations a neglected outpost of the Spanish empire. Its establishment as a small settlement did not come until 1581 and after more than half a century of discouraging struggle by a number of conquistadors who failed in their attempts to subdue the Indians. They did not, like their contemporaries Pizarro and Cortez find on this flat costal plain any Aztec or Inca empires of high civilization and great riches which could easily be overthrown. The hinterland which now pastures millions of head of cattle was sparsely populated by nomadic Indians who grew no crops and lived off the flesh of wild animals and birds. Their hatred of the foreign intruders was as fierce as that which the Apaches directed against our own encroaching settlers.

Many of the early Spaniards were killed and in spite of their superiority in arms and knowledge of organized warfare at least one company of conquistadores was massacred.

Long before the place had been freed of danger from Indians a few Spanish settlers left the mining regions of Peru and Bolivia and began to settle around the present city of Buenos Aires. It was not unlike our own migration from New England to the West, though almost three centuries earlier. These migrants were not swashbuckling adventurers in search of easy wealth. They knew that there was no gold or silver to be found at the end of the journey and that with each mile that they traveled they were making more difficult any return to their old homes. But they did know that the land was fertile beyond anything they had ever dreamed of in Europe. A few horses and cattle which had escaped from the Spanish soldiers or been stolen by the Indians had flourished and multiplied on the always green pampas and now they appeared to be countless. There was fine meat to be had at the expense of a bullet; horses to be lassoed and tamed; and crops could be grown with a minimum effort. After the rainless and soilless Andes where gold and silver could be found but a man would die of hunger and thirst, this was the promised land. They came here to make their homes. Spanish wives came with them and in this small settlement there was very little mixing of white and Indian blood.

These pioneers were from the beginning treated harshly by their government, and were alternately exploited and neglected. The settlement of Spaniards was so poor and despised that the church ignored it and the priests remained near the rich mines of the Andes. Spanish colonies were looked on as the personal property of the sovereign and their first and most important function was to produce quantities of gold and silver for one fifth of all produce went to the crown. In order to make sure that there were no leakages all trade was very strictly controlled. Settlers in places like Buenos Aires were not allowed to sell their produce or buy their European supplies in the open market—only in the distant port of Panama. Everything had to be transported overland across the Andes to Peru and then up the west coast and across the Isthmus to the only port where they were allowed to trade. Supplies had to be bought in the same way. A round trip from Buenos Aires to Spain by this difficult route required two years. Settlers in Buenos Aires were forbidden to sell their hides or tallow to the Dutch and British trading ships which occasionally made calls at the port in defiance of Spanish regulations. The law also denied them the privilege of buying European goods they needed from these enterprising sea traders although they were offered at a fifth to a tenth of the prices they would have had to pay for supplies brought from Panama. Everyone in Buenos Aires therefore became a smuggler for it was only by smuggling that they could exist.

As he makes this historical review the Argentine cannot overlook the striking manner in which the social as well as the economic position of his country has been changed. As humble farmers and cattle raisers the original pioneers were far below the official class at Lima. They were in fact little more than a colony of squatters despised by the elder and wealthier communities of Spanish America. They were not considered important enough to be governed directly by the authorities at Lima and could deal only with minor officials in what is now Bolivia. The little colony of a few hundred constituting the nucleus from which the great Argentine nation of the present has grown started at the bottom.

In their present social position they are not only at the top but occupy a position that is unique. The present-day Argentine considers himself as being the only true representative of the Latin-American racial group—the only survivor of the original Spanish settlers. The Argentines who date from colonial times are pure creoles.[1] In all the other countries there are groups of Indians and mestizos and in some mixtures of negro and oriental blood. The citizens of pure white blood constitute at best only a small minority. With unimportant exceptions Argentines are all of white blood.

Maintenance of the purity of his racial strain is not the only justification for Argentine self-esteem. From the poorest of the colonies it has become the richest and most powerful of the Spanish American countries. This has come about rapidly and within the memory of some men who are now living. Less than sixty years ago Argentina and Chile had the same population but now the Argentines outnumber the Chileans by just a little less than three to one. A part of this increase has come about through the migration of Chileans themselves, a larger part through the influx of millions of Spaniards and Italians. Whether they came from Chile, Spain or Italy they found Argentina a better place and the second generation are true sons of Argentina. It is no wonder that the Argentines get a bit heady when they contemplate the progress they have made and the great future which undoubtedly lies before them. They think thoughts as satisfactory as those with which the Pharisee fed his own self-esteem.

[1] It should not be necessary to explain that the use of the word creole does not in any way imply any mixture of blood. A creole is anyone of Spanish or French blood born in either of the Americas.

Buenos Aires, one of the largest, wealthiest and most beautiful cities in the world, is a symbol of Argentine accomplishment. It is not on a natural harbor and occupies its present location principally because of the will of the Argentines to build a city there. The port is kept open only by constant dredging far out to sea. If for any reason the dredging stopped the city would soon be isolated to all sea-borne traffic. Even with the dredgers always at work, ship's keels often scrape the mud and are shoved into the harbor by powerful tugs. Next to New York it is the biggest port in America and yet as nature endowed it, it is one of the poorest. Nor did nature contribute anything to the beauty of the city. There wasn't even a little hill which a lookout could see—just a flat expanse of muddy shore. Rio would be beautiful even if the Carioca range of mountains looked down on nothing but a palmthatched village or the beach. The beauties of Buenos Aires are all man-made. I do not want to say too much about the absence of mountains and scenic beauty around Buenos Aires for I feel that if the local residents ever got real mad about it they would go out and build a few mountains just as they have built a big beautiful city in a place where there was no reason a city should exist.

In the city itself there are no buildings with the antiquity of those to be found in other cities. At a time when there were century-old cathedrals, palaces and universities in Lima, Santiago, Quito and Bogotá, Buenos Aires was nothing more than a sprawling village of less than 300 inhabitants. It did not begin to grow until the year of our independence for in 1776 a viceroy was sent to govern the place, the trade restrictions which had been in force for almost two centuries were removed and a man could be a merchant without at the same time being a smuggler. By the time the Argentine Declaration of Independence had been adopted, July 16, 1816, the city had a population of about 50,000. From that time it began to outstrip the other South American capitals.

These Argentine pioneers who turned their backs on the mineral wealth of the Andes for the more solid but less alluring wealth of the pampas were more farsighted than they realized. They suffered poverty and hardships and few of them lived to know anything else, but the foundations which they laid have supported a structure of constantly increasing wealth and prosperity. With every decade since their migration the relative importance of products of the plantation has increased while that of mining has decreased. That is true of all of the countries except Chile. Colombia is now leading the continent in the production of gold and yet her export of bananas amounts to three times as much as her production of gold. Many large and fine diamonds are found in Brazil—about one million dollars' worth are exported every year. But that is one half of one per cent of the value of her annual coffee exportations. Exhaustion of the easily worked gold and silver mines did not put an end to the search for bonanzas in different countries. Money was made in sugar and then the sugar mills were deserted for cocoa. Then cocoa was deserted for rubber until with reckless exploitation the rubber trees were exhausted. A great deal of South American enterprise reminds one of the old time gold seekers who would abandon a paying streak when he heard of another which he thought was better. The Argentine alone has remained aloof from all this opportunism and his country is the wealthiest of them all.

That wealth has been spent on the city of Buenos Aires —on the creation of plazas, broad boulevards, statues, parks and fine public buildings. Skyscrapers are springing up now—as modern as any in the world. From an apartment on the twenty-seventh floor of one of them I got a bird's-eye view of the city and across the estuary saw the shores of Uruguay. The famous *subterraneos* have proven that even a subway can be artistic. The entrances and waiting platforms are so beautifully decorated with tile mosaics that they would provide suitable foyers for movie palaces. After years of familiarity with New York subways those of Buenos Aires appear theatrically unreal. After you are seated on a train it would not surprise you for an orchestra to strike up and show girls singing greetings at each station. They might even put on a performance in the train itself for while they are not entirely noiseless they are not so deafeningly noisy as the New York subways.

Buenos Aires is almost as hustling a place as the Brazilian city of São Paulo. It is to Rio what Chicago is to New Orleans. There are not so many men as in Rio sitting at the sidewalk cafés during business hours. The bootblacks who are seen everywhere do their work quicker. You cannot walk a block without someone trying to sell you something—a spring which will hold a coat collar in shape or a special knife for peeling potatoes. The scene is as lively and noisy as a country fair. Tramcars, taxis and the little motor busses, which are called *colectivos*, jam the streets. To add to the confusion the little *colectivos*, which dart about the city like a lot of excited water beetles, seldom come to a complete stop when letting a passenger off. Local people seem to be taking pride in being able to hop off or get on while the bus is still going. There are no taxi stands and these vehicles constantly cruise the streets looking for fares. In addition to the streets which run in checkerboard fashion there are newly built diagonal streets giving the pedestrian six corners instead of four to watch. There isn't a traffic light in the city. They were installed some years ago but no one paid any attention to them so they were just abandoned. It was not until I had been there for a week that I finally figured out a fairly safe method of walking from the City Hotel to the American Club.

The contrast between city and country is striking in all parts of the Southern continent but more so in Buenos Aires than in any other. In a half hour drive from the center of metropolitan Buenos Aires one is out in the monotonously flat grass country—scenery which only a cow could love. It is like driving from the central part of Manhattan over any northern route and finding in Westchester County pastures and wire fences and tumbleweed exactly as in Montana or Western Texas. Only in the spacious and well-kept parks can the people of this great city come into contact with anything remotely resembling pleasant life in the country. But of course there is no pleasant country life in any South American country.

Considering the very small number of Britons, about 50,000, who made their homes in Argentina, they have had an important and widespread influence on the life of the people. They were outnumbered by the Germans almost two to one but without making any attempt to do so they have gone much farther than the Germans in creating an English social atmosphere—as they have all over the world where they settled in any number. The Germans established breweries and a few restaurants and some important business houses and that is all the casual observer can see of their contribution to the life of Buenos Aires where most of them live. The influence of the British is seen everywhere and runs much deeper than surface observations would indicate. The Argentines have gone in wholeheartedly for all British sports; polo, football, golf. As in all other places where there is a settlement of three or four British families who are on speaking terms with each other they organized a country club. The Hurlingham, about twenty miles from the center of Buenos Aires, looks like an English estate which has been set down like a square of turf in strange surroundings. Here the British played all the British sports and without either plan or purpose changed the life of a nation.

Argentines of the better class adopted British sports so enthusiastically that their life took on a British tinge. The young man of good family who could not play polo, golf or football was looked on as a person who is somewhat odd, just as in the British Isles. They have gone in for outdoor sports so thoroughly that on a fair Sunday afternoon it appears that half the population of Buenos Aires is out-of-doors either playing games or watching them being played. There are football clubs in all the provincial towns as there are also in Brazil. All the sports draw big crowds. There is no baseball played here or in any other South American country, but the Argentine small boy follows polo with the fervor of the youthful baseball fan at home. One of them who sat next to me in the stands at Hurlingham shouted his advice to the players all the time a game was in progress.

This wholesale adoption of British sports by the Argentines has set the pattern for the social life of the country and especially of Buenos Aires. The strength of this influence is nowhere better illustrated than in the German community itself. In order to make themselves agreeable to their Argentine hosts, and be accepted socially, the Germans have had to simulate the British sportsman and learn to play polo and golf and football. They have done this with typical German thoroughness, but without what might be called complete success. Somehow a German in jodhpurs and a riding crop looks as if he were dressed for a fancy dress party as does a Japanese wearing plus fours and carrying a golf club.

Whether or not it was British influence or the power of British example I do not know but certainly the two great morning papers of Buenos Aires, *La Prensa* and *La Nacion*, are more like the London *Times* than like any other paper with which I am familiar. It would probably be a little more accurate to say that they are more like the ideal toward which the London *Times* has striven but has never attained. Without a slogan to emblazon its righteous principles before the world *La Prensa* makes a calm and dispassionate approval of the news it considers fit to print and leaves out all mention of many events which would be recorded in any other newspaper. Divorces are ignored, as are suicides. When a very prominent official killed himself the most *La Prensa* would do was to say that he "died suddenly." Family scandals as revealed in divorce suits tried outside of Argentina are, so far as *La Prensa* is concerned, family matters and there is no reason why the public should pry into them. In the make-up and the handling of news both papers are much more conservative than any newspaper in the United States has ever been. The lamented Boston *Transcript* was, by comparison, positively sensational.

Neither *La Nacion* nor *La Prensa* indulges in any typographical tricks or uses sensational headlines. The news is carefully and dispassionately presented for those who care to read it and it is evident that a great many people do. The Boston *Transcript*, after following a similar policy for more than a hundred years, was finally compelled to suspend because of lack of public support. The London *Times* would have been closed by creditors decades ago had it not been for the fact that the owners of the paper have been able and willing to meet the deficit from operations. Several generations of Englishmen have boasted about their famous paper but they never gave it enough support to make it a profitable publishing enterprise. In sharp contrast, the two great newspapers of Buenos Aires have large circulations, have piled up colossal fortunes for their owners and today constitute two of the most valuable newspaper properties in existence. It is illuminating to reflect that while Boston could not support a single paper of this character, Buenos Aires gives most liberal support to two.

The Argentines know that a great future lies ahead of their country. It is easy for a patriot to visualize the time when Argentina will no longer be just the wealthiest of the Latin-American states but will be a world power. With the exception of Brazil she has outdistanced all the neighboring countries in point of population. There may be temporary setbacks such as those caused by the present war in Europe but a country possessing such great agricultural wealth must go ahead. So far this wealth has been exploited principally by the inefficient methods of big-scale stock breeding. The land is held by only a few people. There has been very little distribution of national lands as in the United States but huge tracts have at various times been given to army officials. The wealthy cattle barons fight the incursions of farmers, just as the cattlemen of Texas and the Western States fought the settlers a few generations ago. But it is a losing fight. Slowly but steadily the big landholdings are being broken up into smaller and more efficient units. It has been estimated that if the country were divided into small farms as in our Middle West, it could easily support a population of 100 million people.

These natural ambitions of Argentina provide the background for our troublesome relations with that country, and the stupidity and selfishness of a group of Western senators has sabotaged the work of the State Department. Argentines look on themselves as the leaders of South America and on Buenos Aires as its political as well as cultural capital. By reason of the differences in language Portuguese-speaking Brazil must always remain in a certain isolation—a part of South America but separated. This leaves Argentina as the natural leader. But we stand in the way. To put the matter bluntly there is envy and jealousy of our power and wealth and resentment at any move toward leadership that we may make. There are few legislative sessions when some hotheaded patriot does not rise from his seat to demand why Argentina doesn't courageously assume the leadership in Latin-American affairs instead of playing the part of tail wagger to the big Yankee dog. At one conference after another it has been Argentina that has led the opposition or alone has held out against proposals advanced by the United States. The attitude, which has become traditional, has the appearance of being a fixed policy of statecraft.

At the moment the meat controversy bars the approach to any better understanding with Argentina. This question has been surrounded by so much politics and propaganda that I had to spend several days of investigation before I got at the truth of the matter. Argentine meat and especially beef is produced so cheaply that if there were a free market it is more than probable that our own livestock industry would be wiped out completely. Even the present high import duty of sixteen cents per pound would provide little protection. But all Argentine fresh meat is barred from shipment to the United States because of the indisputable fact that the Argentine herds suffer from *aftosa*[2] This malady, which is better known as the hoof and mouth disease, is a scourge affecting cattle that is as mysterious as infantile paralysis. By the expenditure of a great deal of money and the slaughter of a great many herds we managed to stamp out the disease. It is prevalent in almost all other parts of the world. Our Department of Agriculture by the enforcement of sanitary regulations prevented the recurrence of the disease by prohibiting the importation of meat from affected areas. This included Argentina and fifty other countries.

The protection of our herds should have been left in the hands of the Department of Agriculture. But when the Smoot-Hawley tariff bill came up for consideration Western Senators managed to get written into the measure a clause prohibiting the importation of frozen meat from any country where herds suffered from *aftosa*. This was an injustice to Argentina for the cattle and sheep of Patagonia are free of the disease. If the problem of protection had been left where it belonged—in the sanitary regulations of the Department of Agriculture—imports from this section of Argentina could have been allowed. They would not have been large enough to work any hardship on our own livestock growers and there would have been no cause for controversy. The Argentines protested at the unfairness of enforcing a quarantine against the entire country because one part of it was affected.

One of the early tasks undertaken by Secretary of State Hull was to rectify this manifest injustice. This was done by negotiating a pact with Argentina which would allow the importation of meat from Patagonia under the control

[2] Contrary to popular belief *aftosa* does not affect the quality or the wholesomeness of the meat.

of the Department of Agriculture. Argentines were jubilant over the negotiation of the pact. It would not have allowed the shipment of any vast quantities of the frozen meat to us but would have removed what they looked on as an unjust stigma applied to meat—which is their most important product. The administration, which was promoting the good neighbor policy, was also jubilant because it removed the only legitimate cause for friction.

But neither side was jubilant very long. The same selfish interests that had managed to get the original quarantine provision written into the tariff bill managed to sabotage the work of Secretary of State Hull. The pact negotiated with Argentina was, as a matter of routine, referred to the Senate Foreign Relations Committee. There it has been accumulating dust for years while Argentina accumulates a growing distrust.

CHAPTER XI

## *Chile, Long and Lean*

THERE was a longer stop than usual at the Panagra airport of Mendoza. While the flight to Santiago is a short one it is one of the most difficult in aviation. Mendoza on the western edge of the Argentine cattle country lies at an altitude of a little more than 2000 feet and Santiago, the capital of Chile, is a little lower. But between them on the route which all travel must follow is the high Andean range often swept by the same terrific winds that a few hundred miles farther south make the navigation of the Straits of Magellan so difficult. The Andes have been crossed on foot, on horseback, by train and now by plane. The journey on foot required months, on horseback weeks, by train days and by plane hours. The trip has always been difficult.

As seen from the air, a few irrigation ditches gave the arid upland plain of Mendoza stripes and spots of green but in a few moments all that was left behind us. The bleak ranges of the Andes were all about us and before us, the stark scene sharply illuminated by bright sunlight. Only a few hours ago we had left the lively streets of Buenos Aires but now it was as if we were in another world, had closed the door to the more familiar world behind us. Could this lifeless place be a part of the same spinning globe in which people lived? There was nothing to recall any familiar scene, no tree or patch of grass or friendly wisp of smoke to indicate that somewhere below us was human life. We flew over high mountains only to see ahead of us still higher ranges of mountains which appeared cold and forbidding even in the warm sunlight. It looked as the world must have looked before the work of creation was completed and God had planted trees and grass and flowers and made it a place in which men could live and love and work and kill each other in needless wars.

As it was a clear and windless day we flew through a pass, climbing higher and higher, but not so high by several thousand feet as would have been necessary if fog or clouds would have forced us to go over the range. There were mountains on each side of us and other mountains below us. I knew it wouldn't happen but it did look as if the wing tips might brush against the rocky sides. At every seat there was an oxygen tube and the Argentine steward showed everyone how to use it. My seatmate slumped in a faint and the steward revived him with oxygen and he got very sick.

A high rocky wall ahead appeared to shut us in a rocky canyon with walls so high it would be impossible to climb them. Then we veered to one side and saw a clear passage ahead and the giant statue Christ of the Andes below us on the left—a symbol as well as a landmark for we were back in the world again. In a few minutes we were losing altitude rapidly and then the beautiful vale of Chile came into view and the city of Santiago which lies in the early morning shade of the Andes. We had left the Argentine capital after breakfast and were in the capital of Chile in time for tea or cocktails.

It is difficult to imagine a city any more beautiful than Rio de Janeiro or one with a grander setting than Santiago with its background of the Andes with their snow-tipped summits. I suppose that some day a Hollywood producer will present a composite picture of South American cities that will excel any dreams of fairyland. By means of trick photography he could set the hills and beaches of Rio de Janeiro against the grandeur of the Andes as seen from Santiago. For close-up shots he could show the decorated pavements of Rio de Janeiro and the beautiful subways of Buenos Aires. The life and color of street scenes could be taken from any of these cities and all would be interesting and all would be different.

Rio and Buenos Aires give the impression of being always tidied up for visitors. Like the well-dressed women who parade in the shopping districts and the freshly barbered men who ogle them, they are just a little too well groomed. Santiago is not. It is a beautiful city with generous plazas, broad avenues, well-laid-out parks, and some very fine buildings. But older parts of the city have not been ruthlessly erased and rebuilt at great expense just because some visitor might make a dirty crack about them. There is little pretense of a prosperity which does not exist. It looks like a city that has been lived in and is still being lived in with vibrant intensity.

With shop signs projecting into the street, and with the narrow sidewalks of the older sections packed with people it somehow reminded me of the casual construction of a Chinese city in which no one bothers about the purely ornamental aspects of life. Santiago would not form a suitable setting for its residents if this were not true. One does not see here dapper little men with handkerchiefs peeping from coat pockets; the odors of bay rum and shaving soap are not so noticeable as they were in other cities. Chileans are poor and they make no attempt to conceal the fact. In Brazil or Argentina a clean shirt or even a new shirt may conceivably cover an empty belly but if a Chilean has on a clean shirt it is a moral certainty that he bought food and very probably drink before he spent any money on laundry work. That, again, reminds me of China.

Chile is a long, lean, string bean of a country with residents who are certainly not fat. The easy exploitation of natural riches played out here earlier than elsewhere and as a result the Chileans have gone through an evolutionary period which has not yet begun in other neighboring countries. For a time the population of Chile actually stood still and if there is any great increase in the future it will be supported by the development of industries and factories. There is no more vacant land to be put under cultivation and there never was very much, for this long strip of a country is like a slice of very lean bacon in which only small patches of fertile land are indicated by the fat.

The size of the estates held in feudal fashion by the landlords of Chile gives a false impression of wealth. The individual family may own several thousand acres. But this will not consist of fertile pasture land as in Argentina or of plantations of coffee trees as in Brazil. There will usually be a few hundred acres of bottom land which can be cultivated by means of irrigation and the remainder will be hillsides providing a sparse pasture. Chile has never been able to produce enough beef to supply its own demands, and imports meat from Argentina. It has been estimated that by intensive cultivation and extension of the irrigation systems Chile could supply food for a maximum of 6 million people. By much easier methods Argentina could feed a population more than a dozen times that number. The Chileans who reflect on this cannot be unconscious of the fact that if Argentina had had a preponderance of population like that of a few generations ago when there was fighting over boundary disputes, the map of the continent would be very different from what it is. They wonder if the greater Argentina of the future will be content with her own boundaries when she will have the strength to enlarge them so easily.

Chileans talked to me about the industrial development of their country as offering the only escape from stagnation but all were confident of the future. It would not be so easy to build factories as to grow coffee or cattle but they have already proven that they can do it. American and British businessmen who have lived long in the country were enthusiastic about the capabilities of the Chilean workman. Just why it should be true I will leave others to puzzle out but it appears that the Chilean has a sense of mechanics and a manual deftness not to be found among his neighbors. There is water power in abundance, raw materials, low living costs, cheap and efficient labor—all of which adds up to high hopes for the future of Chile as an industrial nation.

On the surface it might appear that the backwardness of South Americans about the establishment of factories was due entirely to their own lack of initiative plus certain difficulties about securing the necessary capital but that was not the only reason. In the past few decades there has been a great development of small manufacturing enterprises in all parts of the world. This is partly due to the expiration of patent rights which while in existence enabled individual companies to monopolize certain manufacturing processes or gave the manufacturers of certain countries a decided advantage over others. We were among the first to benefit by these new opportunities and have made the most of them. We now produce more enameled cast-iron bathtubs than all the rest of the world but in 1884 no American manufacturer knew how to make them. The few that we had were imported from Germany or Scotland.

With the expiration of basic patent rights vast new fields were opened up to the manufacturers of machinery who now made and placed on sale all kinds of appliances that would enable the man with small capital to go into manufacturing of one kind or another. The advertising pages of trade magazines are full of announcements of opportunities of this kind. At the same time there was a simplification of manufacturing processes and more general knowledge about them. It is in many ways fortunate for South Americans that their industrial development was retarded as it has enabled them to draw on the experience of others and avoid their mistakes.

The power of the feudalistic landlords was threatened earlier and more successfully in Chile than elsewhere. There are a few of the big landowners left but their struggles to maintain their old dominant positions now amount to little more than futile gestures. Chilean women, the most charming on the continent, have been emancipated from the convent-like seclusion in which they are held in the other nine countries. They take part in public affairs, agitate for social reforms, hold public office, work in shops or go into business for themselves. The young women are proposed to by men who fall in love with them and accept the men of their own choice with no more parental interference than in the United States. In the public parks boys and girls may be seen together without a chaperon in sight and more than that—they neck and they spoon and sometimes they kiss right out in public. You may be sure that there are no such scandalous goings on as this in strait-laced Buenos Aires, from feminine participation in public affairs to feminine participation in public kissing. If a Buenos Aires policeman ever saw anything like this, there would be some arrests made unless he died of the shock.

The rights of labor were first recognized in Chile and here the first labor organizations were formed, several generations before the dominant ruling classes in any other part of the continent had indicated any consciousness that labor existed for any other purpose than to be exploited by the employer. These early labor organizations did not concern themselves entirely with the matter of wages and hours and other concessions from employers but also tried to promote temperance among their members in which they do not appear to have met with any great success.

The social legislation of Chile is more comprehensive than that of most other countries. It embraces not only minimum wage and maximum hours of labor but many other things including medical care, housing and hospital care. Some say that a great impetus to this movement, which had already been started, was provided by the operation of the mammoth copper and nitrate companies in which about $750,000,000, mostly money from the United States, has been invested. The management of these companies provided their thousands of workmen with good houses in sanitary surroundings and hospital and medical care. All this was provided without legal compulsion and in conformity with a practice followed by most American companies operating in countries where there are low standards of living. The social reformers of Chile were quick to point out to the legislators that if big foreign corporations could afford to be so considerate of the health and well-being of their employees there was no reason why more selfish or less enlightened concerns should not be compelled by law to do the same thing.

How far the example of the American companies influenced the legislation I do not know but the code which was adopted is a comprehensive one. Among other things it provides that factories coming within certain classifications shall provide a place where the babies of women employees will be cared for during the hours that the mothers are at work. The law provides that a cot be provided for every sixty women employed whether they are married or not. One of the most interesting sights I saw in the continent was the light and airy nursery on the top floor of a cigarette factory in Valparaiso where some sixty or seventy youngsters were cared for under the personal direction of the best child's doctor in Chile. As has happened elsewhere as a result of social reforms of this kind being enacted into law, this tobacco company is doing much more than the law requires. The British manager of the company was proud of the modern machinery and the cleanliness of the factory but we hurried through some of this in order to get up to the nursery and see the babies. The code requires only that they be cared for until they are one year old but many were past that age because the manager knew they would be better cared for there than at home and because he just didn't want to miss an opportunity to go up to the nursery and have a look at them every day.

The provision that single as well as married women be counted in making provision for the babies is a very sensible one. According to statistics for the year 1935 out of 1000 children born in Chile 360 were of illegitimate parentage. Although the percentage varies in each country it will be found that in all of them there is a surprisingly large number of illegitimate children in all of the ten republics. But, as a Chilean friend pointed out to me, no one should take statistics too seriously. In order to illustrate his contention he said that there are more deaths per capita in hospitals than in the most dangerous of factories.

Certainly the figures showing the number of illegitimate children born in South America do not prove the existence of the moral laxity they may appear to indicate. In a great many, if not in practically all cases, they mean only that the parents have just neglected to go through the troublesome legal formality of getting married. In the rural districts it may be very difficult to get in touch with officials and priests. In the cities a marriage is at best a very expensive affair involving a fiesta with food and drink as well as fees to priests and officials. With many of the poorer people even the cost of new clothing would be an excessive financial burden. And so couples who have decided to live together just slip into the marital relation quietly with no fuss or bother and no one thinks anything about it. Throughout South America it costs a great deal to get married and a great deal to die if one is to be buried in decent fashion. But birth is always cheap.

It is difficult for people who have been brought up under more rigorous conventions to accept this condition as tolerantly. A few years ago the newly arrived New England manager of a big copper mine discovered to his shocked surprise that among his employees there were about a thousand parents who had never been married. The crop of illegitimate children was large and was increasing every year. He talked the matter over with his wife and they decided that something had to be done about it.

The only proper and decent thing to do was to get them married as expeditiously as possible. With that end in view the New Englander arranged to take care of all of the legal formalities such as securing licenses and the registration of the marriages and then made a deal with the local parish priest for a mass ceremony at wholesale rates. The couples who had been more or less unconsciously living in sin all these years were not particularly grateful for the blessing of respectability that was going to be bestowed on them but since the boss desired it they agreed. There was of course to be a fiesta.

After the arrangements had been practically completed and the couples had had time to think of all the social complications their marriages would involve a new difficulty arose. A delegation representing the workers informed the boss that while they were willing to fall in line with his new ideas and get married, it didn't seem right that they should be legally married when their papas and mamas were not. Arrangements were made to marry this generation when another one was heard from for the grandfathers and grandmothers hadn't been married either. And so, after a few weeks of delay, three generations were married all at the same time while a fourth generation watched the ceremony.

In the production of native humor there are barren spots in South America and spots of great fertility. The Brazilian has a gay wit, the common man of Chile a salty humor, the Peruvian a fine appreciation of the ridiculous. Humor does not thrive in the rich soil of Argentina. This is in spite of the fact that Molinas Campos is an Argentine and an artistic genius worthy to be compared to Walt Disney. Since humor is outside the pale of pure culture Colombians will have little to do with it except in a clandestine or shamefaced way.

The point of view of the Chilean common man is much like that of the Chinese. Poverty has made him a philosopher and he is more inclined to laugh at his superiors than to revile them and join the Communist party. There are Communists in Chile as there are representatives of almost every conceivable school of political thought. But the man with a sense of humor must be an individualist whose thoughts cannot be regimented and made to fit into a political machine.

An American friend told me about a conversation he overheard between a couple of Chilean workmen who had stopped on a railway siding to have a look at a huge electric transformer which filled most of the space on a flat car. They walked all around the car several times examining it from every angle and finally one of them said:

"I wonder what that funny-looking thing can be?"

"I'm not sure," said the other. "But it might be a North American canary cage. These Yankees always make things as complicated as possible."

The career of a rising young Chilean politician was cut short by the wisecrack of another workman. He and his companion after a hearty meal of beans and a glass of wine sat down in the sun on the pedestal of a statue in a plaza and promptly went to sleep. In the meantime a crowd gathered about them for the spot where they were enjoying their siesta had been chosen as the meeting place for a political rally. When the candidate's speech began one of the sleepers woke but the other slept on, snoring comfortably. In the midst of what the orator had intended to be an impressive pause the sleeper outdid himself with a snore that echoed through the plaza and he jumped up with a start. The orator suspected a trick by a political opponent.

"Who is this man," he cried, "who brays like a donkey?"

"Come on," said the snorer to his companion. "Let's get out of here. That fool doesn't recognize the sound of his own voice."

That was the end of the speech and the end of the politician's career. Every time he tried to make a speech after that someone affected a snore which was the signal for the party to break up.

CHAPTER XII

## The People Pizarro Conquered

IF WE should ever put on a publicity campaign to attract tourists from Lima and other coastal cities of Peru we can go rather light about sunshine and flowers because, year in and year out, they have a lot more sunshine than they can use and they wouldn't get very excited about our inferior flowers. But we should give great emphasis to the fact that the visitor will not be in the United States very long before enjoying a good rain. An experience like that would give the residents of Lima something to write home about because it is something they have never seen. And if you have never seen a heavy rain it certainly should be a very impressive spectacle. Added to that we should try to get the visitor to stay long enough to see a good snow storm. We could be certain that after he had seen both of these strange and unusual manifestations of nature he would have something to talk about all the rest of his life.

The streets of Lima have a dry and dusty odor and for the very good reason that they have not been moistened by a heavy rainfall within the memory of many fathers and mothers. In fact just a light shower is such an admittedly rare occurrence and is spoken of with such reluctance by local residents that I sometimes doubt if there is ever any rain at all. It is one city where the shops do not stock either umbrellas or raincoats and the only way one can get his feet wet is by sticking them in a bathtub or under a water tap. The only umbrella ever seen in Lima, so far as old residents remember, was carried by a lady attached to the U. S. delegation to the Pan-American conference when it met there. The old lady had always carried an umbrella and no one could convince her that she would not need it in Lima. Local American residents had to explain to the Peruvians what the funny-looking thing was used for.

The matter of rain was under casual discussion by a group of us in the bar of the Bolivar Hotel one afternoon when one old-timer said he had once seen it rain so hard that every square inch of ground in Lima was actually wet and that the accumulated dust of many years had been washed from the great bronze statue of San Martin that adorns the Plaza. He said he remembered the occasion very well because he had gotten his feet wet and caught a cold which had hung on for weeks. After the manner of men who cherish petty vanities he was very proud of the fact that he had enjoyed an experience which no one else could duplicate. No one contradicted him but after he had left someone said to me:

"Don't take Bill too seriously. He is inclined to brag a little after he has had a few drinks."

One is accustomed to think of a rainless spot as one of cloudless skies and undiluted sunshine. Lima is anything but that in the spring months of November, December and January. Every afternoon that I was there great banks of clouds collected overhead—the gray mass streaked with black from which one would expect to see flashes of lightning. Any New England weather prophet would have been willing to place a bet that rain would be falling in half an hour. But it never rained. The clouds gathered again the next day at about the same time and every day. It appeared the height of foolishness to go out without a raincoat. This promise of rain that is never fulfilled finally developed in me an unreasonable irritation that was not relieved until I enjoyed a real rain in Ecuador weeks later. What must it be like to the farmer who sees these black rain clouds day after day but knows that he must keep at his irrigation ditches?

No matter from which direction he approaches Lima by sea the traveler is prepared for rainless Lima. To the north or to the south, for hundreds of miles in either direction no land is to be seen but the cinder-like mountain ranges on which no sprig of green is visible. There is neither soil nor rain in some of the copper-mining towns of the Andes where many Americans live. They have built tiny gardens by transplanting soil thousands of feet up the mountainsides by pack mules. In one place the gardens are irrigated by distilled water.

The fact that it does not rain, must, through the centuries, have proven very provoking to many generations of architects for in a rainless city and one where it never gets really cold all that is needed in the way of a roof is something or other that will keep out the sun. That is about all the Inca architects attempted. The Spanish architects brought their traditions of gabled roofs with them and did not change. I have no doubt but that many an architect with his conscience troubled by the fact that he shouldn't put a gabled roof on a house that will never be pelted by rain has finally said to himself, "Oh, what the hell," and has slapped on gabled roofs anyway. Out in the country they don't bother with such things and on the eight-mile drive from the port of Callao to Lima one passes a succession of houses as flat-roofed as packing cases which they greatly resemble. In Lima three fourths of the houses are of that type, the others are gable-roofed. Each of the plazas is ornamented by a fountain and how pleasant is the sight and sound of falling water!

The rainless years have discouraged mosquitoes for they can find no stagnant pools in which to breed. This has left the field open to fleas which have feasted on generations of viceroys, Indians and white Peruvians. The tourist trade has brought them new epicurean delights. For some unaccountable reason I had been in Lima several days before they discovered me. Then after a restless night I woke to find that a least one very active flea had done a very thorough job of exploration. But that night I slept in peace and jumped to the conclusion that my flavor having proven unsatisfactory the fleas had rejected me. The following night I found out how wrong I had been. I had not been rejected, only reprieved, while the scouts spread the glad news. A visitor was in town, a visitor who for several weeks had gorged on the beefsteaks of Buenos Aires. When I surveyed the wreckage in the morning it appeared that the great number of bites could not possibly have been inflicted by a single family of fleas. It must have been the work of a clan. And from the fierceness of their attacks I feel sure that their ancestors must have fed on the blood of Pizarro. The housekeeper didn't think so. Folded on the bed was a beautiful woolen blanket I had bought in Chile as a present to my mother. The housekeeper eyed it suspiciously.

"Where did you buy that?" she asked.

"In Valparaiso."

"That's where the beasts came from," she said. "They were Chilean fleas, not Peruvian."

She took the blanket away and did something to it and that was the last I ever heard of fleas.

After Pizarro had destroyed the old Inca empire he set about the building of a new city on this coastal plain eight miles from the sea. He drew the plans himself, a task that could easily be accomplished in a few minutes. He just laid out a checkerboard city on a flat plain and spotted in a few plazas. He had no visions of a city that would be either beautiful or large or he lacked the art to express them. The many handsome palm-lined boulevards have been the work of recent times. He could not have devoted much time to planning the city for on the same day he laid the cornerstone for the cathedral where his mummified body is enshrined in a glass case looking like nothing so much as a huge dead cockroach. He destroyed the Inca empire by treachery and murder and a few years later was fittingly murdered by his own soldiers.

The Incas were the Nazis of South America and gained their dominance over other tribes by methods identical with those later followed by Hitler. Populations of conquered areas were shifted so as to prevent insurrections; the Incas assumed a racial superiority over all others, compelled acceptance of their political and religious ideas by force. The state controlled everything, just as in Nazi Germany. The fact that the people were so thoroughly regimented and disciplined made it easy for the Spanish conquerors to enforce their rule which to the people meant only a transfer of authority. A Peruvian student of history with whom I discussed the matter said that Hitler was preparing the German people for alien rule just as the Incas had been prepared—that while it would be impossible for a German governor-general to rule the British Isles it would be a comparatively simple matter for the British Colonial office to take over and operate the machine which Hitler has built.

Lima was not an industrial city, not even an agricultural market town, but an imperial capital from which the far-flung empire of Spain in the New World would be ruled. Even distant Buenos Aires was subject to Lima. The residents were not as in other places colonists who conquered a wilderness and made it productive but officials who had the easy and not unprofitable task of looting the subjugated Indians of their wealth. The Spaniard had fallen heir to the great and wealthy Inca empire with riches that made Europe appear poor. Control of the riches of the New World by the officials at Lima was ensured by laws restricting all trade to that city. Great wealth flowed into the treasury and galleons freighted with gold and silver sailed from the port of Callao to the mother country. Lima became the richest city in the New World. It was a big and important city when Buenos Aires, Santiago and Rio de Janeiro were small and struggling settlements. Its officials and residents lived the most courtly and luxurious lives. In the many curio and antique shops one finds occasional bits of old Spanish jewelry which give a hint of what life in Lima must have been like in those rich colonial days when Spain was mistress of the world.

The past has been preserved in the architecture of Lima in spite of the fact that the city has been frequently damaged and once was almost completely destroyed by earthquakes. Time has not healed these gastric disturbances in the bowels of mother earth and rarely does a fortnight pass without a quake. There are few buildings without cracked walls and broken cornices though Lima has not in recent years suffered so severely as neighboring Callao which a few years ago was almost completely destroyed. A number of modern buildings are now being erected but many generations just copied the architecture of the past.

When the Moors conquered and occupied Spain they brought their harems with them and built balconies on their houses so that the oriental beauties could look through the lattices at the life outside without being seen from the street. After they had driven the Moors from their homes and America was discovered and the Spaniards began coming to the New World, they brought the Moorish architecture with them though without the harems. As they had no harems the institution of the latticed balcony was unnecessary but they built them just the same so that the señoras and señoritas could look out. As the architects of Lima could not justify themselves for playing with the roof lines of the city they leapt at the opportunity to tack on balconies. According to history there were some very fine ones of carved stone but they were destroyed by the great earthquake of 1746 and the present ones are unpretentious wooden affairs but there are a lot of them. Even the church dignitaries ignored the voluptuous significance of the Moorish balcony. The finest one in all Lima is the one on the palace of the Archbishop overlooking one of the most important plazas.

There is of course no way of telling how many señoritas may at any given moment be peeking from behind the wooden grilles but at almost any hour of the day plenty of them may be seen leaning over the balconies, where their view is restricted to what they can see in a street thirty feet wide—the roadway usually well filled with American motorcars. One would like to imagine that they lingered there at dusk while some handsome young man strummed on a guitar below them in the best Hollywood manner. As a tourist attraction it would be a wow. But cities rarely live up to tourist expectations. Elephants do not pile teak in Rangoon and so far as I know there is not a guitar in all Peru. The only one I saw in all South America was played by an old blind man in Santiago while his wife held a tin cup in which the charitable threw coppers. Was he once young and handsome and was this the guitar with which he courted her?

The most pleasing features of the architecture of Lima are the courtyards which are partially concealed from the visitor, though one gets charming glimpses of them from the street. All of the old residences consist of one- or two-story structures built around patios or courtyards much like the Chinese houses in Peiping. Handsome grilled gateways, some of which look as if they might have been brought over by Pizarro, mark the entrances but do not shut off the view of a neat square which may be either tiled or sodded and invariably contains some growing plants. Trees and shrubs are planted in the patios so that while Lima is a compactly built city it has from the air a surprisingly parklike appearance. In the days of the viceroys these houses built around a courtyard constituted the aristocratic residences of the place but now it has become fashionable to live in one of the suburbs where a modern motor road winds carefully between gnarled olive trees that are said to be several hundred years old. Some of the beautiful old courtyards are still maintained in something like regal style but others are neglected and used for the storage of cargo.

The many wars and revolutions which have marked the history of Peru have had their effect on the architecture of the capital city. With a few exceptions most of the old shops and residences of all cities in South America are at all times prepared for riots and rebellions. The old boast that an Englishman's home is his castle is, in the country of its origin, only a figure of speech but in Lima it is a physical reality. All houses are built flush with the street, the windows barred by iron grilles. The only entrance is by the front door or the gate to the patio and there are peepholes so that the caller may be inspected before the door or the gate is unbarred. The doors and windows of shops are equipped with steel shutters and when shops are closed the shutters seal the place with bullet-resisting armor. That is the conventional pattern for a majority of the shops and private residences of South America. Crowds may riot and patriots may fire rifles and revolvers but the shop and the house are fairly safe from disturbances. The political security which every city has enjoyed can be measured fairly accurately by the proportion of shops which have unprotected show windows where displays are on view on Sundays and holidays. There are few of these in Lima although protection does not go to the extreme it does in Santiago where all of the windows of a four- or five-story building are securely shuttered. That was a government building housing many officials and therefore would be a tempting target in case of a revolution.

The Peruvians have not only suffered from their own revolutions but still smart from the effects of an invasion by their Chilean neighbors. In Sherman's march to the sea he was a kindly conqueror compared to the Chileans who not only destroyed private and public property but sacked the national library. It may be for that reason that the books in the library are now guarded like the securities in a bank vault. I wanted very much to have a look at the stacks but all I was allowed was a distant glimpse of them through iron bars.

Pizarro would have been a queer Spaniard if he had not thought of plazas, when he sketched them in on his checkerboard city just as it would have been a queer Englishman who would not have thought of a village green in planning the villages of New England. With no rain Pizarro's plazas must have been sorry dusty places until a comparatively recent time when an adequate water system was built by impounding in reservoirs the water from the snow-fed streams of the Andes. The water is expended lavishly on the turf of the plazas and on the shrubs and flowering trees which are almost as beautiful as those of Burma. At the beginning of December the trees were in full spring bloom. The most gorgeous one, the hucharda, is covered with purple flowers which after a few weeks fade to a lighter color and drop on the lawns, giving them, at a little distance, the appearance of being covered with violets. Flowers do not follow the seasons but appear to bloom at their own sweet will so that you see in the same garden spring and autumn flowers.

The plazas are full of life and color all the year round. The principal one, Plaza des Armes, faces the cathedral and is under the constant surveillance of a greatly over-sized statue of Pizarro on horseback.[1] A great deal of the shopping of the city is done in the neighborhood. Around the plaza the second stories of the houses extend over the broad pavement affording protection from the sun. Here the well-dressed women come to do their shopping—though not so smartly attired as their sisters of Chile or any of the east coast cities. Mingled with them are Indians for more than half of the population of the country are pure Indian, and four fifths of the remainder are half-breeds leaving a half million, or one tenth of the population, of pure Spanish descent. For four hundred years they have held most of the offices although there are now a few Indians in official positions.

Most of the pure-blood Indians live in the mountains where they eat dried mutton or salted llama meat, weave their own clothes and drink their own home brew of fermented corn. Spanish rule has not changed them. A few visitors are usually to be seen in Lima where they stand in front of show windows transfixed by the sight of merchandise for which they can see no conceivable use. They do not remain long. The sophisticated city slickers of Lima cheat and tease them and they are glad to get back to the highlands with the herds of llamas. Some of the Indian women sell herbs which look much like the merchandise of that sort sold to the country people in China. To the layman it looks like a basketful of dried weeds but who knows what hidden treasures it may contain? It was from such rubbishy messes as this that ephedrine was discovered in China and quinine in Peru.

[1] This statue is the work of an American sculptor, Charles Carey Rumsey and was presented to the city of Lima by his widow. After being shipped from the United States it was unveiled in 1935 as a part of the ceremonies in connection with the celebration of the four hundredth anniversary of the founding of the city.

The attitude of the pure-blood ruling classes toward the predominant Indian population is a curious combination of fear and contempt. They affect to despise all forms of Indian art and laugh at visitors who buy the very interesting hand-hammered silverware or the handmade fabrics. Their term for this kind of merchandise is the Spanish equivalent of "Indian junk." On the other hand they are definitely uneasy about this great mass of silent Indians in the mountains above them who after all these centuries are still aloof, unassimilated. Secretly they speculate on what this mass might do if awakened by education or aroused by a racial appeal sounded by an impassioned leader. Japanese were encouraged to settle in Peru because of the profits that could be made from their labor. Now the rulers wish they weren't there for they might arouse and organize the Indians. Perhaps this is nothing more than the workings of an uneasy conscience slowly becoming aware of the fact that Pizarro's oppression of the Indians has changed in form but has never ceased.

It is with reluctance that I speak of the architecture of the many churches of Lima. The good fathers who followed Pizarro must have had very dim memories of the Baroque churches and cathedrals that had been built or were building in Europe for they only made poor copies of the decorative features, achieved size without majesty and added decorations like frosting on a cake. When the hideously overdecorated churches were destroyed by earthquake in 1746 they were rebuilt with all of their old faults. With very few exceptions they provide striking examples of the length to which bad taste will go when not restrained by considerations of cost of construction. I wonder what our New England ancestors would have done if, like the Spaniards, they had found a country rich in building materials and a population of skilled artisans who could be easily enslaved. New England architecture would probably have been lost to the world because it never would have existed, and we might have started off with a semblance of the atrocious scroll-saw work that came with a later period.

As one travels from Lima into the Peruvian Andes the churches and shrines are progressively more barbaric. According to eminent historians the Spanish priests who sought to convert the Aztecs around Mexico City made the acceptance of the new faith easier by incorporating in the altar decorations some of the familiar emblems of the older Aztec religions. The same thing was done in Peru but it is rather surprising to find them there after more than four hundred years. High up in a village of the Andes I saw a roadside shrine in which Inca and Christian symbols were curiously intermixed. The familiar form of the cross was completely obscured by figures of a crowing rooster and the Inca symbols for the sun and the moon, and other emblems with which I was not familiar. I would not have known it was a Christian shrine had it not been for a blood-smeared face of Christ.

At the foot of the cross were three dice just as they might fall after a cast in the game of Bidou, the popular dice game of the east coast. The origin of this justly famous game is obscure but it is played with three dice just like the game played in Greece and Rome before the time of Christ and from what is known of that ancient game some of the points in scoring are the same. Does the presence of these dice in an altar decoration indicate that this was the game with which Pizarro's followers gambled for the loot they stole from the Incas? And does it possibly signify that Bidou was the game played on an earlier and more tragic occasion and thus it became a symbolic emblem of an altar decoration?

Lima is one of the many cities in South America which has honored the memory of Washington by erecting a statue and naming a plaza after him. Apparently there were other and earlier plans to commemorate the names of great citizens of the United States, but something went amiss. In one of the many aimless strolls I took around the city I caught a glimpse of what appeared to be a marble statue in a main courtyard given over to cheap rooming houses and a dressmaking establishment. It was about the last place one would expect to find a marble statue but throughout South America statues are almost as common as filling stations and one finds them in many unusual places. Investigation confirmed the existence, not of one, but of two statues: of Washington and Franklin. Washington's sword hilt had been broken off and Franklin's belly was covered with childish scrawls in colored crayon. Even when they left the hands of the sculptor they were pretty poor. I can't imagine any committee ever accepting them but I would like to see the mystery of their existence explained. I dread the thought of what conclusion might be reached by archaeologists a few hundred years from now, especially if the Axis powers should succeed in destroying the things that Washington and Franklin stood for. If I ever go back to Lima I propose to investigate this matter but in the meantime if any traveler is interested the address is 338 Ica.

Peru has followed the lead of neighboring countries in social legislation and has adopted maximum hours for labor without, however, doing anything about a minimum wage. The problem of providing better housing and cheaper and better food for workmen has been attacked very successfully. There are many government-sponsored restaurants where the workmen can get a good wholesome meal for a few cents. On the other hand the government offers protection to established industries against wasteful and unnecessary competition. It is common in all countries to protect manufacturers against competition from abroad but the Peruvian policy goes much farther than that. For example the cotton mills now in the country are considered to be quite sufficient for present needs. So the government has moved to prevent any immediate competition by temporarily prohibiting the importation of textile machinery for any new enterprises.

There is a curious division of labor in the sale of the daily papers which appears to be the result of following old custom. When the big morning paper *El Commercio* and its rival *La Prensa* appear on the streets just after early mass, huge piles of *El Commercio* and smaller piles of *La Prensa* appear on the stands of the news dealers. If they are hawked about the streets at all it is in the suburban district with which I am not familiar. There are no newsboys on the streets in the central district. If you want a copy of either paper you go to the newsstand and buy it.

When the afternoon editions come out there is an entirely different machinery of distribution. No copies are piled on newsstands which shut up shop early in the afternoon. Instead there are hundreds of ragamuffin boys and a few dozen cheerful ragamuffin girls who appear on the streets selling the papers and apparently having a whale of a lot of fun. The boys, who make a game out of it, hunt in packs so that you may have half a dozen on a single corner or walk several blocks without being able to find a paper on sale. The little girls, most of whom show traces of Indian ancestry, are by far the better merchants for they work alone and for some reason appear to dominate the best centers of distribution such as the Plaza San Martin on which the Hotel Bolivar is located. If there is no lottery drawing the papers appear on the streets about three o'clock, and on the days when there is a lottery about two hours later for the list of winning numbers constitutes the most important news on dull days. In fact from the number of lottery ticket vendors who are always underfoot one would assume that everyone in Lima was a regular purchaser of tickets. At about seven o'clock the young merchants assume that the market has reached the saturation point, just as their small stomachs have reached the exhaustion point, so they go home to supper and to bed and if anyone wants a paper after that hour he will have to wait until the morning papers are published.

The Lima police are mostly short, stout and dark. At first I got the impression that they were tall but soon found that they appeared tall only because of the very low average height of the Peruvian. Even in the daytime they are very smartly attired with high boots, khaki uniforms with white facings. But when the sun goes down behind the saw-tooth Andes and the temperature drops they appear in all their glory—a khaki cape with red facings always worn open so as to give the best theatrical effect. But the most striking piece of his equipment is the traffic whistle which has trumpetlike qualities and in the hands of an expert is able to give expression to strong emotions. I have heard the whistle in the lips of an enraged policeman express unprintable remarks to a chauffeur who passed a red light.

Of course Pizarro could not have foreseen motorcar traffic in his day but with the narrow streets he laid out he did not even make adequate provision for heavy carriage traffic. The result is that most of the streets are one way and a taxi trip requires many detours. However the rate is the same so long as you do not get outside a certain area. Everytime I asked a policeman how to get to any place he invariably advised me to take a taxi and then ran out into the street and blew his whistle at the first taxi driver he saw. The poor driver thinking he had violated some traffic regulation would pull to the curb with a frightened face only to find that he had picked up a fare. It must have been an old joke to both the driver and the policeman but they always laughed about it.

After an association with taxi drivers in many parts of the world I think I would rate those of Lima as the most friendly. Unlike others of their calling who look on the traveler as some lesser person they are quite willing to accept him as an equal, a fellow man whose ignorance about such simple matters as the direction to take to the cathedral should be looked on in a charitable way. My first experience with the Lima taxi drivers was a very pleasant one. My Spanish was at the moment completely understandable involving as it did no more than the number and name of the street to which I wanted to be driven. Instead of starting the car the driver turned in his seat and protested:

"But, Señor, you don't need to take a taxi for a short trip like that. Here, I will show you."

I was already seated in the car but when I got out he pointed and said:

"You see that Kodak sign down there? The place you want to go is just across the street."

That was all but it started my all-too-brief Peruvian experiences very happily for me. Confucius would have loved this taxi driver but I don't think Pizarro would have thought much of him. The great conquistador's policy was to take every advantage of the weak and defenseless.

I loved the democratic way Peruvian waiters, taxi drivers and even the petty shopkeepers assumed that everyone was on the same economic level as themselves. At the Maury Hotel where I enjoyed the best food in South America I was often tempted by that combination of good food at absurdly small prices and ordered much more than I could possibly eat. After a few days the waiter became familiar with the differential between my eyes and my stomach and just conveniently forgot to bring dishes I had ordered which he knew I would not eat. When I went to a shop to buy a package of Gillette razor blades the clerk brought me a single blade. The Peruvians are not only poor but they're thinly whiskered and a good blade will last them a long time.

The gay dog of a Peruvian just like his fellows in Brazil and Chile has a marvelous time on what is to American standard a very small amount of money. Like the Chilean, he spends less money than the Brazilian or the Argentine on haberdashery and barbershops and shoe-shining stands; is less odorous with the pleasing scent of bay rum. To him alcoholic products can be used to better purpose than that of anointing the hair or rubbing over a freshly shaved face. The Brazilian who is comparatively unfamiliar with alcohol sits in the café and sips his one-cent cup of coffee. The Argentine who is always inclined to keep his head about him also drinks coffee which comes from Brazil but he is sure it is better because it is made after the Argentine fashion. The Chilean enjoys a glass of his own very good wine for a few cents and gets a big glass of very good beer for three cents.

But for real devil-may-care men about town one must

go to Lima where the boys in the corner saloon whoop it up on their Pisco sours. No headwaiters ever opened a bottle of vintage champagne with more adroit showmanship than that displayed by the Peruvian bartender when he mixes what is, in its price class, one of the finest drinks in the world. With great care he puts in the tot of Pisco rum, sugar, lime juice and a bit of the white of an egg. The cocktail shaker is shaken violently, then given three resounding smacks on the open palm of the left hand. A little more shaking and three more smacks and the drink is served. The cost is six cents in the more expensive places. Only a seasoned veteran will spend more than a quarter at a sitting. Full of good spirits and at peace with the world he tips the waiter 4½ cents and says:

"*Comprose una casa.*" (Buy yourself a house.)

CHAPTER XIII

## Where Time Has Stood Still

THE advertising booklets issued by steamship and travel agencies say little or nothing about it, but one of the most interesting sights in South America is provided by the approach to Guayaquil, the principal port of Ecuador. There from the comfortable shaded deck of a Grace Line boat one may turn back the pages of history and see the lush tropical west coast of South America just as it was when first seen by white men more than four hundred years ago. Only the presence of another steamer or the white sail of a pleasure boat will mar the illusion that you are living in the days of Pizarro and Cortez. The long approach to the harbor is through the mouth of the Guayas River and for an hour or more after entering the mouth of the stream there is no hint of the existence of anything the Spanish conquerors did not see when they pushed on here soon after the conquest of Peru had been completed. In other places stuffy museums give hints from which one can reconstruct the past but here the past is revealed in real life—a new thrill for the tourist.

There are no modern buildings of any sort around the mouth of the river but through the tropical foliage which partly conceals the muddy shore the primitive huts of the Indians can be seen, unchanged through the centuries. They consist of nothing more than a rough floor supported by stilts driven into the swampy ground—just high enough to keep the floor from being submersed at high tide. The roof is of palm leaves which may keep out the sun but affords little protection from a heavy rain. Rarely are the occupants of one of these jungle shacks able to step from them onto dry land. But even this has its compensations for he can catch fish without leaving his own doorstep. When he does leave his house he steps into a canoe made of the carved-out trunk of the balsa tree. The wood of this marvelous tree is almost incredibly light, weighing only seven or eight pounds to the cubic foot. It is much lighter and stronger than cork. For many centuries the only use made of this wood was in the construction of that most primitive form of transportation, the canoe and now it is used in the construction of the most modern, the airplane. With canoes carved from solid trunks of this material generations of Indians paddled up and down the rivers and ventured on excursions to the sea coast before they saw the sails of the first Spanish ships. They probably paddled out in friendly fashion to meet them just as they paddled out to see the *Santa Elena*, the corklike little boats tossed about by the waves the propellers made.

Only a half-dozen canoes were met in the cruise of a little more than thirty miles, but many others could be seen moored about the huts. The animal life on the river could have been little more abundant in the heart of the jungle itself. Though the noise of the propellers drove them away and we did not see them it was easy to believe what more experienced travelers told us of the existence of sharks and alligators. Some small boys on the *Santa Elena* saw sharks and alligators and huge snakes in the trees, or thought they did, which was just as thrilling as the actual sight. At any rate this was just the kind of a spot where one would not be in the least surprised to see huge snakes in the trees. The presence of myriads of fish was evidenced by the thousands of birds competing in the exploitation of the only industry they know. The trees along the bank were lined with herons sometimes perched so thickly that at a little distance the trees looked as if they were covered with patches of white flowers. Unlike their competitors the herons appeared to have hours for fishing and hours for contemplation and digestion for while hundreds were busy diving into the water and emerging with a fish other hundreds loafed in the tree tops.

There was no loafing for the pelicans who were constantly flying slowly over the water like heavy bombers. They always had a keen if solemn eye out for any fish that might be swimming too near the surface. When he spotted one the pelican hit water like a dive bomber and by the time he had righted himself there was one less fish in the river. For a moment he would rest on the water looking ridiculously sober and stiff-necked, like one to whom life is but one continuous earnest endeavor with no time for lightness or frivolity. Either appetite or industry always nagged him for he never rested more than a few moments before he was cruising again just as the Royal Air Force cruises in search of enemy submarines.

High overhead the long winged frigate birds cruised as if they were just flying about for the fun of it and were completely disdainful of anything but the sky above them. These are the beautiful birds which attracted so much attention from the English sailors when they made their first voyages into tropical waters and it was the sailors who gave them their name. It was more appropriate in the days when frigates with pirate flags cruised the seas than it is today. The bird is not so celestial-minded as he appears to be but is as crafty and unscrupulous as any pirate that ever sailed the seas. Like the always sobersided pelican he eats fish for breakfast, dinner and supper but disdains to catch them for himself. As he sails about in the sky nothing that transpires in the water below escapes his attention for he is always on the lookout for a chance to rob some other more hard-working bird.

The pelican gobbles his fish before he leaves the water and so does the heron but the brown-spotted Peruvian booby having caught a fish, will for some reason known only to boobies, attempt to fly away with it. This is what the crafty frigate bird has been waiting for. As soon as he spots the booby his leisurely slow-winged flight becomes a projectile aimed at the booby with the accuracy and swiftness of an arrow. Before he knows what happened the fish has been snatched from his beak and the frigate bird is again sweeping the sky with his great long wings. There is nothing for the hungry booby to do but go back to work. The booby is a fool and a fool is a booby. But most dictionaries are silent as to whether a fool is called a booby because he acts like the bird; or the bird is called a booby because he acts like a fool. The frigate bird might have been named after the Spanish conquerors or the English pirates who saw this river just as we see it today for they did no useful work but robbed the Indians and each other.

The whistle of a steam launch signaled a change in scene and brought our thoughts back from the ancient and primitive past to the less interesting present. Rounding a bend in the river the unimpressive sky line of Guayaquil came into view to the musical accompaniment provided by a sawmill. The steam launch whose whistle had disturbed us was towing a barge loaded with bananas and was racing to get to the quay in time to start loading by the time we had docked. This was the first of many barges and before the day's work was done we had loaded 45,000 bunches. Cocoa is the most important export of Ecuador but the more-than-a-million bunches of bananas shipped every year bulk large in the volume of freight carried by American vessels. If ample refrigeration space was not provided, and an elaborate system of air conditioning maintained, the cargo would arrive in New York a rotted mass of pulp. They are watched as carefully as an incubator baby and as a result the bright green bananas which are loaded at Guayaquil arrive in New York a beautiful yellow and ready for the table.

The loading is done by negroes and the way they worked revived in me half-forgotten boyhood memories of colored roustabouts loading cargo on a Mississippi River steamer at old Ste. Genevieve. It was the kind of work that appeals to the negroes' sense of rhythm and appreciation of the theatrical. The bunches of bananas were lifted from the barge, swung onto the back of the waiting negro and trotted into the refrigeration rooms with the timing of a tap dancer and something approaching the tempo. Such work produces symmetrical muscles and fiercely beautiful bodies as was pointed out to me by a spinster schoolteacher from New England.

After the gay and beautiful Rio, pretentious Buenos Aires and the colorful cities of Santiago, Valparaiso, and Lima, Guayaquil appeared a sorry place but full of color and atmosphere all its own. Some have said that Buenos Aires reminded them of Chicago but Guayaquil reminds one of nothing else he has ever seen. But there was something strangely familiar to me and finally I remembered. Here for the first time I saw a realization of the banana belt towns pictured in some of the O. Henry stories. It was just the sort of place where you could imagine a lonely consul drinking himself to death, or desperate characters plotting crimes or patriots plotting revolutions. There is little that is pleasing to the eye, no architecture to lift one's thoughts above the ground. Only a few public buildings which appear to have been designed by architects. Many of the others looked as if they had been picked up at bargain sales all over the world—secondhand houses that their old owners had discarded—and set up in Guayaquil.

Poverty is inclusive but not depressing because it does not involve such physical distresses as cold or hunger. It is different in the mountains but here on the coast it is always warm and foodstuffs are so plentiful that anyone who has spent years in the Far East would be shocked at the food allowed to go to waste in the public market, not even conserved for the chickens and the pigs. It is true that for many people bananas provide the staff of life and if one has been weaned on bananas it is a very satisfactory food. Our own doctors of a past generation warned mothers against allowing their children to eat bananas but now they recommend them.

In the knicknacks and gadgets of life the people are poor. Curio vendors who came on board shamelessly begged for cigarettes. There were few neatly dressed men on the street, none well dressed, many who were shabby. In contrast to the shops in villages in neighboring Peru the shops of this important port are poorly stocked with the kind of shabby goods that only Japan can produce. The entire stock of one shop consisted entirely of flashy buttons and cheap jewelry. There were hundreds of finger rings set with glass imitations of every known jewel and all for sale at less than ten cents each. Huge imitation diamond brooches, necklaces and bracelets could be bought for the same price. All of the surprisingly numerous pawn shops appeared to be busy but most of the transactions involved loans of less than a dollar. Many pawn articles on which they get only ten to twenty cents.

Guayaquil is one of the places where American sailors ashore frequently get into trouble. The settings for a nosebleeding combat are ideal. A great deal of the locally grown sugar cane is turned into molasses which in turn is converted into rum carrying as much punch per nickel invested as any devil's brew to be found in this sinful world. The other ingredient for a good soul-satisfying brawl is supplied by the awkward young policemen. Few of them appear more that twenty years old in spite of the fact that service of at least one year in the army is an apprenticeship required before one can join the police force. Their uniforms are dirty and there is nothing military about their bearing. As an added provocation to the sailor whose emotions are being churned by shots of very bad rum the policemen carry absurdly long swords. I do not wish to appear to condone any interference with civil authority but at the same time I must admit that I can readily understand why a crowd of sailors on pleasure bent would want to take the police department apart.

Military service of one year is compulsory at the age of twenty though the figures of military strength do not indicate that more than a very small percentage of the men available for duty are ever called to the colors. The last available figures showed that there were only 3,492 privates on active duty but a surprising number of officers. There were almost 1,000 sergeants, more than 500 captains and lieutenants, 125 colonels and majors and 5 generals. The small over-officered army absorbs almost 20 per cent of the total revenue of the country. Much more is spent on the army and the navy (one gunboat) than on education.

There are in fact almost five times as many high-ranking army officers as college professors in spite of the fact that there are four officially recognized universities. This would appear to provide very liberally for higher education in a country with a population of a little more than 3 million people but the total number of students enrolled in a recent year was 670. One of the four universities had only twenty-two students and a teaching staff of six. Official statements about education leave plenty of room for wonder and speculation. Primary education is free and compulsory and yet the total number of students enrolled is only a little more than 100,000. Students in secondary schools which correspond in a way to our high schools number 2,007.

It is interesting to note how ancient and modern customs follow the same patterns in far-distant parts of the world. The many canals which run out of Ningpo and other parts of Chekiang provinces are served by flat-bottomed passenger boats on which the Chinese ride from

one market town to the other. There is nothing they can
see but the enclosing banks of the canal. To relieve the
tedium of the trip there is a blind storyteller on every
boat. This was a service for passengers maintained in
China centuries before the de luxe trains of the United
States installed radios in their club cars so that some per-
verse passenger could tune in on a soap melodrama when
others are waiting to hear the news. From ancient China
to the United States to Ecuador is quite a jump but it has
been attained. As the busses travel through the streets of
Guayaquil the radio blares forth constant entertainment
consisting principally of American phonograph records
played at the local station.

It is not only by providing musical entertainment for
passengers that the busses put the Fifth Avenue Coach
Company to shame. The busses are not only numbered
but are also given names like Pullman cars. One is named
Shirley Temple, another Henry Ford. But I don't think
the Detroit tycoon would be especially flattered for the
car is the product of a rival manufacturer and is in a
decrepit state. South Americans have been much more
liberal and discriminating than we are in bestowing personal names or names of historical significance to streets
and places as well as to motor busses. Every great historical
event has been commemorated over and over again by a
street with a date or a name, such as "Avenue July 17" in
Montevideo. It is too bad we have never adopted this
pleasant Latin-American custom. From their point of view
there is only one appropriate name for Fifth Avenue. It
should be called "Fourth of July Avenue." The greatest
date in our history and the greatest street would be
jointly honored by bearing the same name.

We must strike them as being a most prosaic and materialistic people when they note that we call some of our most important thoroughfares main street or market street, number them or merely designate them by a letter of the alphabet. So far as I know there is not a main street or a market street in all South America. Names all have historical significance so that the map of every city tells a story of the past. This is but one of many indications that the peoples of South America are more conscious of their histories than we are of ours. As with us most of their heroes are those who have served their country most unselfishly. One thing that would convince them of our lack of taste or historical perspective or both is the fact that while many of our cities have named streets after Washington or Lincoln or Jefferson some of them are sorry streets which do no honor to the great names they bear.

The entertainment feature provided by the busses cannot be duplicated by the competitive American-owned tramcar company. But any headaches American investors suffer because of competition by the busses are mild to those they suffer because of the general depreciation in the value of all South American currencies. It looked like a good idea when their directors bought these properties and for a few years the dividends which were regularly paid made everyone happy. Then the value of the milreis, sucre, sol, bolivar and the numerous variety of pesos began to slip—and ski. In the meantime the fares which could be collected remained the same because of franchise conditions fixed in those now seemingly fabulous days when a franc was worthy twenty cents and no one thought it would ever be worth any more or any less. With the fall in value of currencies it has come about that in South American countries some tramcar companies carry passengers long distances for less than one cent. Under such circumstances dividends are impossible and the companies have difficulty in maintaining their properties. The decrepit condition of most of the tramcars is due to the same reason that the Ecuadorian is usually dressed in shabby clothing—there is no money to buy anything better.

This drop in the value of currency and fear that it may drop further has given Guayaquil and many other cities on either coast a deceptive appearance of prosperity. People with idle money in the bank have watched its purchasing power grow constantly less and are now investing it in real estate and putting up houses which will have a solid and dependable value. In the days before the first World War the Ecuadorian sucre like the Mexican peso, the Japanese yen and the Russian rouble was exchangeable for about fifty cents in U. S. currency. After some fluctuations it had that value in 1920. Then it began to slip, being worth only twenty-five cents in 1925 and sixteen cents a year later. It is now worth only about seven cents. With differences in detail that has been the story of almost all South American currencies.

Just south of Ecuador, in Peru, scientists are carefully and anxiously watching the boobies who are so persistently robbed by the frigate birds. Supplying food for the craftier frigate bird is not the only useful function this stupid bird performs for because of him and his remote ancestors market gardens all over the world have been supplied with a new fertility. For many centuries the rocky island off the coast of Peru provided a resting place for the boobies on their annual migrations and here their droppings formed the great deposits of guano. On their visits they feasted gloriously on schools of anchovies. For some years these deposits were carried away by any skipper who wanted to fill his holds. The supply was so great that it appeared to be inexhaustible. As has been remarked by others a great many families owe their fortunes to the bowel movements of the sea birds which built up these vast deposits of guano. The great American shipping firm of W. R. Grace & Co. started in business in this way. Young Mr. Grace was employed as a clerk in a ship chandlery concern in Callao and visited the guano deposits with a ship stocked with supplies for sale to men on the guano boats. As a result of this the first Grace enterprise was a square-rigged windjammer built for the guano trade. About thirty years ago the Peruvian government took over the deposits as a monopoly and put into effect a system of conservation, allowing the deposits on various islands to be collected only after intervals of two or three years. The ancient deposits were gone but it was thought that in this way there would be a steady supply available.

Then the unexpected and unexplainable happened for the boobies quit coming in their former numbers. Maybe after a century or so they had learned to resent the visits of man to islands which were formerly their exclusive possession. In its anxiety to bring the boobies back, the Peruvian government has made all kinds of regulations, one of which prohibits trap shooting from the decks of steamers in Peruvian waters but the birds still stay away. Some say the area is no longer popular with them because the anchovies no longer come in such large numbers. This has led to the speculation by some that the Humboldt Current has changed and the schools of anchovies now swarm in other places. As a young lady on the boat sagely remarked:

"If the Humboldt Current has changed, I suppose there is nothing anybody can do about it."

Any idea that the Ecuadorians are affected by the indolence that is supposed to characterize countries lying in the banana-producing zone would be dispelled by the character of the goods brought on deck for sale or offered by peddlers who loiter about the landing place. The one article most persistently offered is the Panama hat, which is not made in Panama at all but in Ecuador and Colombia, the best ones coming from Ecuador. It got its name from the fact that in the gold-rush days miners found the hats on sale at Panama. The principal point of production is a town with the clog-dance name of Jipijapa, eighty miles from Guayaquil. But in dozens of other places the villagers spend their time at the tedious work of fashioning the hats. It is a difficult work that requires a deft and well-trained hand though they are not woven under water as they are generally supposed to be. More than a million of these hats are exported every year, most of them going to the United States.

This is the least colorful of many handicrafts. If northbound travelers have any money left after they have completed their purchases of furs and silver in Peru they usually spend what is left of it in Guayaquil. There are baskets woven of colored fiber, table mats of the same material, remarkable mosaics of wood in natural colors. These are not just curiosities of craftsmanship but articles of real artistic merit. All of these things are sold at such cheap prices that even after freight and duty is added they would be looked on as bargains at home. There should be a good sale for them but in the development of this business the New York importer would run into the same difficulties that beset the exploitation of so many South American products: lack of adequate supplies and no dependable standard of quality.

When displayed around the swimming pool on the steamer, the display is as crowded as an exhibition booth at a country fair. But an order for any item which would justify an importing house in sending out samples or even in circularizing the trade could probably not be filled. And if it were filled by drawing on all available sources of supply, there would be almost as many standards of quality as there are individual items. Handicraft products like this do not play a big part in the foreign trade of the world but it was by starting in this modest and painstaking way that Japan began to build up the foreign trade which eventually grew to such huge proportions.

Among the few but growing number of industrial establishments in Ecuador is a factory producing 750,000 pairs of shoes a year. This is not a very large number of shoes to supply the needs of more than 3 million people yet it must do that for imported shoes are too expensive for any but the very wealthy. It was with this figure of Ecuadorian shoe production in mind that I saw a one-legged man getting his shoe shined on a street corner in Guayaquil and there suddenly flashed on me what I think is a logical explanation for the vast amount of public shoe shining that goes on in every place in South America. It wasn't because the man had only one leg but because he was so obviously poor. I wondered if he had to pay full price for having a single shoe shined and then I wondered why he would pay what was probably the equivalent of the price of several ripe bananas when shining shoes is such an easy job to do as I know from personal experience.

I remembered having seen hundreds of other shabby

men in the cities of half a dozen countries getting their shoes shined and realized that this was in a way a kind of distinction. It is not everyone who can do this for every-one does not own shoes. In fact a rather accurate social and economic division might be made of the people of South America—the shoeless and the shod. It is a distinc-tion which in places like Guayaquil and other places on the tropical coast has been imposed by the privileged classes. In Guayaquil where it is never cold they would be much more comfortable if they would, like Burmese ladies and gentlemen, go barefoot except for heelless sandals that can easily be kicked off. But as the privileged classes bought and wore shoes that became a badge of distinction that definitely marked one as having been born out of or escaped from the lower levels. And so men get their shoes ostentatiously shined whether they need them or not, giv-ing a great deal of employment to a great many people of the shoeless class and providing what is probably the world's largest per capita (shoe wearers only) consump-tion of shoe polish.

Undeterred by what others may say the residents of Guayaquil call their city "the pearl of the Pacific," fol-lowing the same line of reasoning that makes the Chicago *Tribune* call itself "the world's greatest newspaper." No matter what passengers may think of the place it is the favorite port with the waitresses on the Grace Line boats for here they have the privileges of a local sports club. As soon as the boat drops anchor a surprisingly large number of attractive girls appear, ready to go ashore. They are the same girls who have been serving our meals and giving the dining saloon such a cheerful and homey atmosphere, but hardly recognizable in their snappy sports clothes. They all carry tennis racquets and long before the port is reached matches and schedules of play have been arranged. All the courts are free to them for when the Grace girls are in port the local residents give up their games so that the visitors can enjoy every minute of the precious hours of relaxation.

CHAPTER XIV

## *Colombia—Our Nearest Neighbor*

THE geography of Colombia does not conform to the limitations of the map maker. There are few flat surfaces to depict and no amount of contour lines will give an accurate mental picture of the country. Rivers do not flow serenely to the sea but rise high in the mountains, leap down waterfalls and tumble along rapids for many miles before they are quiet enough to be entrusted with a boat. The coastal plains on both the Atlantic and the Pacific are succeeded by hills and they by ever higher mountains so that Colombia suggests a pyramid rather than a flat surface—a pyramid with a number of peaks and plateaus and thousands of corrugations where little valleys provide small areas of fertile land. No one of these is large but in the aggregate they amount to millions of acres. There is such a variety of climate in the range between the lowlands and the mountains that if you wanted to travel all over the country you would have to provide yourself with almost every kind of clothing from sun helmets to heavy overcoats.

The Spanish settlers spent little time on the coast regions where the cities of Barranquilla and Buenaventura now stand. They pushed on to the higher levels for the same reason that modern tourists spend little time in these places. They are most damnably hot. And in former days they were also most damnably unhealthy. The largest upland plateau was found at an elevation of 8,600 feet not far from the center of the country as it is now constituted. Here the city of Bogotá was founded, capital and principal city of the country.

It was almost as isolated from the area surrounding it as a penthouse without elevators or staircases. Navigable rivers do not flow at elevations of a mile and a half. The waters from the fertile plain on which Bogotá is built plunge down one 425-foot fall and many smaller ones before reaching the sea. A journey to either coast was tedious, uncomfortable and difficult. Before the establishment of airplane travel the journey between Bogotá and Barranquilla could not possibly be accomplished in less than a week. Usually it was ten days and it might be three weeks. This was in modern times, after the crooked and fickle Magdalena River had been improved and railways and highways built. That is the time it takes a traveler today unless he goes by plane. It must have been worse than that in the centuries following the founding of the city in 1538.

Some of the Spaniards (I presume of the lower classes) married Indian women. Others did not and so perpetuated a Spanish creole population of pure blood but isolated—a mountain oasis surrounded by tropical jungles. The lowlands were populated by negroes, Spanish soldiers, and mestizos; the highlands by Spanish who settled there in medieval times and they and their successors came into little contact with the outside world except through books. Isolated from the rest of the world the aristocrats turned to education not as a useful tool of accomplishment, but as something to cultivate for the pure intellectual enjoyment of it. Schools and libraries and learned societies were founded but there were enough roughnecks to maintain a bull ring.

This devotion to culture has become a characteristic of the country. Erudition appears to drip from the pores of the Colombian. With the questions restricted to highly cultural subjects there are thousands who could, with credit to themselves, appear as guests on the "Information Please" program. If a visitor is not careful he will find himself dragged into a discussion about the influence of Proust or the form of the French novel or be compelled to betray his ignorance by a confession that he is not familiar with the works or even the names of any of the long list of eminent Colombian poets. It came as quite a surprise to me to learn that the greatest American poets never wrote a line in English but composed their immortal works solely in Spanish, the only language they knew. The per capita production of poetry is probably greater in Colombia than in any other Spanish-speaking country. The stirring events of history have been recorded over and over again in epic poems of a length which can adequately embrace events of great detail. Every time a notable man dies the public is told in measured meter that the trees bow their heads in grief, the grass lovingly covers the form of our dead brother. Religious poems do not add anything to the gaiety of the literary scene. After these refined amusements it must be a great relief to go to a bull fight, see a few horses gored and the arena crimsoned by the blood of a half-dozen slain bulls. Even a good barroom brawl would tend to ease the atmosphere. The Colombians appear to assume that they alone are interested in the pursuit of literature for in no hotel could I find a decent writing desk.

It is in keeping with the academic character of the people that there should be great zeal in the compilation and publication of statistics. They carry this to a point that to an unacademic gringo appears a trifle absurd. For example the yearbook of the "Institute de La Salle," a very fine school maintained by the Christian Brothers, publishes a complete record of each of its hundreds of students. If anyone is interested in the matter he may learn that in his sixth scholastic year Ernesto Santos Silva was graded 84 in conduct and 80 in scholarship and did not receive a diploma. So poor Ernesto is held up to shame before future generations. Of course he must have been a very bad boy to get such a low grade in conduct. Very few of his schoolmates got less than 95 and a surprisingly large number of them got 100. The group photographs published in the annual indicate that there are many of just that type.

Other publications reveal the fact that there are a lot of Ernestos in Colombia. The annual statistical report of the government is a very voluminous affair but in the dull-looking pages of figures there is more human material than I have ever found in any similar mass of figures. Statistics of deaths are given in such detail that we learn that seventy-five died of alcoholism in the year 1939. By far the largest group died between the ages of fifty and sixty, which should be a warning to a number of fellows I know. But a few of the old soaks lived on past the seventies and one hardened old reprobate died after passing the age of eighty. The statistical report gives no indication that old age had anything to do with it.

On the same page there is the revealing figure that 1,286

died of homicide. I had always been under the impression that with about 10,000 homicides a year we led the world in this sort of thing but if we slaughtered each other with the persistence and efficiency of the Colombians we would average well over 50 per cent above that figure. The same isolation that has bred family feuds and given Kentucky a high homicide record leads provincial Colombians to kill each other. Families which live in the same neighborhood for centuries get on each other's nerves and inherited grudges grow with each generation. These less cultured people do not compose poems but they do distill and drink *chicha* which is as potent as anything a Kentucky moonshiner ever produced. That provides the lubricating oil when old family feuds are thrown into high gear.

Participation in these feuds must start at an early age for more than a hundred or approximately 10 per cent met their deaths before they reached the age of twenty. These mortal combats in Colombia are much more sanguinary and also much more sporting than in Kentucky. There the feudist often takes down his old squirrel rifle, draws a bead on his adversary and lets him have it. It is only by a figure of speech that his hands could be called bloody for he shoots from a safe distance. In Colombia they go to it with machetes and if the victor survives without some wicked gashes, he is either very lucky or very expert. American manufacturers who are interested in the maintenance of our prestige as the producers of superior articles should be glad to know that the feudists prefer machetes made in the U.S.A. The cheaper German knives may be all right for chopping brush out of jungles but when it comes to the serious business of homicide the keener American tool is preferred.

There can be no doubt about the power of the church

in Colombia. The struggle in every country to break the monopoly of the church in matters of education was a long and bitter one but nowhere as long and bitter as here. The constitution gives the church a certain control over education and as no one would dare to propose a change in the constitution all reforms have had to be worked out within its framework. The country is looked on as one of the last remaining strongholds of medieval clericalism. Religious issues still provide political footholds. The Liberal party which is now in power has always taken the lead in moves to break up the great property holdings of the church and provide a more liberal system of education than that offered by the pitifully inadequate parish school. There was never any confiscation of church property or other harsh measures, but at every opportunity the rival Conservative party denounces its opponents as oppressors of the church. An election appeal of this sort does not go unheeded but it is no longer so potent as in the past. Only a few years ago it would have been impossible for any candidate to be elected president of the country if the archbishop opposed him. That is no longer true for the voters have come to a realization of the fact that there are many issues more important than the preservation of the ancient privilege of the church and that even an archbishop may be wrong in his political judgment. Unfortunately at the moment many of the high church officials are nursing a grudge against the United States and unwittingly helping the Nazi propagandists. The principal if not the only cause for irritation lies in the provocative activities of a few crackpot pope-hating American missionaries who do not represent any of the well-known missionary organizations.

With their conception of the world as it was constituted

in the Middle Ages the priests of Colombia have had a very difficult time adjusting themselves to the modern world of radio and cinema. These are looked on as works of the devil which distract the attention of the young people from their devotions. Having fought them rather vainly for years the church is now offering competition. I happened to be in Bogotá during Christmas week when there was the inevitable problem as to just how far holiday gaiety might go without interfering with the appropriate religious observance of the season. The churches were crowded at the daily services, so crowded that I sneaked out of several of them because of the physical discomfort. But the churches presented a strange appearance. The familiar altar decorations were hidden by stage settings depicting the flight of the holy family. The ancient organ was supplemented by a string orchestra in the choir loft. The music was not Gregorian though I did not recognize what it was until I heard the gay "Jingle Bells" familiar to every American child. A few minutes later the climax of the musical program was reached as the orchestra broke into the strains of the rhumba. That was the church's answer to the radio and cinema.

Unlike the churches of Lima those of Bogotá are never vacant, with white women and Indians of both sexes making up a majority of the worshipers but with a much greater proportion of men of white blood than in any other place I visited. The only explanation I heard of neglect of the church by the male population in other countries was not entirely satisfactory. I asked a Peruvian why it was that so many of the churches in Lima were, most of the time, completely deserted and only sparsely filled at any time. He said that the churches were primarily intended for the women and the Indians. The Indians were a pretty wicked lot and although he didn't say so I inferred that he put the women in about the same class. He continued that so far as he was concerned he had attended divinity school in his youth, was thoroughly familiar with all the rites and ceremonies of the church, and so did not look on it as necessary to attend services regularly.

The well-dressed men and women of Bogotá appear much better dressed than they really are because they are seen surrounded by the Indian population, poor, barefooted, with clothing that is usually ragged and often dirty. The Indian men all wear ponchos—even the little boys. It is an overpowering garment. With the upper part of the body encased in it the existence of a shirt is only indicated and trousers fade into obscurity with only the lower part of the legs revealed. There are many handsome Indian men and I hoped to see a dandy with a gorgeous new poncho but was disappointed. The nearest approach to dandyism I saw were a number of Indians with Hitleresque mustaches. There was no significance to that beyond the fact that they, like Hitler, had upper lips on which mustaches would grow.

The Indians one sees around Bogotá bear no kinship to the savage uncivilized tribes in the interior who occasionally manage to pot an American oil man with one of their poisoned arrows. There are many kinds of Indians in Colombia and those around the capital come of ancient civilized stock. The great savanna where the Spanish settled has an area of about two thousand square miles completely surrounded by towering mountains. Like the coastal plain on which Lima is situated this level expanse of fertile land was inhabited by a tribe of highly civilized Indians, who were neither Incas nor Aztecs though their culture was somewhat similar. Their civilization must have reached a very high stage of sophistication for they had taught parrots to say prayers for them and when a man died his praying parrot was buried with him. How the Buddhist priests of Tibet would leap at a pious fraud like that if they only had some parrots! As they haven't they use the device of writing prayers on flags which flutter in the breeze or enclosing them in wheels which are revolved by running water.

With the barefoot population in the majority, shoe shining was more public and ostentatious in Colombia than in other places except Ecuador. Here the business is monopolized by barefoot boys in incredibly dirty pants who are to be found in every plaza. Spotting me as a gringo they shamelessly soaked me six cents for a shine but charged only three cents to shine the shoes of their fellow countrymen with bigger feet. In each case they cleaned our shoes with half a lemon. It reminded me that in Santos they always brought me finger bowl with half a lime—a portion large enough to provide one of the ingredients for a gin rickey.

In its policies the government of Colombia is most progressive but in many of its activities and especially in police regulations it is as antiquated as the Inquisition. Permits are required to enter the country, permits to leave, permits for a businessman to go to another town. It would appear that a good part of the population of Colombia consisted of officials engaged in weighing applications and passing on the question of whether or not their fellow countrymen should be allowed to go some place or other in pursuit of their lawful business. If the records of the police are as complete in fact as they are in theory it should be possible for them to tell just where every one of the more than 9 million citizens was on any given date and why.

The construction of the Panama Canal marked the beginning of a new era for Colombia. During the period that the canal was building and for some time after it was opened for traffic the Colombians nursed their resentment against the United States because of the way in which title to the Canal Zone was acquired. The facts connected with the whole matter were such as to provide each side with endless material for arguments. But soon after the canal was opened to traffic the practical benefits which Colombia received began to offset the old resentments. The canal has been of more value to Colombia than to any other country including our own. It solved a serious problem of transportation in the only way it could be solved. Colombia is the only South American country with ports on both the Atlantic and the Pacific but before the opening of the canal that was just something that looked nice on a map. Actually it required a great deal more time and cost a great deal more money to ship a ton of merchandise from Barranquilla on the Atlantic side to Buenaventura on the Pacific side than from New York to San Francisco. With the opening of the canal the two ports were linked by water and for the first time in history were able to trade with each other. Barranquilla was a sleepy banana belt town with the principal sign of activity being provided by a mule-drawn streetcar system. The opening of the canal made it a boom town which grew from less than 50,000 to more than 150,000 and is still growing.

A measure of the prosperity of Colombia is found in the figures showing our purchases of coffee. In 1909 before the canal was opened it amounted to 448,000 bags. With the opening of the canal in 1916 it increased to more than a million bags. In 1938 it amounted to 3,413,000 bags. Contrary to popular belief we are and have been for years the most important customers in most of the South American countries but in no other are our purchases so important. We take 60 per cent of all of Colombia's exports, four times as much as Germany.

The growth of commercial activity in his country threw on the Colombian businessman responsibilities he was ill equipped to face. When the Spaniards settled in Bogotá they declined to do any manual labor and they never have to this day. Their mental labor was not along useful lines. A knowledge of French authors and an ability to compose verses is of no particular value in setting up a business organization. As a matter of fact few Colombians take a very active part in the conduct of the business of their country. A large part of both imports and exports are handled by German concerns which have been long established here. The Colombian is something of an amateur at business. He has yet to establish a business code and when he does it will undoubtedly be a very fine one like that of his Spanish ancestors. In the meantime he is, to say the least, provoking. Several American businessmen assured me that they were the most impractical people in the world when it came to the negotiations of any kind of a business deal. One said that if you quoted him a price for cargo which he knew to be well under the market value he would inevitably haggle and delay and demand still lower prices. Another said he had found that the only way to do business in Bogotá was to live in Barranquilla and make occasional visits there. If one lived there the Bogotá customers could never make up their minds to place an order. This list of unexaggerated complaints might be continued indefinitely proving nothing but the caution and timidity that comes from a lack of business experience.

The fact that there are practically no steel-shuttered windows in the capital at Bogotá provides an encouraging indication that the country will make progress and develop steadily in the future. Expensive plate-glass show windows are not left unprotected if there have been recurrent revolutions in the past or if there appears any danger of them breaking out in the future. Colombia has been singularly free from political upheavals of this sort. Elections are fair and orderly and are participated in by a large proportion of the voters.

The present population of about 10 million is but a fraction of what the country could support. With its wide variety of climates Colombia produces everything that is common to both the tropical and the temperate zones—coffee, bananas, wheat and a wide variety of other products. Vast areas have never been planted and the land under cultivation is worked by the most primitive methods. Some experts have estimated that the country could pasture 50,000,000 head of cattle, which is 16,792,713 more cattle than Argentina has according to the latest available statistics. The most recently developed source of wealth is oil. Colombians are completely justified in looking on their country as the treasure house of South America and they believe that with the industrial development that will accompany more thorough cultivation of the soil the country could easily support a population of 100,000,000.

CHAPTER XV

## *Nickel and Dime Stores in Brazil*

WHEN I began looking around for the largest and most successful retail establishment in Rio de Janeiro, I had no idea what I would find. I thought most likely it would be a Brazilian imitation of an American department store, just as I found in other journeys, German imitations in Berlin and Japanese imitations in Tokyo. And it would not have surprised me to have found a German or a Japanese store struggling to look like a Berlin or a Tokyo imitation of an American store. I had heard so much about German and Japanese initiative in all parts of South America that I was prepared for anything. Conversely I had heard so many stories about the blindness of my own fellow countrymen to the obvious possibilities for the trade in this part of the world that I sometimes wondered if I would be able to buy Gillette blades, or Kolynos toothpaste. In any event the store I found was the very last thing I expected to find.

There wasn't any question about where the taxi should take me. Ask a hundred Brazilians in Rio what is the largest and busiest store and you will receive one hundred identical answers. It is the *Lojas Americanas*. Having been in South America three days I was too sophisticated to be deceived by the name. One of the first things the North American has to learn is that we have no monopoly of the name "American" which is the common possession of the citizens of every one of the twenty-one republics. But in this case the name meant just exactly what the greenest tourist would expect it to mean. It is an American store, founded by Americans (I mean North Americans) and managed by them. It is located on a street just off the Rio Branco, the great street of Rio. But if the Portuguese signs were replaced by English, the extra zeros cut off the milreis prices and a few more blondes mixed with the predominantly brunette sales force, the visitor might think he had stepped into a five-and-ten-cent store just off Fifth Avenue or off any one of a hundred streets in a hundred cities of the United States. It is as American as Woolworth's and in fact a kind of collateral descendant of the Woolworth chains.

I had just recovered from my surprise at this discovery when I was told that this is only one of a growing chain of identical stores already constituting the biggest retail-selling organization in all of South America. There are now eleven units in the chain and each one is larger and busier than any other shop in its trade area. The smallest unit would be considered a large and important store in any city south of the Panama Canal. It all started when James E. Marshall found that he had to use Spanish as well as English signs in a Woolworth store he managed in Florida. But he wouldn't have seen these signs if he hadn't already served his apprenticeship in the Woolworth organization. And the Brazilian enterprise would not have been the great success it is if he had not spent a few more years in preparation for the venture. Like W. T. Grant, F. W. Woolworth, S. S. Kresge, F. M. Kirby and a number of others who have made names for themselves in the chain-store business, Jim Marshall's home was in Wilkes-Barre. But that is not the reason he got into the business. His ambition was to be a bookkeeper, sit at a desk and add up figures and wear a white collar—draw his pay check every Saturday but wear a white collar seven days a week. That was the life. Most of the boys in Wilkes-Barre worked in the coal mines and white collars were out of the question. Young Jim wasn't sure about the other talents he might have but he knew that he could add and subtract and multiply and that appeared to indicate that he was a natural-born bookkeeper. He was so anxious to get going on this career that he graduated himself from high school just about the time the teachers had gotten well acquainted with him and he took a course in a commercial college. Then came the bookkeeping job and he was all set for life. All set until a boy friend who was a little older came back to spend his vacation in Wilkes-Barre and told Jim what a swell job he had working in a Woolworth store some place in North Carolina.

There was life and movement there. Customers came in. Every day you opened up cases of new merchandise—all of it interesting. Suddenly Jim realized that the life he had chosen for himself was one of monastic seclusion. A book-keeper in a cage, with no daily human contacts except the boss who might not be pleasant. In the impulsive way of boys he changed his career overnight. He was eighteen.

"I knew I was on the right track when I got in to see the boss of the Woolworth store," he told me. "There he was in business hours getting his shoes shined while people came in and he told them what to do. I decided at once that was the life for me. Sit on a stand and get your shoes shined and have people come up and ask you what they are to do next."

During the time that his shoes were being shined the Woolworth boss questioned Jim and just as the bootblack put on the final flourish with his polishing cloth, said:

"All right. We'll hire you as an assistant at eight dollars a week."

Jim rushed home to tell his mother that he had been hired as assistant manager of the Woolworth store.

His first surprise came when he found that he was not to work in the Wilkes-Barre store but in the one at Sunbury.

"That was the longest journey I ever took in my life," Jim told me. "I was leaving Wilkes-Barre for the first time and I wondered if I would ever get back."

The second surprise came when he learned that in the Woolworth vocabulary "assistant" is a very flexible term. He was assistant in the sense that he assisted everyone else, especially in the manual labor of opening cases and unpacking merchandise, carrying it upstairs to be placed on the display counter. Once in a while they let him stay after hours and decorate windows.

The only chance he ever got to wear a white collar was on Sunday for on all the other days he wore corduroys.

At the end of the year he got a raise of a dollar a week. It began to look as if he might die of old age before he got to the point where he could have his shoes shined during the business hours and tell anyone else what he should do. Maybe the bookkeeping job was better. Certainly he decided he was a failure as a merchandise man and he was getting on in years for he would soon be twenty-one. He had a vacation coming and was so anxious to get back to Wilkes-Barre and stay there, that a week before the vacation was due to start he bought a Wilkes-Barre ticket, just to carry around in his pocket and look at it. At the appropriate time he was going to inform the boss with as much dignity as is possible in a twenty-year-old, that the great and growing Woolworth chain would have to get along without him.

Maybe it was chance. The day before he was going to leave there appeared in the office mail a blue letter which meant that it was for the personal attention of one of the staff. The letter was for Jim, the first indication that the executives of Woolworth's knew of his existence. Pinned to it was a check for twenty-five dollars, almost a month's salary. He was courteously invited to go to Atlanta, Georgia, at an increase in pay. Jim went and kept the ticket to Wilkes-Barre as a souvenir. From there he was shunted all over the South, usually to new or struggling units of the Woolworth chain where a young fellow who had ideas and didn't mind working ten or twelve hours a day would be useful. He began saving money because every good Woolworth man was supposed to have money in the bank.

As manager of the store at Ybar City, Florida, the first exotic influence came into his life, the first indication there was anything of interest or importance outside the United

States. Ybar City had been a great center for the manufacture of cigars; the residence of many Cubans whose wives and daughters spoke Spanish. All the signs in the store had to be in Spanish as well as English. This was strange business to Jim and he was cautious and careful. He would give each sign to three girls and ask for independent translations which he would compare letter by letter. If all three translations agreed he would give the three Spanish texts to three other girls and ask them what the English meaning was. If they all agreed that the translation was correct Jim assumed that no mistakes had been made. Then he had the sign printed. That was the way he worked and the reason that he traveled fast in the Woolworth organization—plus the fact that he worked fast.

Those Spanish signs fermented in his mind. Cuban women came into his store speaking a language he couldn't understand, but they made the cash registers ring. It was fascinating to him to hear them speak Spanish to the sales girls and then pay out money for the goods they had selected. He had traveled a long way from Wilkes-Barre and with the great distance that exists between Florida and Pennsylvania the terror of being so far away from home had disappeared. He was on his way to Brazil and didn't know it.

The World War intervened. The recruiting officer wouldn't take him as a rookie because he was underweight. So he joined the officers training camp and finally became a sergeant. Not a very high rank, but better than not being in the army at all.

When the Armistice was signed he had his mind made up to another career. He was going to be a traveling salesman, carry samples, have an expense account, stop at good hotels and sell spaghetti for a New Jersey concern. After the stress and excitement of army life, a chain store appeared small and cramped. A traveling salesman had some scope and action. The spaghetti manufacturer hired him on sight. But a few days before he was going to start on this new job he went into a Wilkes-Barre bank to cash a check for his mother and he ran right into one of the Woolworth bosses.

"How long have you been home, Jim?" the boss enquired.

"About a month, sir," said Jim.

"Then why haven't you started to work?"

"I'll be around in the morning," said Jim.

There followed more years of coddling new stores and nursing sick ones and Jim got all he wanted of hotels for he was constantly transferred from one place to another and had to leave each store as soon as its problems appeared to be solved.

"It really wasn't fair to me," Jim told me. "I didn't get much of a chance to learn from other people. Only once in a while I worked under someone who knew more about the business than I did and learned something from him. I had to tell people what to do when I wasn't too sure myself."

He worked in much bigger places but all the time the memory of those Spanish signs in the Ybar City store kept coming back in his memory.

Woolworth opened stores in Cuba and if they had sent Jim there he might have remained with them. But they didn't and he began thinking about going to some Spanish-speaking country and opening a store of his own.

In 1926 he had earned a long vacation and he and his brother took a trip to South America. They thought that maybe they would find a place where a dime store was needed. At any rate they would have a look. Jim was thirty years old and for that age had traveled far. He could look forward with confidence to increasingly important jobs in Woolworth's and he had found that while the lower-grade employees were paid very small salaries those in the upper brackets were very well paid indeed. All that he had to do was to stay with the organization and he would be a very rich man, possibly a millionaire. But he was sure it would be more fun running a store of his own. The place he had in mind was Buenos Aires. After his experience with the Spanish signs in Ybar City he had been reading books about the countries south of Rio Grande and had learned that Harrod's of London had established a very successful store there. If a store the type of Harrod's would succeed there seemed good reason to believe that a dime store would have a good chance. Late in the summer the two brothers returned and their plans were all set to open a store in Buenos Aires. There was only one difficulty. Jim would have to save some more money. He knew he would have to start on a shoestring but he wanted the string to be as long as possible. Then something unexpected happened—Jim fell in love so suddenly and so violently that he proposed to the girl four days after he met her, was accepted in September and they were married before Christmas.

"I waited until after we were married before I broke the news that she was going to spend the rest of her life in South America," Jim told me. "Maybe I shouldn't have done this. But it has worked out all right."

Anyone who visits his home and meets Mrs. Marshall sees that it has worked out all right in every way. Atlantic City was the appropriate place to go for a honeymoon and Jim thriftily arranged to be transferred there for a few months. He needed all his dollars for the great adventure in Buenos Aires. The honeymoon trip lasted two years for Jim stayed on in the Atlantic City store for that time. Then in 1929 he counted his money and decided it was time to go. In the meantime he had taken on two partners. One of them had money to invest. The other had no money but he was so enthusiastic about the whole venture that he was counted in. Jim sold his Woolworth stock, took his money out of the savings bank, sold his furniture, and with his bride and the two partners set out for Buenos Aires.

Another bit of luck too for if he had waited just a little longer the stock-market crash would have hit him and cut his little shoestring in half. Jim never got any farther than Brazil. A Brazilian they met on the boat urged him to have another look at Rio de Janeiro before they made a final decision. He did and Jim saw a lot of things he hadn't seen on his previous trip. As a matter of fact he hadn't paid very much attention to Rio. Those provocative signs he had seen in Ybar City had been in Spanish. His imagination had been stirred by the idea of Spanish-speaking customers and he had actually learned some Spanish. No Spanish was spoken in Rio—only Portuguese. But Rio was a big city, the streets full of people who were neatly dressed, and had money to spend. There were thousands of government clerks, army officers and employees of big companies who did not earn very much money but the pay checks were regular and dependable. There were very few wealthy people. Almost everyone belonged to the class that had to figure the family budget pretty carefully —the class that would have some respect for a dime and would not spurn a nickel.

There were hundreds of individual shops, some very

fine ones. But the shops which had the most imposing displays and the best locations stocked only the goods that the very wealthy could buy. Many a shop had several hundred thousand dollars' worth of merchandise on the shelves and never more than two or three customers in the place. Jim couldn't help thinking of the thousands of customers who would come to a shop in that location every day if it were stocked with articles selling at five and ten cents.

The Brazilian customers who make small purchases but make them every day had been overlooked by the Rio shopkeepers. All the attention was centered on the rich who every now and then might buy a diamond ring or a fur coat, purchased at a profit that would pay the day's rent for the vendor. The housewife in search of a saucepan or a package of hairpins was forced to go into some untidy store and deal with a trousered salesman who might or might not be respectful—especially if she happened to be a young and pretty housewife. If she had a dozen items on her shopping list she might have to go to half a dozen places before she bought all of the items and often take what the little shop had in stock, rather than what she wanted. With every item she bought she had to argue about the price and after she got home she was never sure she might not have done a little better if she had argued a little longer.

Jim's enthusiasm for Buenos Aires shifted to Rio. As a matter of fact he has enough enthusiasm to cover a good many cities as he probably will before he gets through. And Mrs. Marshall liked Rio. She had never complained about having to leave all of her friends and relatives but Jim's conscience had always hurt him a little about waiting until after the marriage ceremony before telling her that she was going to go so far away from home that she couldn't get back very often.

Rio was decided on as the headquarters for this strange new attack on the Brazilian retail trade. But after leasing the premises there for the first store Jim decided that he would make his initial venture in Niteroi, a smaller place across the bay.

"I knew I was going to make a lot of mistakes," Jim told me. "So I thought it would be better to start in a place where the mistakes would be smaller and wouldn't attract so much attention."

The goods which had been ordered in New York for shipment to Buenos Aires were diverted to Rio and everyone worked early and late getting ready for the day when the goods could be unpacked and put on sale. Everyone got up at four o'clock in the morning so as to get the first ferry from Rio. Jim had a lot of help and advice. The local American community was very much interested in the enterprise, though doubtful about its success. Quite a number of Brazilians got interested in it, not because they expected to profit by it but just because the Brazilians are a kindly and helpful people and because they are intensely interested in anything that is new.

As the result of the Brazilian contacts which he established, Jim played a role he had never thought of, that is, he introduced what was practically a new word into the Portuguese-Brazilian language. A Brazilian doctor who had studied the history of the Portuguese language was responsible. There are two words which can be applied to a retail establishment, just as we may call a place a shop or a store. One of these words is *casa* and the other is *lojas*. For some curious reason every merchant who had ever set up a business in Brazil had called his establishment a *casa* and no one had ever used the word *lojas*. Some say that probably the first Portuguese merchant who set up a little shop several centuries ago called it a *casa* and everyone else followed his example. It was as much as if in America every retail place would be called a shop and none referred to as store. The Brazilian doctor argued pontifically that *lojas* was really the right word to use. Jim didn't bother about the learned arguments but the idea of giving his store a name that would set it apart as different from all others appealed to him and so the name *Lojas Americanas* was adopted.

It was the first *lojas* in all Brazil but now there are hundreds of them.

In fact whatever the word *lojas* may mean in the Portuguese dictionary it means in Brazil a store which sells dependable merchandise at a cheap price.

The executive staff was pretty evenly divided between Brazilians and North Americans who had a hard time talking to each other. The Brazilians knew little English and the North Americans knew less Portuguese. But they had to work together and in their daily contacts each learned the other's language. Jim is very proud of the fact that all the members of his staff speak Portuguese. He says that he is not very good at it but as I sat in his office and listened to him at work over the telephone I noticed that he could change from one language to the other and back again without pausing to shift gears.

One thing about which there was no argument was that the entire sales force which would come in contact with the customers should be composed of girls. In Brazil as in all other countries, it is the husband who brings home the pay check, but it is the wife who spends it. Jim had seen the male Brazilian salesman at work and knew that the customer he had in mind would feel more at ease with sales girls. But there were no shop girls in Brazil. The general idea of Brazilians of every layer of society was that girls should lead a secluded existence. In theory she should be kept hidden from prying eyes of the predatory male until some young blade began coming along on the pleasant nights strumming a guitar under her balcony. If he strummed persistently enough or if he stuck it out in rainy weather, it was assumed that his intentions were serious and papa would make some inquiries. If everything worked out all right a marriage would be arranged. Historical accuracy compels me to add that most of the guitars in Brazil were owned by the grandfathers of the present generation and most of them are without strings. But even without guitars the theory of seclusion remained the same.

Lucky Jim! Just at the time he decided to spend the rest of his life in Rio a revolution was brewing in that beautiful city. No troops were called out and no blood was shed but it was a revolution. It was a quiet but determined revolt of the girls who had been seeing Hollywood pictures and through them learning that there are other things in life beside sitting at home and waiting for some young fellow to come along and marry you. They wanted to play tennis. They wanted to wear bathing suits, even if the men did look at them. They didn't want to be like the girl who married dear old dad but like the girls who live such glamorous lives in the films.

Jim became an agent provocateur in the revolt and sent it speeding on its way. He announced that the *Lojas Americanas* would use only sales girls, that an increasing number of jobs would be open to them. It was difficult getting the first few, but his Brazilian friends helped him.

After that it was easier. There were doubtless many anxious family conferences where papa and mama gravely considered the strange new life the willful daughter proposed taking up. She would have to sit in a shop where any man who came along could stare at her, would have to quote prices, and sell merchandise to strange men. Nothing of the balcony seclusion about this.

The first shop across the bay from Rio was opened with all due ceremony. It was customary for a priest to bless every new enterprise and the baby *Lojas Americanas* was brought into the world with all the customary rites. The shop was opened for business at eight o'clock on the following morning. All the sales girls were at their counters, the stock display and the price signs in place. Jim and his assistants lurked in the back of the place, trying to look unconcerned. An hour went by and no one came. A great many stopped and looked at the show windows but that was all. Some of his fellow countrymen had told Jim that the Brazilians are a proud people who would be ashamed to be seen entering a cheap shop and Jim was beginning to think they might be right.

Maybe he had been a fool to quit the exceptionally good job at Woolworth's. Finally just a few minutes after nine o'clock a little Syrian girl after pressing her nose against the windowpane for a long time came into the *lojas* and bought a ten-cent doll.

"I wanted to grab her and kiss her," Jim told me.

That was the beginning of a trickle of customers that soon became a stream which has grown larger every year. It was a good thing it was just a trickle at first. The girls had no idea about the way they should conduct themselves. The Americans had to apologize to indignant customers, explain to the girls that they shouldn't argue and talk back even if they knew they were right and the customer was wrong. The idea was to sell goods. There were other troubles. The original stock of goods had been a typical Woolworth selection, just about what one would have found in any Woolworth store located in the South where, as in the coastal regions of South America, one does not meet extreme cold. Jim had studied the market as best he could but he learned something new the first day he started in business and tells me he is still learning.

At the time he selected the stock there was a vogue for toy stuffed elephants at home and Jim bought a few gross of them. The elephants were made with the trunk hanging down because they packed better that way.

When he unpacked his stock the sales girls didn't want to handle the elephants. His Brazilian advisers said no one would buy them. Why? The figure was an unlucky one. Why? Because his trunk was hanging down. If the trunks were up in the air in the position an elephant assumes when trumpeting, would that still be unlucky? No, that was a lucky omen. One of the axioms of the chain-store business is that merchandise must be disposed of and Jim sold the elephants. In their spare time the girls performed major operations, skillfully dismembering the trunks and sewing them on again sticking straight up in the air. The elephants sold and Jim ordered more of them, instructing the puzzled manufacturer that toy elephants intended for sale in Brazil had to conform to certain standards of conduct. The way things worked out was that the trumpeting elephant was a much more intriguing figure than the other and the manufacturer who grumbled about having to make a special breed of elephants for the Brazilian trade soon found his sales of elephants at home increased. Because this was one of the first things he learned about the spe-

cialized tastes of the Brazilian customers, Jim has always
stocked toy elephants and you will see them in every one
of his shops—just so no one will forget that, no matter
how unreasonable he may be, the customer is right.

Dolls have an even greater symbolic importance than
trumpeting elephants and anyone who has a lot of cheap
dolls to sell will find Marshall's sales resistance practically
negative.

But there was one assortment of merchandise he didn't
salvage. It consisted of cheap ornaments, ribbons and other
doo-dads in which purple was the predominant color.
There was no reason why Jim or anyone else in the United
States should know that in Brazil a dark purple is the color
of death and that while women will wear dresses in which
black is the predominant color, no one would wear a hat
in which there was the smallest purple flower or a bit of
ribbon.

The sales girls learned their jobs and after a little while
there was no difficulty about getting all the help wanted
in the store, or rather in the stores, for it wasn't long before there were several of them. The girls and their papas
and mamas soon learned that when it came to the all-
important business of getting married, a job in the *Lojas
Americanas* was a good deal more effective than sitting
in a balcony and wondering if the handsome young man
would risk bringing his guitar out in the rain. All of the
original employees are married and many of those who
succeeded them. There is in fact a continual turnover in
the stores although no girl has ever been known to quit
her job except for the one purpose of getting married.
Most of the girls make very good marriages with young
men who come into the store. Instead of playing the guitar
they buy merchandise.

I don't know whether Jim does it or not but it wouldn't surprise me if just by accident the prettiest girls should be put at the counters where the most difficult merchandise happens to be stocked. I spent a lot of time in the various stores and I remember one day seeing a very well-dressed young man buy a potato masher for which he obviously had no use. But the girl was very pretty. I asked Jim if they lost sight of the girls after they were married.

"No," he said. "They always come back to see the store they worked in and in fact they are just about our best customers."

At the time the first *lojas* was opened the Brazilian milreis was worth about twelve cents. Jim invented a sign which he had copyrighted and protected in every way. It read:

### NADA ALEM DE 2$ooo

Translated into English this meant that nothing in the store was priced at more than two milreis, or at the time, about twenty-five cents in U. S. currency. This was in spite of the fact that more than 75 per cent of the goods had been imported from home, had paid the Brazilian duty and each article bore a revenue stamp. Then the milreis began to fall in value, slipping down to its present level of about five cents. With each fall it became more and more difficult to find goods and it began to look as if the *Lojas Americanas* would have to go out of business not through lack of customers but because of a lack of goods to sell to the customers.

In the original stock a few articles of Brazilian manufacture had been included. There were not many articles because ten years ago there were very few articles made in Brazil. Jim set out to find other things that could be made here and feed the constantly growing demands of his customers. There was some very good pottery produced near Rio according to designs that had been brought over from Portugal a long time ago. Jim cajoled the manufacturer into producing pottery according to his designs and placed with him the largest orders he had ever received. In the same way he hunted up manufacturers of glassware and porcelain and others who were making crude and poorly designed pots and other kitchen utensils. By this time the *Lojas Americanas* had grown and Jim had brought down from the States a number of young bachelors with chain-store experience, mostly in Woolworth's. They were sent in search of struggling Brazilian factories —and most of them were struggling—and reported on what each could make. Then they returned to the factories with designs and orders. They were insistent on the design, insistent that the quality be maintained, but if the manufacturer could meet their requirements he was sure not only of a large initial order but of a steady stream of orders.

As was the case when he sold his shares in order to get cash for his South American venture and when he hired his sales girls, Jim's timing was just right. Brazilians had just come to a realization of the fact that as an agricultural country they could never compete with the rich lands of the Argentine. Public-minded Brazilians were anxious to see their country industrialized. But it lacked both capital and trained technicians. Ten years earlier he would have run into indifference. Now he found the small manufacturers eager to help, ready to co-operate, and many of them have risen to prosperity through the start that James E. Marshall gave them. In the meantime there have been a number of large manufacturing enterprises started—such as shoe factories and textile mills—with capital investments running into millions in any currency.

But in his modest way Marshall may have made a greater contribution toward the industrial development of Brazil. There are dozens of factories which either came into existence or were placed on a solid financial basis solely because of his incessant search for salable merchandise. And the process is still going on. If any Brazilian has an idea of starting a factory that will produce articles of a small unit value he is sure of encouragement from Marshall's experts and of substantial orders if he can produce goods. Jim himself has never made any attempt to appraise the effect his efforts have had on the development of Brazilian industries. His only interest is in securing salable goods for *Lojas Americanas* and if, as a result of those efforts a certain number of Brazilian manufacturers have been aided and encouraged to build up factories which would supply goods for others and even for export, Jim didn't care. He never tried to make an exclusive contract of any kind with a manufacturer. All he wanted was the first chance to market a design which he or his staff had worked out. After that he was willing to take his chances with any and all competitors. But the results of his work are beginning to show up in the official statistics of Brazilian exports. When the infant *Lojas Americanas* received the blessing of the priest there were not many toys produced in Brazil. The little Syrian girl who was the first customer bought a doll because there were not many little girls of any nationality in Brazil who owned a doll. Jim started specializing in dolls and encouraged the manufacture of all kinds of toys. The industry has now attained such importance that when the Argentine-Brazilian trade conference reached an agreement soon after I was in Rio one of the clauses provided for the sale of Brazilian toys in Argentina.

With the continued drop in the value of Brazilian currency even the articles which were locally made increased in price and soon the old sales slogan was outmoded because there were so few articles which could be sold for two milreis. The signs came down from the stores and the slogan was discarded. But Brazilians still refer to it as the "*Lojas dos dois milreis*" which is the the American equivalent of "the dime store." At the present time articles which sell as high as fifty cents are regularly stocked and occasional experiments are made with articles which sell at a still higher price.

The little trial store across the bay from Rio was still hitting on one cylinder when the main store in Rio itself was opened. There was not on this occasion the long and anxious wait for the first customer. While not exactly waiting for the store to open, there were crowds in the store within a few minutes after the shop girls took their places. In rapid succession other stores were opened so that before the year was ended Jim had not only the original store in Niteroi but four others in Rio itself. On the anniversary of the opening of the first store, he opened one in São Paulo, the bustling industrial city in Southern Brazil. São Paulo is three hundred miles from Rio, but the reputation of *Lojas Americanas* had spread. When the São Paulo store was opened the crowd outside was so dense that fifty policemen had to be called in to keep order and for the first part of the day customers were allowed in only a few at a time.

In the decade that the *Lojas Americanas* has been in existence there has never been a halt in its growth. In fact each year progress has been a little more rapid, sales volume going beyond the quotas set. Expansion has been about equally divided between the establishment of new stores and the enlargement of old ones. In Marshall's office which overlooks the bay and city of Rio there is an impressive display of blueprints and architects' sketches showing how existing stores will be enlarged, just as soon as a new lease can be made. The original sales force of a dozen girls has been increased until now there are more than a thousand. With the rapid growth of the business Jim found his accelerator wasn't working properly because of lack of capital, so he reorganized the company and sold stock to his friends. Liberal dividends have been paid from the start but the dividend figure gives no more than a hint of what has been earned. If the *Lojas Americanas* were liquidated tomorrow the stockholders could reasonably expect to receive many times the amount of their original investment.

Jim learned about the peculiar tastes of the Brazilians in the matter of merchandise and he learned a lot of other things about them that make him what might be called an enthusiastic pro-Brazilian. When he started there were plenty of hard-boiled old Brazilian hands—Americans who had lived there for years—who were prophesying failure. One argument they advanced was that the Brazilians would be ashamed to be seen going into what was openly and avowedly a cheap store. Another school of gloom dispensers said that the plan to display the goods on unprotected open counters was not only suicidal but wicked. It would encourage petty thievery and Jim would not only lose his profits through what is known politely as "inventory shrinkages" but he would encourage crime. As in all chain stores the inventories in the *Lojas Americanas* units are watched with meticulous care, not only to learn the bad news about shrinkages but also to avoid that great tragedy of being out of stock of salable merchandise. You would think that Jim was a Brazilian patriot defending the honor of his native land when he shows you figures over a period of years proving that his losses from petty thefts of customers and the pilfering of his employees amount to less than half of similar losses in the chain stores of the good old United States.

Jim Marshall has never gone to Buenos Aires, the place he started for. Maybe he will get there some day. But he has a lot to do in Brazil.

"There are 45 million customers in this country," he told me, "and there are a lot of them that I am not selling anything to."

CHAPTER XVI

## Can We Hold Our Export Trade?

SOME future historian who happens to compare statistics of American foreign trade of today with the books and magazine articles of contemporary writers will find himself confronted by a very puzzling problem. He will have to decide which of two directly contradictory statements of facts he should accept as correct. The figures show that American manufactured products have a wider distribution than those of any other country; that in many lines we have a virtual monopoly of the field. If the records are still available he will find that this is true in spite of the fact that from toothpaste to tractors, the products marked "made in U.S.A." are almost invariably sold at a higher price than those of competitors. A little further research will disclose the fact that in the decade of 1930-40 there were American banks, selling agencies, branch factories and assembly plants all over the world, that in the years of peace all of them were busy and most of them were prosperous.

On the other hand numberless books and magazine articles will state directly or infer that American businessmen of this decade were rank amateurs in the field of foreign trade and were constantly losing business to competitors and especially to the clever Germans. In support of this statement he will be able to read dozens of anecdotes in which it is revealed that this order, or that order, or both orders, slipped from the hands of an American salesman to fall into the hands of a German—and always because of the stupidity or stubbornness of the American manufacturer or exporter. The authors of these books and magazine articles are sincere and patriotic Americans who are genuinely grieved. They offer the manufacturer much kindly advice, but he continues to make the same old mistakes. The historian born after the year 2000 will find it very puzzling that a group of businessmen should be so dumb and at the same time so successful.

So far as I have been able to discover, the authors of these stories are all writers whose business experience has been confined to collecting pay checks from editors or publishers and spending the proceeds. Certainly none of them ever made a living selling or promoting the sale of American goods in foreign fields or they would never have recorded so many unimportant and wholly misleading incidents. As popular writers they have a keen eye for the picturesque and the unusual. As men without merchandising experience they are often blind to the uninteresting but significant facts about export trade. As a result they have quite innocently built up and continue to perpetuate the great myth that when it comes to export trade our manufacturers are sadly inefficient.

Having said this, I may as well admit that I once made a modest contribution to this myth myself. At the time my sole business experience had been confined to usually futile attempts to make my pay check as a police reporter last from one pay day to the next. A series of fortunate circumstances sent me on a long vacation trip to Mexico, my first visit to any foreign country. I spent several days on the Isthmus of Tehuantepec where like other visitors I was amused to find that the ladies wear a headdress looking very much like a widow's veil except for the fact that it is white, beribboned and fringed with lace. A young mining engineer from Colorado who was living on the isthmus told me the story of the origin of the peculiar headdress—and a very good story it was. He said that in the sailing ship days a French frigate had been wrecked near the spot and the natives enjoyed a period of prosperity by salvaging the wreckage. They found many casks of brandy or wine and other useful merchandise which they either drank or sold, but several huge cases were packed with articles which puzzled them. The contents of the cases consisted of many gross of infants' dresses consigned to shops in Buenos Aires. The natives could find no use for these garments because it had never occurred to them that an infant should ever be clothed in anything but the dirt which their skins accumulated without effort or expense. But one of the ladies put the little bodice over her head and the skirt, covered with ribbons and lace, fell down her back. The effect pleased her as it did all the other ladies and so a new style was started. The fortunate possessors of the cases full of infant dresses prospered in the millinery business—until they ran out of stock.

About this time that ubiquitous German salesman, who always seems to be on the spot when there is a piece of business to be picked up, appeared on the scene and with characteristic enterprise collared the millinery business of the place. He sent instructions to his factory in Hamburg and in no time at all they were turning out infant dresses for sale to the millinery trade of Tehuantepec. The young mining engineer, who was about my age, was all burned up over the fact that some American manufacturer hadn't grabbed this golden trade opportunity—and so was I. They may have overlooked a bet but I didn't. I collected a few photographs and wrote an article about it for which a Chicago trade magazine paid me thirty-five dollars. A newspaper editor in Des Moines wrote an editorial based on the facts as set forth in the article, sternly warning American manufacturers that this was the sort of thing they would have to look out for if they ever expected to get anywhere in the field of foreign trade. As for myself, I not only earned the price of a new suit of clothes but had a warm and satisfactory feeling that I had given American manufacturers something to think about.

At this late date I doubt if there was any truth in the story the young engineer poured into my equally youthful ears. I see that a travel handbook refers to the headdress as an old Aztec costume. There may be some doubt about that. But there is no doubt about the fact that I wrote the story of the German salesman in the most complete ignorance of anything connected with manufacturing and merchandising. This was impressed on me a few years later when I got into the merchandising profession myself and learned something about what keeps the wheels of factories turning. The total number of ladies affecting this curious costume is only a few thousand. As styles do not change they wear the same garment for years. A very simple calculation will show that the replacements could not possibly amount to more than 500 units annually. As the unit price is about a dollar, a monopoly of the business would hardly justify any manufacturer in buying a new sewing machine.

That silly story of mine is typical of hundreds which have been written by men who, like myself at the time, knew nothing about trade. And I am inclined to think that many of them took the same mildly venomous delight I did in showing up the American manufacturer. Young newspapermen, and many experienced writers, revel in stories of this kind because of a rather general belief that the average businessman is not as smart as he is supposed to be—certainly not as smart as a good city editor. And it must be admitted that in the past the American manufacturers have provided them with plenty of material.

It was not until about twenty-five years ago that we really got into the export business for ourselves. Before that time the overseas sale of American products had been handled by export agents of other nationalities and by a group of commission houses which operated in New York. Some of the foreign firms, principally British and German, had been in existence for generations and were well known and trusted by the merchants with whom they dealt. Their executives spoke and wrote the language of the country whether it was Spanish, French, Portuguese or Hindustani. They were familiar with local currencies, import duties, trade regulations and business practice. When they took an agency for an American product it was assured a fair distribution and the manufacturer found a profitable export trade with no headaches or worries. Many of them not only didn't know anything about how their products were sold abroad but didn't care to know anything beyond the figures showing the profits they had made.

The New York commission houses operated on a slightly different basis. They did not represent manufacturers; but with branches or correspondents in all the principal commercial centers of the world they acted as purchasing agents for local dealers. If a merchant in some South American city wanted to purchase, let us say, a hundred Oliver plows, he would place the order with a commission house. The latter would purchase the plows for him at the best possible price, attend to the packing, shipping and insurance and charge the merchant a commission for the services performed. A good many American manufacturers did quite a big and profitable business through these commission houses with only a vague idea as to where their goods were being sold.

As he was making money out of the export trade and had no worries about it the manufacturer might have continued this inefficient system of distribution for many years. But the World War destroyed the old machine. The moment the war started the British and German agencies began to lose their usefulness and when we joined the Allies the German connections which had lasted that long came to an abrupt end. The New York commission houses continued to operate throughout the war and in fact most of them made a great deal of money. But for one reason or another, most of them went into bankruptcy when the armistice was signed and the few which remained soon passed out of the picture. The manufacturer had to handle his own export business or see it perish.

The mistakes he made were grotesque in character, gigantic in size. In many cases he didn't even know how to use a cable code. He didn't know that ocean freights are computed by volume as well as by weight. He had to learn from experience how roughly stevedores can handle a case of fragile merchandise. Each country had different currencies, different methods of computing customs duties, different regulations to which exporters must conform. There were a thousand little tricks of the trade and he didn't know any of them. To make matters worse he often employed as export manager some Central American whose only asset lay in the fact that he knew the Spanish language. Sometimes he wasn't even good at that.

In all ports of the world local merchants who had ordered merchandise from the United States awaited the arrival of the cargo with a certain amount of trepidation. When it did arrive it was often found that things were even worse than had been feared. I didn't have to read about these mistakes in a book or hear about them second-hand for I saw them in China. Merchandise was broken and worthless because of poor packing. A thousand pounds of candy arrived in sticky masses of chocolate, sugar, cardboard and sea water. Documents necessary for clearing cargo through the customs were often missing. Freight charges were excessive because packing cases were unnecessarily large. As China was a foreign country they shipped goods packaged for Mexico or Cuba, with nice Spanish labels that no one could read. They sent us catalogues and advertising matter in Spanish. Just for a change we would get some in German or French. I suppose the only reason they didn't send Chinese catalogues to Brazil and Argentina was that they hadn't gotten around to printing them in that language.

All the mistakes made in the Far East were duplicated in South America with local variations. Brazilian businessmen who speak nothing but Portuguese were insulted by the receipt of letters in Spanish, a language they affect to despise. Residents of Argentina were equally incensed at receiving letters in Portuguese. In some countries import duties are computed on a basis of gross weight and some importers had to pay twice the normal duty because of the unnecessarily heavy packing material. South America probably suffered the most because the merchants there were suddenly cut off from their usual supply of merchandise from Europe and had to take what they could get from the United States or do without. Some manufacturers took advantage of the opportunity to get rid of faulty goods, figuring that with the customer so far away distance would soften the blow when his kicks came back.

The British and Germans who had been making steady profits handling the sales of American products had always contended that we couldn't do this for ourselves and they found plenty of evidence that they were right. The stories of what happened during those adolescent days of our foreign trade are still told with relish. Colossal mistakes were inevitable. Instead of building up the machinery slowly over a period of years and generations as the British and the Germans had done, the American manufacturer had been compelled to do it all at once.

As might have been expected he never made the same mistake twice. This is true in spite of the fact that mistakes are still being made—just enough of them to keep the old myth of American ineptness alive. But they are made by *new* manufacturers. The only significance they have is that they indicate the growing interest in the export trade. Every month, or every week, or possibly every day, some manufacturer decides to see what he can do about selling his goods abroad. A good many of them fail to make a thorough study of the procedure they should follow and learn by the old trial and error method. But they learn.

As soon as the American manufacturer began selling his own goods abroad he saw that under his old system he had only skimmed the surface. In most cases the agents or commission houses had not sold his goods but had only filled the orders that came their way. In dozens of countries there was an undreamed of volume of business to be done. The curly-headed export managers who wrote such nice long letters in Spanish were replaced by American sales managers with clerkly assistants who could translate their letters for them. With this new setup and with most of his mistakes things of the past the American manufacturer began to give his competitors a race in which he soon took the leading position and has never given it up.

The basic idea of the American manufacturing and merchandising system is quite different from that of other countries. The British, and to an even greater extent the Germans, manufactured for the export market lines of unbranded merchandise that could be sold on a basis of price competition. For many years the British dominated the cotton goods markets of the world principally because of the cheap labor employed in the Lancashire mills. During the same period the Germans flooded the world's markets with cheap hardware. Then the Japanese came along with even cheaper labor and took both markets away from them.

Price competition is something the American manufacturer has always tried to avoid. In the development of his domestic business he has always tried to create a product of outstanding merit and distinctive design. His ideal was a piece of merchandise enjoying such a high reputation for quality that it would sell regardless of the fact that competitive articles may be offered at a lower price. Having perfected his manufacturing processes he called in advertising men to help him and as a result he built up a single product or a line of products which would sell by brand name. That was not an entirely new idea. But Americans were the first to adopt it generally, the first to appreciate the power of advertising, and have done more than all other nations combined to develop and perfect the system so that it might well be called an American innovation. In any event it places our selling abroad in a class by itself.

Long before the American manufacturer became aware of the possibilities of overseas sales, the reputation of many of his brands had spread far beyond the boundaries of the United States. It was for this reason that the agents of other nationalities were so keen to represent them. It was easy for them to make a profitable volume of sales as all that they had to do was to satisfy the demand which already existed. When the American began selling his own goods he believed the methods that had enabled him to build up markets at home would also succeed in remote parts of the world and built up his selling organization accordingly. He established agencies whose principal business was to sell his goods and began backing them up with advertising. It wasn't long before some of the big New York advertising agencies found they had foreign accounts large enough to justify them in opening branch offices not only in Europe but also in such relatively remote places as Buenos Aires, Rio de Janeiro, Calcutta and Alexandria. These were well staffed by merchandising experts who made market surveys and planned and executed sales campaigns that left competitors gasping. It is a very significant fact that while these agencies were all started originally to serve their American clients many of them have secured growing amounts of British and German business. In passing it may be remarked that in many parts of the world, and especially in Latin-America, American advertising appropriations provided the local newspapers with the first substantial legitimate revenue they had ever received and thus contributed to the building of an independent press.

The Department of Commerce came to the aid of the exporters and among many other useful services, provided them with an easy method of surmounting the difficulties of handling shipments abroad. Through a series of handbooks covering every country in the world the exporter can now familiarize himself with all he needs to know about packing, currency, customs duties and other official regulations. There is no longer any reason why any of the old mistakes should be repeated. No other government has covered the ground so thoroughly in official publications and it is a fact that these invaluable handbooks are treasured and used by British and German businessmen who are fortunate enough to possess them.

At home we had been educated to purchase goods by brand name and, thanks to the spread of this American idea, the whole world is falling into the same purchasing habit, which means a demand for the well-known products of American factories. It is true, of course, that there are a number of world-famous British products, many of which had been manufactured decades before any of us were born. There are also a number of branded German products which enjoy well-deserved reputations for superiority. But for every British or German brand which enjoys this distinction there are dozens of American brands. For example in Latin-America there are more than two hundred products of American factories which are supported by what might be called national advertising campaigns. Even before the present war curtailed their activities there were less than fifty combined British and German products advertised in this way. The advertised American products have an alphabetical range which starts with abrasives and ends with zippers.

As the export business of the American manufacturer grew and as various countries raised tariff barriers, he hurdled them by setting up assembly plants for machinery and motorcars and manufacturing plants for many other products. Again, this was not a new idea but again American manufacturers carried it out in a new way and with more thoroughness than those of any other country. For example there is a German dentifrice which thirty or forty years ago was probably the leader in world markets. As sales were restricted by high tariffs in various countries the proprietor of the brand made deals with local factories whereby he turned over to them his trade-mark rights and formulas and collected a royalty on all sales made. It was easy money while it lasted but it didn't last long. The local manufacturer, unable to resist the temptation to use cheaper ingredients soon brought the brand into disrepute, and it dropped from a leading position to a place very near the bottom of the list.

With branch factories located in many parts of the world the American manufacturer keeps a watchful eye on his products by an elaborate but effective system of remote control. In Buenos Aires I visited a very interesting little establishment where several dozen señoritas pack and label a line of well-known toilet articles—nail polish, deodorant, etc.—more than a million bottles a year. Most of the raw materials are shipped from home and those bought locally are subjected to the most rigid inspection. In addition to that, samples of every mixture made up are sent by air mail to the laboratories at home and nothing is bottled until a cable of approval has been received. If the mixture does not come up to rigid tests it is not used. Every American manufacturer with branch plants abroad uses similar methods to make sure that his product is kept up to standard. The result is that while Kolynos toothpaste may be packaged in Shanghai or in Rio de Janeiro the product is just the same as that produced at the home laboratory in New Haven.

American products covering a wide variety of lines are either manufactured, partly manufactured or packaged in various South American cities. That old household favorite Sloan's Liniment is produced in three countries. Gillette blades are shipped down in long rolls of steel ready to be cut into proper lengths. Both General Motors and Ford maintain huge plants where some parts of the motorcars are manufactured and assembly lines work just as in the plants at home. The Otis Elevator Company has manufacturing and assembly plants in several important cities, each of them employing hundreds of workmen. The list could be extended indefinitely. These branch manufacturing plants give the sale of American products abroad a volume which is never reflected in trade statistics.

Thanks to the American idea in manufacturing and merchandising the American salesman abroad is the most favored of his profession. He sells a product with which the retailer is already familiar and for which there is a steady demand. He looks on the merchandise he sells with respect and affection. He is frequently a highly trained technical expert. If he is selling a machine he can operate it and, if necessary, repair it. In the case of machinery or such highly specialized products as abrasives, his customers rely on him for advice. With most salesmen making their regular calls it is not a question of whether or not he will get an order but what the size will be. In a great many cases, in fact, his only competitors are other Americans. This is true of motorcars, of much office equipment, of electric refrigerators. It is also true of many toilet articles and cosmetics. In all countries outside of Europe a great majority of the ladies use American lipstick, rouge, nail polish, toilet powder and soap.

In what a different position is the poor German salesman who is selling unbranded merchandise! If it should happen to be, let us say, a line of men's shirts he must demonstrate the quality of the merchandise and then fight out the question of price against all other lines of unbranded shirts. It is taken for granted that the first asking price is not the last and the purchaser, after a deal has been closed, never knows whether or not he might not have secured another discount if he had held out a little longer. The American salesman has only to mention the brand and the question of quality and workmanship are automatically answered. The question of price rarely comes up because it has been standardized over a period of years and is subject only to slight variations. He had only to discuss color and weight and style. Compared to him the German salesman is like the old-fashioned peddler who used to tramp the country roads with a pack on his back!

In machinery and builders' hardware and an endless line of mechanical accessories the American manufacturer also has the advantage of an established reputation for superior products. He is the favorite of the architects of South America who almost invariably specify Yale locks and hinges and always Otis elevators to mention only two of many items. But as is the case all over the world the cost of erecting a building is usually greater than the estimate. Only when it is necessary to readjust the specifications to make the cost fit into the budget are cheaper materials used. Of course, this is not invariably true but in almost all cases the installation of German hardware is because of necessity rather than choice. The same conditions govern the sale of machinery. Almost all, if not all, German machinery sells for much less than American machines but it is well known that they wear out quicker and require greater replacements. The manufacturer who can afford the investment buys American machinery; if he cannot he contents himself with German equipment.

There have been a great many newspaper stories and some editorial comment on the fact that Germans give long terms of credit and some appear to believe that for this reason they are able to take a lot of business away from us. This may be true in the purchase of machinery for capital investment. But when it comes to all classes of consumer goods German and American products are on quite a different footing. Unbranded shirts, for example, may move slowly or rapidly from the merchant's shelves, depending on what shirts the merchant across the street may have in stock. On the other hand there are regular customers and a steady demand for Arrow shirts, just as there is for B.V.D. underwear and other standard, branded merchandise. Barring some unforeseen disaster or trade depression the merchant knows and the salesman knows, just about how long it should take to turn over the stock. Credit terms are arranged on an equitable basis under which the financial burden is shared by the merchant and the manufacturer. Liberal credit terms given by the Germans is not the result of a well-considered merchandising policy. They are compelled to give these terms in order to make sales.

Every now and then some inquisitive traveler makes the discovery that the Germans or the Japanese—or somebody—are offering a machine of some kind or other at a price very much less than that charged by the American manufacturer and hastily jumps to the conclusion that this means the beginning of the end of some phase of our manufacturing industry unless something is done about it. A New York correspondent a little more than a year ago discovered that the Germans had a big stock of sewing machines in South America which they were offering for about half the price of the Singer. At about the same time a famous columnist discovered that there had been an alarming increase in the sale of German motorcars in a South American country. There was a lot of viewing with alarm. Editorials were written. Now, as a matter of fact, the Germans have been making this sewing machine for many years and the Italians and the Japanese have been making even cheaper machines. Yet from the Rio Grande to the Straits of Magellan fully three fourths of all the sewing machines are Singer and all of them have been bought at prices twice and three times higher than that paid for the competing machines. As for the German motorcars, they were Opals made by the General Motors factory in Germany and the only people who bought them were the local German residents. They bought them as the result of official pressure.

There is no need to get unduly alarmed about cheap German sewing machines or motorcars or anything they have produced in the past or will produce in the future. There will have to be a much greater economic upheaval than even Hitler plans before Germany or any other country will be able to make the kind of quality goods on which our export market flourishes. This is not alone a matter of technical skill, manufacturing and merchandising. We can produce these articles at a profit only because of the large market at home. No other country has this home market and hence the manufacturers of other countries have no incentive to make quality products. German

trade in the future, as well as in the past, will be confined
to what might be called the underprivileged customers—
those who cannot afford to buy the superior American
products unless and until we are reduced to the German
standard of living and they are elevated to ours.

German factories are not in competition with us except
in a very few lines. But with each year that passes they
are facing a growing competition in the form of rapidly
developing local industries. There are thousands of big and
little establishments throughout South America—most of
them new—making just the kind of cheap consumer goods
on which German, and, to a lesser extent, Japanese trade
has thrived in the past. These native products embrace
varied lines such as cheap hardware, knitted goods, cotton
cloth, glassware, porcelain, toys and aluminum ware. Many
of the factories require a small investment and do not demand a high technical skill. The products come within
the low-quality and low-price range for which there is
practically no demand in the United States. Price considered, they are better than the German and Japanese
products and over each of them has been placed the protective umbrella of a high protective tariff. The successful
operation of this rapidly growing number of factories
raises local standards of living, adds to the number of the
middle class and so creates a greater number of possible
customers for the quality products of the United States.

As is the case with German propaganda, and even with
the German military machine, there has been more sound
and fury than actual accomplishments in the field of export
trade. In 1933 Hitler announced his intention of increasing
sales of German products abroad and coined the menacing
slogan "export or die." After six years of effort in which
every device the Nazis could think of has been used the

editor of the *American Exporter* points out that German exports increased only 15 per cent. During the same period Secretary of State Hull was **making efforts to increase** world trade in which we would share with other nations. Our exports increased 84 per cent. That was the increase for our total trade. In South America, where the Nazis were devoting their best efforts, we actually increased our sales 162 per cent. It was a very satisfactory business not only as to volume but as to the class of products sold. More than four fifths consisted of fully manufactured goods.

In 1938 when the German high-pressure methods were presumably at the peak of efficiency our sales to South America amounted to more than $300,000,000 or 27 per cent of the total while German sales were less than $200,000,000 or 17 per cent of the total. We did an even greater proportion of the business in Central America. It may surprise many readers to learn that in 1938 our sales to the twenty Latin-American republics amounted to more than the combined sales of our only important competitors —Germany, Great Britain and Japan.

It is only when they run into a government-controlled economy of one sort or another that the American manufacturer and salesmen have to admit defeat and during the past few years there has been a lot of that. In one country after another they have been faced by import control, exchange permits, blocked currencies and barter deals. Germany has actively promoted these deals as a means of securing new products without the payment of cash and also to force the purchase of German goods. Other countries have followed the German example. Chile alone had seventeen different barter agreements with various countries when I arrived in Santiago and made an additional one when I was there.

The twin devices of blocked exchange and exchange control provide artificial stimulants to trade which the Germans have used to the utmost. We may reasonably expect the system to be extended to every country which falls within the sphere of German economic influence. Each extension of this system of trading of course closes certain avenues to the American manufacturers but even the complete development of the system would not destroy our trade in South America or anywhere else. All that we would have to do would be to adopt the same selfish tactics ourselves, insist that all countries from which we make purchases take payment in our products—just as Germany has done and—to a lesser extent Great Britain.

This is entirely contrary to the American principle of free competition and the open door in trade. But if we are forced to adopt this system it would, in a great many countries, work to our advantage and to the very serious disadvantage of those who have done most to promote this totalitarian system of promoting their foreign trade.

For example we bought from Brazil in 1937 approximately $75,000,000 worth of her products but sold her less than $50,000,000. This was not an abnormal situation. In every year since 1921 we have bought a great deal more from Brazil than we have sold her, the adverse balances in most years running from $50,000,000 to $100,000,000. During that same period Germany and Great Britain have each sold to Brazil a great deal more than they have purchased from her. We have, of course, the bulk of the trade with Brazil and have retained it without the use of these high-pressure methods—but if we should apply those methods the increased purchases we would compel Brazil to make from us would be sufficient to cut the sales of British and German products in half.

It is to be hoped that we will never be compelled to adopt these totalitarian methods but, if we do, we could, at the expense of our South American neighbors, apply them with profit to ourselves. Probably due to the fact that we do not buy frozen meat from South America there is a general impression that we are not good customers. I was under this misapprehension myself until I spent several hours going through trade statistics which present quite a different picture. The year I chose for analysis was 1936 as at that time the various barter deals and blocked exchange arrangements had had little if any effect on trade. The tabulation reveals that in that year we bought more than we sold from every country except Bolivia and Peru. The actual figures show that we bought from the ten South American countries approximately $300,000,000 worth of products and sold them only $204,000,000 worth. As in the case of the Brazilian figures quoted above this was not an abnormal year. Tabulations for other years will show differences in detail but the picture remains the same. In some years we sell more to Argentina than we buy. In a few countries the trade is fairly evenly balanced, but we consistently, year after year, buy from Brazil, Chile and Colombia more than we sell.

No matter under what conditions the German manufacturer returns to his export trade in South America he has a lot of new headaches waiting for him. As a part of the wartime economy which preceded the actual hostilities, the Nazi party took over control of German industry. This program was to produce goods just as fast as possible and get them to market at any price that would provide foreign exchange or stocks of war supplies. As the supply of raw materials was limited, every factory was required to submit a monthly inventory of all stocks on hand. If one appeared to be well supplied and production in another was lagging because of lack of supplies, the Nazi economists arbitrarily transferred the material. The result was that the factories turned out finished products as rapidly as possible. If they didn't use the material it would be taken away from them and they would be unable to make anything. All down the east coast and up the west coast of South America I heard stories of recently installed German machines proving defective, of electric fans becoming useless in a few months. These were not cheap unbranded goods but the product of the world-famous Siemens-Schukert factory. It will be years before this fine old German concern can regain its old reputation for honest and dependable products. The outstanding example of this Nazi-controlled manufacturing is found in Chile where a large fleet of German airplanes, obtained by barter, are still on the ground. They look all right but no one has been able to fly them. Even if Hitler wins the war German manufacturers are going to have a hard time explaining that away.

In spite of the really phenomenal success of the American manufacturer and exporter, stories of ineptness continue. During the past three or four months I have read every book about South America I could lay my hands on and in almost every one of them there are one or two stories just as absurd as the one I wrote about the headdress of the women of Tehuantepec. One very well-known authority on the history of Latin-America commented acidly on the fact that American manufacturers trying to do business in the Andes did not pack their goods in the hundred-pound parcels which can be carried by the llamas, those picturesque beasts of burden. The inference was that we were losing a lot of valuable trade through ignorance of the requirements of an important transportation system. The truth of the matter is that one might travel all through South America and visit every town of any commercial importance and never see a llama. They are only found in the high Andes where the local population is composed exclusively of Indians with about the lowest purchasing power on earth. In fact, I have made a good many inquiries about it and no one has been able to tell me of anything in the way of American goods these Indians do buy or could possibly buy. The total possible American trade in which llama transportation could play any part would probably be about as important as the Tehuantepec millinery business.

Another scholarly traveler discovered a German salesman whom he held up as an example for Americans to emulate. He met this paragon in a remote village in Peru and learned from him about the way to introduce a new product to the Peruvian market. The German, he said, traveled in canoes from one year's end to the other, spoke the native languages, lived in the native villages, distributed samples of his pills and booked orders for them. No American salesman, said the author, ever did that. Quite right. He wouldn't be so stupid. The American merchandise expert knows that the only way to introduce a new brand of goods, whether it be a pill or a radio, is to start at the center of distribution—not in the wilderness. If an American wanted to sell pills to the Peruvians he would start in Lima, knowing that if he could build up a market there the people of Cuzco and Pisco and all the other towns would follow the lead set by the capital. What this German was doing was old horse and buggy days stuff—developed and discarded as wasteful two generations ago.

One of the stock criticisms of the American manufacturer is that he insists on selling the kind of goods that he produces and that he will not make the slightest concession to the desires of his foreign customers in the matter of design or detail of construction. The classic example, which has been quoted as having occurred in a half a dozen different cities, is about plumbing supplies. A South American merchant who had been stocking German or French or Belgian plumbing supplies and as he was no longer able to get his orders filled, in whatever country it was, offered an American manufacturer a very large order if he would only make the parts to specifications which would fit the stock the merchant had on hand. The American not only refused the order but would not even discuss it. In contrast to his conservatism and stubbornness it is pointed out that German factories will without question make spare parts and fittings for any well-known brand of American plumbing.

Now it is inconceivable that any American manufacturer could have executed an order of that kind with any profit to himself. The sizes of the pipes and the threads of the joints used in Continental plumbing are not the same as those used in America. Before executing the order the manufacturer would have had to install a lot of new equipment which he probably would have difficulty finding in the United States. It is not extraordinary that German factories would be able to supply imitations of American plumbing, just as Japanese factories are able to supply imitation spare parts for American motorcars. Factories in both countries have machinery for duplicating standard American products which they offer for sale at cheaper prices. There is nothing clever about this. At best it is a business which exists on the crumbs of another industry.

In Bogotá I met a Colombian importer who repeated the old complaint about the stubbornness of American manufacturers. He was ready to place an order for 10,000 enamel washbasins and all he wanted the manufacturer to do was to punch a small hole in the edge of the basin so that it could be hung on a nail when not in use. He thought the manufacturer who refused to do this was very unreasonable and at the moment I was inclined to agree with him. But the manufacturer of a similar line of goods set me right.

"Of course a hole shouldn't be stamped in the edge of an enamel basin," he said. "The nail would soon wear off the enamel, the hole would get rusty and a basin that should last for years would be ruined in a few months. We wouldn't fill an order of that kind. It is not good merchandising."

That is just the sort of an order the Germans—and the Japanese—would fill.

The visitor to any South American city does not have to call on the American commercial attaché or read a book of statistics to see that the products of American factories have a very wide sale. The chances are better than one hundred to one that he will be driven to his hotel in a motorcar made in Michigan. On the way he will see many familiar signs advertising Goodyear, Kodak, and Palmolive, to mention only three of dozens. At the cashier's desk in the hotel he will see a National Cash Register and very probably an Underwood typewriter. He will ride to his floor in an Otis elevator and if the hotel is located in the tropics he will very probably find in his room either a G. E. or a Westinghouse fan. If he wants to spend the evening at a movie there will be several Hollywood productions in local theaters from which he can make a selection.

If the theater is a modern one it will be air-conditioned by the use of American equipment.

In most hotels only a continental breakfast is served, but if the American visitor wants a cereal he can always get Quaker Oats, Kellogg's Corn Flakes or Shredded Wheat biscuit. In a quarter-hour stroll through almost any of the larger cities he will see on display in the show windows Stetson and Knox hats, Arrow shirts, Holeproof socks and Paris garters. In every first-class jewelry shop as well as stationery store he will be certain to find a representative selection of Parker or Eversharp pencils and pens. If his wife is traveling with him she will have no difficulty in getting the kind of lipstick, face cream, nail polish or any other beauty aid she would find in a New York shop. In fact a visit to any pharmacy will present a familiar sight. Except for the Spanish or Portuguese signs it will have much the same appearance of any drugstore at home, with the same familiar products on the shelves. The chances are the visitor will run into a special offer on Gillette blades or Colgate toothpaste.

The American manufacturer and exporter have done a good job in the export field—one that should make all of their fellow countrymen proud. They keep the factory wheels turning and give employment to many thousands of skilled and highly paid workmen. They have introduced into foreign trade the principle of selling on quality rather than price, have in fact established a new system of commercial ethics. Because of the high standards of quality maintained by the manufacturers and because of the high standards of the salesmen they have given us a reputation for commercial integrity enjoyed by no other nation except Great Britain.

The next time you hear anyone say that Americans

don't know how to handle the export business, it would be quite appropriate for you to say:

"If you will pardon me for saying so, I think you may be mistaken." Or, if you want to be really emphatic, you might say:

"Don't talk like a damn fool."

CHAPTER XVII

## Popeye and the Propagandists

ON MY visit to South America I had a professional
as well as a journalistic interest in finding out how
the widely publicized German propaganda machine was working, for I am an old war propagandist myself. As the Far Eastern representative of the Committee
on Public Information I had charge of our own official
propaganda during the first World War and tried to do
in China just what the Germans are trying to do in South
America: create friendship for ourselves and hatred for
our enemies. The Germans were working in China at the
same time, as were the Japanese. It had been part of my
job to keep an eye on them, not only to counteract their
work but also to see if they were using any methods we
could adopt. (The Japanese, of course, were our allies at
the time, but that did not deter them from persistent attempts to sabotage Sino-American friendship.) The British

[ 264 ]

and French propagandists worked very closely with us, and we even consulted our Italian allies at times, and so I had a fine opportunity to observe the propaganda methods of a number of different countries. It was fascinating work.

After this experience I welcomed an opportunity to see the new and important German machine. I was prepared to lay aside national prejudices and admire the machine as a perfect piece of mechanism and possibly pick up a few pointers which might be useful in the event that we should get into war. What I had heard and read led me to believe that I would find something as new and effective as the modern bombers and tanks. Certain newspaper articles and editorials I had read had either said plainly or inferred that by means of free news services, subsidized newspapers, radio broadcasts, and personal contacts the Germans had pretty much of a strangle hold on public opinion all the way from the muddy Rio Grande to the frozen southern tip of Cape Horn. They were doing the thinking for all of Latin America. Every embassy, legation and consulate had its press attaché with the kind of an expense account a newspaperman dreams about. They had agents in every city, town and village. The most powerful weapon was the Trans-Ocean news service, which had correspondents everywhere and even in the smaller places a staff of experts large enough to edit a daily paper. That is the picture I had in my mind from reading New York newspapers and magazines.

On the boat from New York to Rio de Janeiro I heard more about it from fellow Americans returning to their homes south of the equator. I learned that in addition to the Trans-Ocean there was the smaller but still powerful Italian satellite, Stefani news service and the little but energetic Japanese Domei service. Each of these three services was willing to supply its news free to any paper that would publish it. The German embassies, well supplied with funds, would subsidize papers which appeared to be friendly and compel German companies to advertise in newspapers which gave an adequate presentation of the German point of view. Of what avail was the good neighbor policy when it was being sabotaged on all sides by this clever, powerful and unscrupulous German propaganda machine?

And what were we doing about it? Absolutely nothing. What we should do, several shipmates insisted, was to get Congress to appropriate a few million dollars, see if we could find some good American propagandists and fight these clever Germans at their own game. I believe several people have written to Congressmen urging action of this kind.

It is true, my shipmates said, that there are three American news services in South America, the United Press, Associated Press and the International News Service and between them they have several hundred clients. In fact there is not an important newspaper in all of Latin America which does not depend on one or more of these news services. But these agencies sell their reports for cash and if a newspaper does not pay, will at times cut off the service, leaving the paper dependent on the free German, Italian and Japanese services. To those who wish to view things with alarm it was easy to foresee a time when the Germans (aided by the Italians and the Japanese) would dominate the papers with their free services. With no news or opinions other than those supplied by the Axis powers, Latin America would become totalitarian and then it would be too late to do anything.

As for the American manufacturer, what does he do?

He never makes any attempt to influence the editorial opinions of newspapers and magazines in which he places his advertising but spends his appropriation solely with the selfish purpose of creating more customers for his goods. The German manufacturer, on the other hand, demands that the newspapers in which he places his advertising publish articles and editorials favorable to Germany. It was well known that a newspaper which took a nasty crack at Hitler got no German advertising. My shipmates who were returning to their homes in Rio de Janeiro, São Paulo, Santos, Buenos Aires, Rosario and various other places were very much in hopes that I would investigate the matter and write something that would get the folks back home steamed up so that Congress would do something.

As the investigation I made was very thorough and led to surprising conclusions it is necessary for me to describe it with some detail. The day of my arrival in Rio de Janeiro I employed a Brazilian assistant and set him to work on as complete and accurate a survey of German, Italian and Japanese press propaganda as I could devise. I suppose any other advertising man would have adopted about the same system. We selected the nine leading dailies of Rio and collected a file of five consecutive issues. With a blue pencil we marked every item of news that came from the three American agencies, all of it filed from their respective bureaus in New York. With a red pencil we marked all the news filed by Reuters, the British agency. With a green pencil we marked all the news credited to the Trans-Ocean and also all other material that appeared to be a German propaganda handout. We had a yellow pencil for items from Stefani and Domei but found little occasion to use it.

When we got through we measured up all of the news

emanating from these different agencies, that is the number
of column inches published in each paper. In the meantime an American advertising agency had supplied me with
the circulation figures for each paper. By multiplying the
number of column inches by the circulation figure we
arrived at what advertising men call the total "reader
coverage." After breaking this down into news service
groups we summarized as follows:

> 82% of the news coverage is from American
>       agencies.
> 11% is from the British agency, Reuters.
> 7% is German, Italian and Japanese, this
>      figure including everything in the way
>      of propaganda that we could find.

We did learn that a number of small papers up country
relied entirely on these free news services but these papers
were of small importance and were published in agricultural communities where interest in anything beyond the
price of coffee and cattle is slight. If we had made an
analysis of them the relative figure would not have materially changed for the more important provincial papers,
like the important metropolitan papers, rely on the American agencies.

Small as the percentage is, the figure really presents a
flattering picture of German propaganda accomplishments.
Actually only two papers in Rio de Janeiro publish the
Trans-Ocean report. One of these is the veteran *Jornal do
Brazil* which prides itself on its impartial and neutral policy
and feels that it should not refuse to accept the German
service. However, this news report is very carefully edited
and each item is weighed according to its news value; all

purely propaganda paragraphs are slashed by the editor's big blue pencil.

The only other paper that prints a line of Axis news reports is the *Meio Dia* (mid-day) which is frankly a German organ. When the war started the paper was struggling for an existence, owed money to its staff, to the ink and newsprint suppliers. Then it suddenly became prosperous with no increase either in circulation or advertising and at exactly the same time made the discovery that a Hitler victory would be the best possible thing for this suffering world and especially for Brazil. As the editors have been rather cold to the beneficent influences of Italy and Japan the local wisacres figure that the whole subsidy is being borne by the Germany embassy. Of the nine papers surveyed this was the least important. It had a small circulation at the time the German subsidy saved it from bankruptcy and when it became a propaganda organ the circulation slipped still lower. In our analysis we credited it with the former circulation figure of 15,000 but American advertisers contended that the figure was much less than that. Its influence on the public opinion of Brazil is probably less than of the *Daily Worker* on the public opinion of the United States.

But to give the German propaganda machine full credit for a good piece of professional work, *Meio Dia* serves other purposes. When the Axis agreement was signed between Germany, Italy and Japan, warning the United States to keep out of their affairs, the *Meio Dia* came out with an editorial giving the pact its enthusiastic endorsement. By a few lies and some adroit reasoning the pact was presented as a means of preserving the integrity of the South American republics from the scheming colossus of the north. Probably very few people in Rio read the editorial, but in his English language broadcast "Lord Haw Haw" quoted it and referred to the little sheet as "that powerful Brazilian journal." The Trans-Ocean also quoted the editorial in its news report which is sent to various parts of the world. An English friend in São Paulo told me about having picked up this bit of news from "Lord Haw Haw's" intriguing chatter and we made some investigation disclosing the very interesting fact that at the time he was broadcasting this news the issue of the *Meio Dia* in which the editorial was published had not yet appeared on the streets. I am happy to record this as a genuine achievement of the German propaganda machine. To be able to quote in Berlin an editorial which is not published in Rio de Janeiro until some hours later is really a triumph.

After getting through with our analysis of the newspapers, my Brazilian assistant set to work on the magazines of which there are a great number in Rio. In spite of the fact that they are all published in the Portuguese language, most of them also look surprisingly familiar to the American reader for the very good reason that most of their contents are lifted from American magazines. Nick Carter still lives in a monthly pulp and so does Jack London in a magazine of a little better class. *El Detective* was publishing "The Seventh Adventure of Cactus Jack."

Most of these magazines are devoted to fiction and fashion, the stories being translated and the illustrations reproduced from our popular monthlies, while the fashions are all from Hollywood, the patterns from *McCall's*. So far as they are concerned the war does not exist. But some of the publications carry news pictures and here, we thought, was a fine opporunity for some propagandist to put something over and justify himself for remaining on Sr. Goebbels' pay roll. We did find one picture of Hitler but on investigation is turned out to be a part of a regular picture service supplied by a New York syndicate. We also discovered one full page of German war pictures in a rather small magazine but on the opposite page was a similar layout of British war pictures. Nothing could be fairer than that. All the pictures having anything to do with the war were infinitesimal compared to the page after page of pictures of Loretta Young, Norma Shearer, Bette Davis, Clark Gable, Shirley Temple and many other stars. It goes without saying that there were dozens of pictures of President Roosevelt who is the idol of a very large part of the South American public. Before leaving this subject I hope I may be excused for saying that while I was in South America the newspapers and illustrated weeklies published just about as many pictures of the author of *400 Million Customers* as of Hitler or Mussolini and without the aid of a press agent.

It was impossible to put a slide rule on the magazines as accurately as on the daily papers but after checking and comparing and getting the opinions of a good many people we came to the conclusion that at least 80 per cent of the art and editorial material appearing in the Brazilian magazines consisted of reproductions or translations from New York publications. The other 20 per cent consists of articles and pictures of local interest.

As I traveled south to São Paulo and Santos in Brazil, to Montevideo in Uruguay and Buenos Aires in Argentina, and as I traveled west and north to Santiago and Valparaiso in Chile and Lima in Peru and Bogotá in Colombia I had similar investigations made, always with the assistance of a local man who was familiar with the newspapers and who had no incentive to get anything but the facts. To tell the truth I spent a lot more time trailing this elusive German propaganda than I could afford in a busy trip. In every country there were the same stories of the huge machine and the vast amounts of money being used to influence public opinion. These stories were all true. The machine is big and expensive but it has failed to accomplish the one purpose for which it was created: fill the columns of the newspapers with news and opinions favorable to the Nazi cause.

In São Paulo, which has a large German population, there was more Trans-Ocean and other German propaganda published than in Rio. In Montevideo where the *Graf Spee* was sunk and a German plot to seize the spunky little country of Uruguay was discovered, there was about as much presentation of the German point of view as you might expect to find in the London *Times*. The propaganda machine remains and for the sake of the hardworking boys who send out press releases that no one ever publishes I hope Herr Goebbels doesn't find out how ineffective they are and cut them off the pay roll. I thoroughly agree with a young American in Montevideo who said he felt sorry for the German press agents who were looked on with contempt by all the local people; who knew no one would print any of their dope, but still had to keep on dishing it up.

In Buenos Aires none of the old established papers print a line of news supplied by the propaganda agencies. *La Prensa* is famous for the fact that it prints more cable news than any other paper in the world, a full forty columns a day, all supplied exclusively by the United Press. *La Nacion* takes the full Associated Press report with many special cables supplied by the *New York Times* and the London *Times*. These are big and prosperous papers as are *El Mundo* and *Critica* and have no space for colored news or opinions favorable to the Nazi cause. But Herr Goebbels would not be a model of German efficiency if he did not demand some proof of action on the part of his employees in Argentina and they are able to supply it. About the time the little afternoon paper in Rio sprang into an unexplained prosperity a new afternoon paper, *El Pampero*, came into existence in Buenos Aires in an already overcrowded field. Its 365th issue appeared the day before I took the plane for Santiago. It publishes in full the Trans-Ocean, Stefani and Domei news services and no other.

The Germans make a very good showing with this least important of all the Buenos Aires dailies. An observant visitor sitting in a sidewalk café at six o'clock, when the one and only edition of *El Pampero* is put on sale, might reasonably come to the conclusion that it was the leading afternoon paper. The leather-lunged newsboys shout its name louder and oftener than that of any other paper and in the newsstands it is usually on the top of the pile so that it is the only paper to be seen. It would not be unreasonable to find here conclusive evidence of the Nazi fifth column successfully at work with all the newsboys plugging for the one paper which supports Hitler. Indeed some very interesting fifth column stories have been built out of more flimsy stuff than this. But the explanation for this phenomenon is absurdly simple. The newsboy pays only two centavos per copy for *El Pampero* while he has to pay six centavos for all the other afternoon papers. As they all sell for ten centavos (2 ½ cents) it will readily be seen that he makes twice as much from the sale of a copy of *El Pampero* which flays the British daily, as from the sale of *Critica* which just as regularly, and much more expertly, taunts the totalitarian powers. But with all the high-pressure salesmanship and the giving away of thousands of free copies the best *El Pampero* can do is less than 90,000 copies while *Critica* prints more than 400,000 daily.

It is common knowledge that the maintenance of this paper costs the German embassy the equivalent of $11,000 monthly. There are no secrets about such matters in Buenos Aires and if the German embassy should be a day late in paying over the money everyone would know about it. A delay of a week would probably mean a complete change in the newspaper's policy. The paper gets further support from German advertisers who are told what to do by the Nazi party chief. Other advertisers ignore the publication completely. One product which carries a large daily advertisement is the famous "4711" line of toilet articles which I advertised in China over a period of more than a dozen years. When I recall how carefully the advertising manager of this fine old Cologne firm used to watch the advertising appropriation in China, I couldn't help thinking how unhappy he must be at being compelled to throw away good money on this worthless publication.

The editorial opinions expressed in *El Pampero* are about the same as those in *Meio Dia*, being rewritten to appeal to Argentine sensibilities. The editorials are quoted by the Trans-Ocean as representing Argentine opinion. While directing its most bitter attacks against Great Britain the paper occasionally finds time to take a crack at Uncle Sam. When I was in Buenos Aires it was making a vigorous exposé of the cruelties suffered by Argentines who were compelled to work for the hard hearted and rapacious *yanquis*.

The magazine field in Buenos Aires is about the same as in Rio de Janeiro except that the magazines are larger and more prosperous. As the Rio magazines are published in

the Portuguese language their circulation is confined to
the limited literate population of Brazil itself. The Spanish-
language Buenos Aires magazines have large and growing
circulation in Chile, Peru and Uruguay. With the flight
of the intelligentsia from Spain, Buenos Aires is rapidly
becoming the publishing center of the world so far as the
Spanish language is concerned. We could not find in any
of them a trace of influence by German propaganda. The
typographical style, make-up and contents follow the
American model and in fact almost every magazine is,
typographically at least, a copy of some New York publication. They contain a larger proportion of original articles than the Brazilian publications but there are the same
pictures of the Hollywood stars, the same translations of
articles originally appearing in New York magazines.

Here again, the Germans have been compelled to establish their own organ of expression. This has taken the form
of a monthly, *Clarinda*, which has all of the physical appearance of a cheap weekly. Both the text and the illustrations are almost unbelievably crude and vulgar and it is
impossible to think of it appealing to anyone with the
least intelligence. What is left of the poor old International
Jew is exposed in all his various forms and depicted in car-
toons as scheming to get control of the riches of Argentina. Three pages are devoted to what is quite frankly a
black list of dentists, physicians and small tradesmen who
are supposed to be unfriendly to the Nazi cause. The professional German propagandist is capable of doing some
very stupid things but in this black list he exceeds himself.
All that it accomplishes is to add to the growing number
of people to whom Nazi methods are abhorrent.

After describing in this detail the work of the propagandists in the two largest and most important South

American countries, any description of their efforts in other countries is necessarily repetitious. In Santiago, the principal city of Chile, the old newspapers will not publish the Trans-Ocean reports and they are found only in *El Supplemento*, the Spanish-language edition of the local German daily. The task of publishing this unprofitable little sheet was imposed on the German publisher by the Nazi party chiefs who are not very prompt about meeting the deficit. The publisher has been heard to refer to himself as "the only sucker in South America" because while the Trans-Ocean service is supplied to everyone else without charge, he is compelled to pay for it.

A careful search of the papers published at Lima in Peru and at Guayaquil in Ecuador failed to disclose any acceptance of German propaganda. I did not visit three South American countries, Paraguay, Bolivia and Venezuela, but overlooked no opportunity to check over papers published in those countries and talk to residents or to recently returned visitors. The story was the same in every place. The Germans were spending a great deal of money and doing a lot of work but the newspapers published only reports supplied by the American news services.

Colombia was the last country I visited and in the capital at Bogotá I found that an official of a neutral country, a former newspaperman, had made an investigation of propaganda similar to the one I had started in Brazil and carried out in other countries. His analysis was much more complete than mine for he had started it the day after England declared war on Germany and at the time I saw his tabulation of figures they covered a period of more than a year. He had measured all the news despatches just as I had done and reduced them to percentages and his figures were almost identical with the ones I had arrived at in Rio de

Janeiro. At first it was very surprising that these figures should have been so nearly the same, but on analysis it is not at all surprising. In every city the large and important newspapers have refused to publish any propaganda. In every city the Germans have established or subsidized one paper which is really the official organ of the Germans.

After a thorough study of German press propaganda in South America I have failed to find any evidence that any of the boys on Herr Goebbels' pay roll could qualify as a press agent for a second-rate night club in a second-rate town. There are very few of them who could hold down a job as a small town reporter and they are utterly unqualified for the handling of public relations of any sort. As a matter of fact when the propaganda machine started operating there were probably a half-dozen German newspapermen in all South America and the propagandists were recruited from deserving Nazi party members who had been totaling up figures in the German commercial houses. They lack nothing in zeal but are about as efficient as a newspaper staff would be if made up of bank clerks. It is with some hesitancy that I expose the stupidity of these employees of Herr Goebbels for I wouldn't like to have on my conscience the fact that I was responsible for the discharge of some enterprising young fellow who is doing no harm to anything but the Nazi pay roll.

Once in a while they do manage to put one of their stories across in rather a big way. Just before I left New York one of their productions got into the metropolitan papers, only to be followed by vigorous and convincing denials. According to the original story a priest in a remote village in Colombia was quoted as having said that American oil-well drillers had machine-gunned from the air a tribe of Indians living in the neighborhood, killing and wounding quite a number of them. Now the sad part about this story is that even if it had been true it would not have been good propaganda. This particular tribe of Indians is about as popular in Colombia as the followers of Geronimo were in the Southwest a number of years ago. Their favorite sport is to lie in ambush and shoot poisoned arrows into travelers just for the fun of the thing. Anyone who would take a machine gun or any other lethal weapon and exterminate the whole tribe would get a vote of thanks from the government of Colombia which has been trying to do just that for a number of years.

For some reason so elusive I could never pin it down the German propagandists have been more successful in planting their stories in newspapers of the United States than in South America. For example, in the summer of 1940 great publicity was given to the statement that German merchants in Brazil, Argentine and Chile were taking orders for goods to be delivered on October 1st and putting up bonds to guarantee fulfillment of the contracts. They were alleged to have said that the war would be over with by that time and the factories in the Reich were running at full blast. It was a good story and the newspapers and news weeklies played it for more than it was worth but there wasn't a word of truth in it and the South American newspapers paid no attention to it.

Another small triumph of the propagandists is found in the way a number of newspapers in the United States handled the banning of the Chaplin film *The Great Dictator* in cities of Argentina and Brazil. This was presented to American readers as affording striking and convincing evidence of the growing influence of the Axis powers. Actually it was nothing more that a police measure of the kind any sensible chief of police would have taken under similar circumstances if he had power to do so. The big cities of Brazil and Argentina are cosmopolitan with large German and Italian populations. The showing of the Chaplin film would have aroused national and racial hatreds—probably would have resulted in armed clashes and needless bloodshed which the police authorities wisely wished to avoid—for exactly the same reasons they had previously refused to allow the showing of Nazi war films.

After we had completed our survey of the newspapers and magazines of Brazil I showed it to a shipmate who had been trying to stir me up on the boat.

"You have overlooked the radio," he said. "The Germans buy time on the radio for news broadcasts or they bribe the commentators to slip in German news."

All too true, I had overlooked the radio. Radio played no part in the first World War. So we started on a new trail. It is not as easy to measure radio coverage as it is that of newspapers and magazines, but we did the best we could. By checking all the radio stations and listening in on most of them we found the news coverage on the radio stations about the same as in the newspapers. The important stations, like the important newspapers, placed such a high valuation on their prestige that they declined to have anything to do with propaganda. Perhaps one or two of the commentators of the smaller stations were biased in their news reports. But still the Germans do win battles and a truthful announcement of that fact does not make either an editor or a commentator the tool of a propagandist. Forewarned by this, I made investigations of radio propaganda in other cities and found about the same result. There are no commentators in South America of the class of Kaltenborn or Swing whose opinions might conceivably sway public opinion. The man at the mike just reads the news despatches as they come from the news agencies.

To most of the old-time American newspapermen who live and work in South America these stories of German propaganda are either a joke or a pain in the neck. They are daily becoming less of a joke and more of a pain in the neck as more and more special correspondents are sent down with instructions from their editors to seek out this menace and expose it in all of its aspects. The correspondents have followed instructions and as a result we have been given at home an entirely false picture. American diplomatic officials are also partly to blame. From conversations I have had with them I feel sure that the reports they have sent to the State Department have unconsciously exaggerated matters. They have reported on the machine and not on its product. The machine is big and noisy but as my statistical examination shows, produces little of any consequence. In my opinion it has created more enemies than friends for the Nazi cause and that is the opinion of a great many other people who have made a careful and impartial investigation of the matter.

There is, of course, the word-of-mouth propaganda which an agent might slip his unsuspecting victim while entertaining him at dinner or buying him a drink at a café. This has possibilities which it is impossible to explore and it is equally impossible for me to take it seriously. The problem of making personal contact with even a million people in this way is insuperable and there are more than forty million people in Brazil alone. According to all accounts they have been at it for several years but there are no indications that Nazi agents have been able to accomplish very much even with their own Germans.

Naturally a survey of the propaganda sent out by mail

had to be confined to a collection of the literature distributed, as there is no way of learning in what volume the mailings are done. A collection of circular letters, bulletins and pamphlets show that the South Americans are getting the same kind of publicity that is being mailed to people at home—documents showing that the British were about to invade Norway, pictures of German children killed by British bombs, etc. Apparently the mailing lists used are large and well selected. It is probably received with more reader attention there than at home because they are not so deluged with all kinds of printed matter. It would be absurd to attempt to measure its effectiveness, but if it has been effective in creating public opinion there has never been any evidence of it. In fact feeling generally is against the Nazis. I did not see a single swastika emblem of any kind, but every Britisher wears a Union Jack or some other British emblem.

It is true that we are doing nothing officially to combat German propaganda, much of which is directed against us. At a very conservative estimate the German government is spending several million dollars a year, but our government is not spending a cent. Fortunately we do not need to. The expenditure of millions of government money could never have built up a propaganda machine equal to that which has been developed through the individual efforts of American news agencies, feature syndicates, publishers and moving picture producers to supply South America with its legitimate demands for news and entertainment. The American news agencies, on a purely business basis, are providing the continent with practically all of its cable news. As a matter of fact their machinery for news coverage is so efficient and complete that most of the Latin-American countries depend on them for reports on all Latin-American affairs. There is not a news-paper of any importance in South America which does not buy the reports of one or more of the American agencies and in most cases depends on them entirely for complete coverage of all but local news. Dozens of small provincial papers manage to pay for a short skeletonized report of the United Press or Associated Press in spite of the fact that the propaganda reports are offered them free. It would be no exaggeration to say that more than 80 per cent of the newspaper readers of South America have depended entirely on American reports for what they know about the war and the events leading up to it. Even the German language newspapers subscribe to the American news services. The American agencies sell an honest and dependable product—news carefully gathered, clearly and concisely written, and as free of prejudice and bias as is humanly possible.

Aside from presenting readers with complete and un-biased accounts of news events in other parts of the world, these American news services have played a very important part in maintaining peace in the countries which they serve. Tempers are likely to flare suddenly and violently when one of the perennial boundary disputes crops up. If the news about these highly controversial subjects was written by local correspondents, it would be humanly impossible to avoid partisan reporting which would add to the existing irritation. With clients in every country and no interest in political issues, organizations such as the United Press and Associated Press send out neutral and unbiased reports. The result is that many a dispute which might easily develop into a major issue has its day in the headlines and then dies out.

In the field of technical publications an equally good job

is being done by such periodicals as *Ingenieria Internacional*, *El Automovil* and *El Farmaceutico*, all three edited and published in New York. Each of these publications is a leader in its respective field. The engineering publication which has a wide circulation gives detailed technical descriptions of all important engineering undertakings. It is a curious and interesting fact that engineers in all the southern republics learn what their neighbors are doing through reading this trade magazine published in New York. It came as a surprise to me to learn that the standard reference book for pharmacists throughout Latin America is a Spanish translation of the U. S. *Pharmacopoeia*. It was published, like the trade journals, as a business enterprise and, like them, pays its way without subsidy. The Spanish edition of *Reader's Digest*, which everyone I met asked me about, rounds out and completes the list of American publications for which there is a genuine demand by our southern neighbors.

Finally as a part of our machine which the Germans would give millions to duplicate there are the American movies and the comic strips. Even before the war the Hollywood productions dominated the business of entertainment in competition with German and Italian films which were produced with the aid of government subsidies and actively promoted by official agencies. In the good old days there were European opera tours when everyone in Rio, Buenos Aires, and other places wore tail coats and white ties and the ladies brought out all their diamonds. The season was short and exciting but after it was over with, and even while it was in progress, almost everyone went to the movies and four films out of five that they saw were Hollywood productions. South Americans are proud of their splendid opera houses and inclined to be a little boastful about the liberal support they give to the European opera companies but I am inclined to believe that for every centavo spent in recent years on the opera a peso or more was spent on Hollywood movies. These movies are all presented in the English language just as they are at home but running titles in Spanish or Portuguese help to tell the story. Thousands of young people have found a new and compelling interest now in the English language as a means of adding to their enjoyment of the movies. Of course, the presentation of some of these productions may have created the impression that the population of the United States was pretty well divided between gangsters and G-men, but not all of them fell in that category and the gangster films have never been especially popular with our southern neighbors. When I was in Rio *Gone with the Wind* had been running six weeks and looked as if it might keep running for as many months. In Buenos Aires it was equally popular. Maybe the visit of a European Opera troupe is of more value in establishing what is loosely called "cultured relations" but my choice would be for a long run of movies like *Gone with the Wind*. If that doesn't present a gripping and unforgettable picture of the way the heart of the North American beats then I don't know what would.

This is but the latest of a long list of important American movies which have had successful runs in every South American city. There is not a Hollywood song hit with which the South American audiences are not just as familiar as the audiences in any city of the United States. But in spite of all that we have done in the promotion of popular music and popular drama there are some who cling to the old grand opera tradition. While I was in Santiago I received by air mail a clipping from the *New York Times*, an interview with a prominent musician recently returned from a visit in Brazil. He spoke at length of the European operas which were heard "down under" and insisted that one of the very important things for us to do was to see to it that South Americans be made acquainted with our own American music. I couldn't help wondering whether or not he had gone to any of the movie theaters and knew that Irving Berlin is just as well known in Santos as in Sioux City.

At home we get our music from Hollywood and so do the residents of South America. For every hundred who have put on tail coats and a white tie and attended the opera a million have heard Jeanette MacDonald and Nelson Eddy and in fact every Hollywood musical production before and since *Singing in the Rain*. I don't know how they could very well crowd more American numbers on their musical programs. There is rarely a popular concert that does not contain at least one number by Stephen G. Foster, rarely a police or military review that some of Sousa's stirring marches are not played. In fact I was awakened at eight o'clock this morning by "The Washington Post," played by the Santiago police band in the plaza just outside my window.

At most public functions where such a program would be appropriate the police or military band can keep going for hours on selections from American composers. Although the incident happened a long time ago they still tell of a program of this sort played on the occasion when a newly appointed ambassador presented his credentials. The officials who had charge of the affair went to a lot of trouble and when one of them noted that he had been born in Georgia he had what he thought was a particularly happy idea. A special musical program was arranged and although there were many selections all through the program the stirring strains of "Marching Through Georgia" were repeated after every number and worked into a lot of ingenuous melodies. His Excellency flinched visibly when he heard the first strains of the hated tune and with each repetition he grew more morose. After the painful event was concluded the embassy staff took the first convenient opportunity to suggest to the ministry of foreign affairs that it would be just as well to omit that tune. They said the ambassador was lonely and homesick and the sweet old tune brought up memories of his happy boyhood days and made him sad.

So far as the music lovers of South America are concerned, memories of the prewar visits of European opera companies are dim as compared to memories of the triumphal "good will tour" made by Toscanini[1] last year. Although they don't like to admit it, the South Americans know that there was always some second-rate talent in the European opera companies, but there was none in Toscanini's organization. His concerts set a new high in musical circles wherever they were heard. The short wave broadcasts of productions by the Metropolitan Opera House have a very large following in South America, probably very much larger than at home in proportion to the number of radio owners. There is not a month that the "fan letters" received from South American listeners do not number more than three thousand—a hundred a day, and they are increasing in number. While on the subject of music it should be noted that our phonograph records are relatively as popular as our movie productions. Every new record produced at home is heard in South America

[1] According to the Brazilian Information Bureau, Toscanini "began his career as a conductor in the Opera House of Rio de Janeiro 54 years ago."

within a few weeks. When I was in Barranquilla the record most widely advertised was "God Bless America" in Spanish.

Last but by no means least there are Popeye and the other gay or grim little personalities created by the American comic strip artists. The bulging-muscled Popeye marches through the pages of newspapers in every city creating for the small boys an effective demand for spinach. He is better known in Latin America than any of the immortal characters created by Cervantes and Camoëns. The marital troubles of Jiggs are familiar to millions to whom Hitler and Mussolini are but names of doubtful significance. In all of them the redoubtable Maggie throws rolling pins under the name of Ramona. Jiggs, who is usually known as Fausto, doesn't demand an opportunity to go to Dinty Moore's for a satisfying dish of corned beef and cabbage, but he is very insistent about going to the hacienda of his friend McManus to enjoy a meal of "rice and beans." Every New York newspaper syndicate does a big and prosperous business in Portuguese and Spanish translations of their features. More American comic strips are published in Buenos Aires than in any city in the United States. If "Popeye El Marino" should ever decided to challenge Herr Hitler, most Latin Americans would place their bets on him.

The fact that the German government is paying subsidies to a few unimportant papers has aroused both envy and resentment in the hearts of other publishers who would find a subsidy useful in meeting the pay roll and the bills for ink and paper. As a means of reminding Herr Goebbels' representatives that they have been overlooked these publications adopt a cautious anti-Nazi editorial policy which everyone knows could easily be converted into a friendly attitude by means of an appropriate financial arrangement. There are some publishers of this type in every country and many of them in countries where it is customary for politicians to pay newspapers for their support.

I shudder to think what would happen to us if our government should ever make an appropriation for press propaganda in Latin America! It could not add anything to the completeness of the news coverage already provided by the American services and might injure their usefulness by creating the impression that they are propaganda organizations. The establishment of the fund would certainly be looked on as an invitation to blackmail and dozens of publications which at present are indifferent or friendly would find it convenient to snipe at Uncle Sam—until bought off.

CHAPTER XVIII

## Swastika under the Southern Cross

IN THE dreams of the Nazi map makers there is an in-
visible empire in South America over which they believe the swastika emblem will eventually fly bringing
the ten independent republics within the sphere of German domination. Thousands of trained agents are working
to make this dream empire a reality. In spite of clumsy
attempts at secrecy their plans and their methods are well
known to the man in the street, provide material for many
a Spanish or Portuguese quip and wisecrack by local
humorists. Most of the agents talk too much. Anyone
visiting Rio de Janeiro, Buenos Aires, Montevideo or any
other capital can, with no difficulty at all learn the names
and the functions of all the principal plotters. They are
known by sight to many people and are frequently seen in

public places. Like their chieftains in Berlin, they swagger in a way that cannot escape notice. Purely by chance I saw a half dozen of the most prominent secret agents in Brazil. They sat next to my table in a restaurant and everyone in the room knew who they were and all about them.

Not quite all—not as much as our own government knows. I feel sure that in spite of their Teutonic self-assurance many of these agents would be slightly crestfallen if they realized how closely our own unobtrusive agents keep a watch on all their movements. It is typical of the difference in our methods that while most anyone can name all the important Nazi spies in his community there are many old-time American residents who do not know that our own governmental organization includes many workers whose names do not appear on any published roster.

We may dismiss as exaggerated and unimportant most of the stories about the movie-plot activities of German agents. These include stories about secret air fields, clandestine stores of arms and hidden radio stations. Maybe these things are embraced in the Nazi plans and maybe some of them exist, but no one in South America takes these stories seriously. Too many of them are suspiciously like something one has read in a book. They provide good yarns with which to thrill the greenhorn tourist and once in a while they fool a traveling correspondent and one of them gets into print. The fanatical young Nazis are capable of attempting any kind of a monkeyshine as we have seen from their activities in the United States. But there are a good many practical difficulties about laying out a secret air field in the Andes, or setting up and providing electric current for a powerful radio station in the jungle. It would be equally difficult to smuggle supplies of arms past customs officials who have throughout their careers been keeping an eye out for arms which the opposition party might try to smuggle in as a prelude to a revolutionary plot to overthrow the government. The detection of arms smugglers is an old game with them.

The paper plans to make this dream empire a reality are very complete. They provide for the control of the government of every country by a local Nazi party which, like the party in Germany, may consist of a minority but will hold all the offices and wield all the power. It is a blueprint of the strategy first used by Hitler at home and later applied to all conquered countries.

Following the procedure used when the German minorities in European countries received the solicitous attention of their party, the first task undertaken by the Nazi agents was the organization of the Germans in South America. It was on this foundation that they believed their dream empire could become a reality. Of what does this foundation consist?

By the simple expedient of classifying as German everyone who had a German grandparent and then indulging in a little elastic arithmetic, the Nazis have been able to compile some very spectacular figures. By persistently representing that all full-blood, half-blood and quarter-blood Germans in South America are adherents to the Nazi cause they present a deceptive but very convincing illusion of a potential Nazi state within the South American continent —of millions of Nazis who are ready to take up arms for Hitler when the time comes and fight for the glory of the Nazi cause. That is the dream of the leaders but it is a dream that is very far from realization. And on a careful analysis the size of the potential empire shrinks to comparatively small proportions.

Perhaps one reason why the public has so readily accepted the Nazi figures is that no others have been presented. It is not a simple matter to compile statistics from ten countries some of which have never taken a census. Yet it does seem strange that of the many writers who have told of the big German populations none appears to have taken the trouble to consult the *Encyclopaedia Britannica* which is the authority for the figures I will present.

With more than forty million inhabitants, Brazil is the most populous of the South American countries having more than three times the population of its largest neighbor, Argentina. It also has admittedly the largest German population. According to the Nazi figures this is 750,000. This is the same figure publicized by the German propaganda bureaus during the World War when a vain attempt was made to keep Brazil out of the war on the side of the United States. Carleton Beals, author of a number of well-known books on South America, quotes with apparent approval a figure of one million.

No available statistics would justify anything approaching these figures. Official reports by the Brazilian government show that the total German immigrants from 1820 to 1931, a period of 111 years was 209,923. There are no statistics showing how many of these immigrants returned home. In the few years that have elapsed since that total was reached the figures has not changed materially. In 1933 the government placed all immigration on a quota basis similar to our own. This limited the entry of German settlers to 4,642 annually of whom 80 per cent must be farmers, farm laborers or rural workers. In 1938 only 193 settlers qualified under this provision.

A very large number of the early immigrants and many of those who came in later years consisted of single men who married into Brazilian families. This dilution of Nordic blood has continued so that with each generation the number of Brazilians with an admixture of German blood has increased but the number of full-blood Germans has decreased. It is possible that a half million could be called Germans by the Nazi system of classification, but probably not more than 50,000 are full blood and a still smaller amount were actually born in Germany. The number who are legally German citizens is still smaller. Like the settlers who came to the United States, most of the Germans went to Brazil to make their homes and after residence of a few years in their adopted country became naturalized. Of recent years an even greater proportion have renounced allegiance to the fatherland because of laws which give Brazilian citizens certain civil rights not allowed to foreigners. The estimate of Americans living in Brazil is that not more than 50,000 may really be classified as Germans, that is, people whose blood ties to Germany are closer than they are to Brazil. From my own observation that population would just about support the three small German-language daily papers published in Brazil. The total circulation claimed for these papers is 44,000, a figure that is obviously exaggerated. All local advertising men place the figure at less than half of that, about 17,000.

Argentina is also represented as having a very large and ardently chauvinistic German population. The figures usually quoted are 260,000 or 300,000. Official figures show that in the sixty-nine years from 1857 to 1924 inclusive the total number of German immigrants was 100,699. Of the millions of immigrants who flocked to Argentina during that period more than half later returned home. If the Germans returned in the same proportion as the others then the net immigration was less than 50,000. During this period the influx of German settlers was a mere trickle compared to that of others. Italian immigrants numbered 2,600,000 and Spanish 1,700,000. The English were just behind the Germans with 64,000 and the British community is now reckoned at about 50,000. If we assume that the rate of increase has been the same in the German as in the British community the German population would be placed at about 75,000. Again using the circulation of newspapers as a yardstick this is just about the community that would provide support for the one German-language newspaper. As in Brazil a very large proportion of the immigrants become naturalized citizens of Argentina and the number of legal Germans is probably less than 20,000.

The community which is called "Little Germany" in Southern Chile constitutes what appears to be the most convincing evidence of Nazi strength to be found under the Southern Cross. Perhaps it fooled the Nazis themselves. Everyone who has visited the beautiful Chilean lake region has commented on the striking evidence of German influence to be found in the city of Valdivia and in some of the neighboring villages. There are streets with German names, many German shop signs and a great deal of German is spoken. The houses with the gay flower boxes might have been lifted straight from Bavaria. To all appearances it is a bit of Germany uprooted and set down in the shadow of the Andes. Most visitors have contented themselves with descriptions of the pleasant picture. I have never heard a single estimate of the German population of Chile, most of which is concentrated in this region. But the figure could not be very high even by the most reckless Nazi computation. The city of Valdivia has a population of 48,000 and that of the entire province is only 236,000. The German-speaking residents, although leaders in the community and very much in the public eye, constitute but a small section of this small area.

In spite of the fact that this province of Southern Chile exhibits so much German atmosphere it is probable that the Germans here are less amenable to Nazi influence than any other community of German origin South of the Rio Grande. The nucleus of the settlement was formed by Bavarian families who migrated to Chile following the political troubles of 1848. Many of them were political refugees. They were of the same generation as Carl Schurz and the grandfather of Wendell Willkie. In the years that followed they were joined by others, relatives and sympathizers. There was never a heavy German migration to Chile nor extensive settlements by any other nationals. The greatly restricted area of fertile soil offers little opportunity to the homeseeker. There was a later immigration in the first few years of this century when about 14,000 Germans settled in the country. But they did not prosper and two thirds of them returned home while others moved to Peru or Argentina.

The industrious Germans who first came to Chile settled in what was practically a wilderness and lived under much the same conditions as our own pioneers of the same period. They prospered and became the dominant element in the community. In fact their only neighbors at the time were the backward and slovenly Indians. The Germans built their own schools and churches and as far as it was possible in a place ten thousand miles from home maintained their own way of life. The original immigrants were farmers who arrived wearing Bavarian leather breeches but some of their sons and grandsons went into business. Some of them moved north to establish successful business concerns in Santiago and Valparaiso. Others who remained on the land increased their holdings and prospered on the labor of the Indians. It has been stated that these Germans have kept their blood pure, but this is fantastic. The original settlers were small in number and many were of the same families. There has been a great deal of intermarriage with Chileans of Spanish blood and the most expert of the Nazi anthropologists would now have a great deal of difficulty separating the Nordic from the Iberian types.

Nazi agents looked on a compact community like this as one which offered golden opportunities and some of their most intensive work has been done here. It followed the usual pattern of visits by agents who extolled the virtues of the Nazi doctrines and made offers of free trips to Germany. An especial effort was made to get young men to visit the Fatherland and remain long enough to be trained in Nazi political methods. Just how many converts were made and how many young men went to Germany is unknown outside Nazi circles. But German shops in Valdivia still sell the most violent anti-Nazi books, as do all German bookshops in South America that I visited. The only real measure of the accomplishments of the Nazi agents in Chile was taken at the instigation of Hitler himself and it was not in any way encouraging. In one of the numerous plebiscites which punctuated his growth to power he made the gesture of throwing open the ballot to residents of Chile of German blood. A German ship anchored off Valdivia (outside Chilean territorial waters) provided the balloting place. The Nazi agents drummed up the partiots, offered free transportation and refreshments. When it was all over with, it was found that only 350 votes had been cast. Whatever the German population of Chile may be it provides support for only one small daily published in Santiago with a claimed circulation of 9,000 and an actual circulation of less than half of that. This is my last opportunity to appraise German populations by the circulation figures of newspapers for in no other South American country is there a German-language paper.

There are more political parties in Chile than in any other Latin-American country and it is not surprising to find that there is a Nazi party. The headquarters are on a main street just above the office of the American Express Company in Santiago and there the head of the party is willing to discuss plans and prospects with anyone. When I was in Santiago he frankly told friendly visitors of his great difficulty in getting enough funds to keep the party going. The names of the Nazi leaders are well known in Chile and it is significant that they do not include any representatives of the residents of "Little Germany." They are all composed of comparative newcomers who were trained in Germany and sent to Chile for special duties.

Because of their own ineptness Nazi activities in Uruguay have been more completely exposed than in any other country. This has given rise to the belief that there is a strong German community in this little country wedged in between Brazil and Argentina. Until shortly after the turn of the century the population of Uruguay was about a million and since that time it has more than doubled. The increase has been accomplished by means of immigration, much of it coming from the two neighbors, Brazil and Argentina. Among the European immigrants the German provided a negligible quantity—being outnumbered more than twelve to one by the Spanish and Italian immigrants. Brazilians head the list of residents of foreign birth with Germans bracketed at the bottom with the British and Swiss. Although this group of Germans is small in number it differs from other groups in that it probably represents a larger proportion of people born in Germany, since practically all immigration to Uruguay came after a certain amount of political stability was attained in 1910. It is probably because the local community was composed of actual bona fide Germans that the Nazi plotters at Montevideo worked out a grandiose plot to seize the little country and make it a German colony from which German authority could be extended north, south and west. It is also typical of Nazi methods to pick on the weak. It looked fine on paper for naval occupation of Montevideo would control the river Plate and a strong military force could threaten both Brazil and Argentina. The plot was prematurely disclosed—very prematurely for a smashing Hitler victory was essential to its success. The spunky Uruguayan government seized the records of the Nazi organization, but with all the evidence of the plot in their hands it is significant that less than a dozen persons were found to be actually involved.

Colombia is the fifth country said to offer hospitality to a large German community. There are, of course, some Germans living in Peru, Bolivia, Paraguay, Ecuador and Bolivia and in all of these countries there are German business establishments, some very important ones. German agents are also at work, but in none is there any settlement of Germans large enough to be of any importance as a nucleus for Nazi activities. I have heard of no figures as to the number of Germans in Colombia but their presence is obvious to any visitor by reason of the number of business establishments with German names. These are to be found in all of the larger cities where they are not confined to large concerns for many are in the retail business.

In addition there are many German farmers who, like those who migrated to Chile, were genuine pioneers who cut down the forests and made homes for themselves in the wilderness. They have prospered just as the German farm immigrant has prospered all over the world. Many of the descendants of the pioneers are now coffee growers who are much more directly interested in the price we will pay for Colombian coffee than in anything that may happen in Europe. Bogotá, the capital and metropolis, is the home of the largest colony of Germans in Colombia and they cannot number more than a thousand or so. Measured by numbers the German population of Colombia is less than that of Chile, which is less than that of Argentina, which is less than that of Brazil. The total of German immigrants in all the South American countries has never been more than a trickle compared to the number of those who came to the United States. There are now more than a million and a half native-born Germans in our country which is probably twenty times as many as in all South America.

It is from the material provided by these widely scattered communities of Germans and near-Germans that the Nazi agents set out to build a state within a continent, to enlist all of German blood in the struggle to create a Nazi-dominated world. Complete success would mean the conversion of every one of the so-called Germans to their own fanaticism so that many thousands of the sons and grandsons and even the great-grandsons of Germans would become voluntary Nazi agents eager to carry out the party orders. Only a fanatic could have viewed the prospect with any degree of enthusiasm.

As has been shown in the above brief survey a very large proportion of those who are classed as Germans consist of descendants of original settlers, many of them of the third or fourth generation. Of these very few are of pure German blood and an even smaller number have ever had any contact with Germany. Another generalization that can be made about them is that a very large proportion of them are farmers. With their characteristic industry and thrift they are prosperous farmers. They are rooted in the soil and in the absence of agrarian abuses cannot be swept off their feet by new political ideas. The Nazi ideology cannot appeal to them as offering escape from either poverty or oppression as they suffer neither. Still another generalization that can be made about them is that most of those who were born in Germany have renounced their allegiance to that country and become citizens of the country in which they live. My own personal opinion is that there are not many more than 50,000 legitimate Germans in all of South America, that is, men who were German-born and have not been naturalized. Of course the oath of allegiance to an adopted country does not mean any more to other Nazis than it did to Fritz Kuhn. But not all are Nazis by any means.

In preparation of the nazification of the continent an entirely new class of German immigrants began filtering into South American countries a few years ago. They were not homeseekers but political agents sent out to organize the German communities. Most of them were comparatively young men who had been thoroughly impregnated with the Nazi creed, have, in fact, no acquaintance with any political ideas other than the "leadership" of the Hitler or Mussolini type which is established by intrigue and deception and maintained by force. Long before we began to take Hitler seriously he was sending to each South American country groups of young men who by good party work at home had proven their loyalty and abilities. A few of them are descendants of old residents who have been sent on free trips to Germany and given what the Nazis call "party training." They are citizens of the countries they are attempting to destroy. Probably a majority of the agents would have been recruited from this class if that had been possible for they could work much more effectively. But they are in the minority. Most of the agents are newcomers who still speak Spanish or Portuguese with a well-defined accent.

Attempts have been made to organize local Germans in every community, with varying degrees of success. They have been cajoled or threatened into joining a variety of German societies and to contribute to the "winter relief" fund which is popularly supposed to be spent for propaganda and party expenses. In the opinion of everyone with whom I discussed the matter, including a few Germans, the success of the Nazi agents was in direct proportion to their ability to threaten. Individual farmers and small retail merchants could afford to thumb their noses at the Nazi agents and many of them did. Those who had near relations living in Germany did not dare to be independent for fear of vengeance that might be visited on fathers and mothers, brothers and sisters. Big business firms, many of which prosper on American agencies, were easily blackmailed into joining the Nazi party and making liberal contributions to funds. With the close party control of all banks and commercial machinery in Germany it was possible for the Gestapo in any South American city to strangle any firm that resisted. If placed on the Nazi black list it meant that its agents and correspondents in Germany were denied the usual banking facilities and their cargo refused shipment on German boats. With the

growth of the barter trade deals this control became even
stronger for no one but a good party member could share
in this trade. They paid heavily for what was nothing
more than the privilege of doing business.

In some cases German firms were assessed 3 per cent of
the gross on all business done. Many firms were compelled
to discharge old employees and replace them with ardent
young Nazis sent out from Berlin. An effective system of
espionage has enabled the party leaders to know just how
much could be demanded from every concern. The shake-
down has been just as complete as any ever made by a
political boss who provides protection for gambling houses
and the red-light district. Most of those who have had to
knuckle under to these demands were solid, substantial
businessmen who had never taken more than a casual interest in politics. It is impossible to believe that they made
their contributions with any degree of cheerfulness or
that they have any great affection for the Nazi cause.
However, in the face of Nazi threats most of the German
business firms fell in line. With them came their German
employees. In the face of similar threats native employees
were blackmailed into making contributions.

Up to that point the organization work was fairly easy,
but after that it became increasingly difficult. The descendants of German families in Brazil, Argentina, Chile
and Colombia were not absorbed into their respective
communities as were similar groups in the United States.
For one thing, the fact that the Catholic church has sought
with varying degrees of success to keep control of education compelled the Germans to maintain their own schools
and so prolong the use of the German language. But with
each generation the ties to Germany became weaker and
they became more and more of an integral·part of the

country in which they lived. The descendants of the original settlers continue to speak German and send their children to schools where instruction is given in the German language. But they also read and speak the language of the country in which they live and a very large proportion of them depend on Spanish or Portuguese papers for their news. Nazi political ideas are as strange to them as to the grandsons of the Germans who settled in Milwaukee at about the same time.

The Nazi party gained adherents in Germany very slowly in spite of the fact that the public was subjected to the magnetic appeals of Hitler himself and greatly influenced by the mass hysteria, beating of drums and waving of flags. Is it not reasonable to presume that these isolated Germans—isolated by both time and space—would be even more reluctant? From conversations with dozens of American residents I noticed what appeared to me to be a very significant difference of opinion. Those who were recent arrivals or who had no business or social contacts with Germans were ready to assume that everyone with a trace of German blood was a Nazi. Those who had German friends or business connections insisted that the Nazi sympathizers were few in number. Those who knew the Germans best and had the largest number of German friends or associates were the most insistent that the Nazi influence was unimportant and placed the lowest estimate on the possible number of Nazi party members.

My attempt to appraise the strength of the party had not gone very far before I ceased to accept without question the statement that some well-known German businessman was a well-known Nazi. In some cases he may have been blackmailed into pretending a position which he will abandon at the first opportunity. In other cases, some of

which are well known, the spiteful stories of Nazi affilia-
tions have been spread by business competitors. There can
be no doubt that thousands have successfully resisted all
Nazi threats and blandishments. The well-to-do farmer
whose grandfather was a South American pioneer reads
about the war in Europe and for sentimental reasons he
would not like to see a German defeat. But he could endure that with much greater equanimity than a crop failure
or a sharp decline in the price of coffee or wheat or cattle.
The opinion I heard most generally expressed was that not
more than ten per cent of those who speak the German
language have any sympathy for the Nazi cause and that
an even smaller proportion would be willing to make any
sacrifice for the party.

The fact that members of their party and adherents are
smaller in number does not appear to have discouraged the
Nazi leaders. By energy and daring they accomplished
great things in Germany when they numbered but a handful and they believe they can succeed here by the same
methods. Though it is their aim to gain control of governments they have a contempt for the majorities which
the decadent democracies hold in such high esteem.

Perhaps when the paper plans for their South American
empire were first drawn up they hoped for a blitzkrieg
political victory. They may have been naïve enough to believe that by intrigue, promises and threats, coupled with
a series of smashing Hitler victories in Europe, they could
gain control over one or more of the South American
governments. With a start like that they could travel far.
In this they have failed completely. There is not a single
government that is not friendly to the United States, not
one that does not more or less openly combat Nazi activities. Unfortunately American newspapers have given

much more prominence to alleged Nazi successes in South America than to failures. The failures and setbacks have been many and while unimportant in themselves are significant. For example, Nazi influence is admittedly greater in Brazil than in any other country yet it was not strong enough to prevent a recent regulation which will prohibit the publication of newspapers in any but the Portuguese language. While enforcement of this arbitrary regulation will hit a number of small dailies, including one in the English language, everyone knows—and the Germans know best of all—that it was promulgated for the purpose of putting an end to Nazi publications in the German language.

While the Nazis have failed to gain any influence in government circles they have, by their meddling and interference, built up for themselves a great deal of ill will. It is significant that while a Union Jack or some other British emblem will be found on the coat lapel of practically every British resident, one will search in vain for a swastika or other German emblem. The only swastikas I saw in all South America were those derisively scrawled on walls by mischievous small boys.

The fact that the Nazis have neither been able to organize the people they call their own or to exert any influence on the established governments has not left them inactive. They continue their efforts at organization and overlook no opportunity to make friends and influence people. According to common report there is a great deal of pro-Nazi feeling in army circles in several countries, some say all of them. While a number of people who are supposed to be able to speak with authority say that this is true, an equal number deny it. No doubt it would be very difficult for any observer to differentiate between the professional military man's admiration for the efficiency of the German war machine and his acceptance of the Nazi philosophy of life or his willingness to throw the lot of his own country in with that of the Axis group.

At the present moment the Nazi agents are devoting their principal attention to the minority parties in each country. They make particular efforts to gain the confidence of those unfortunate politicians who are out of office and in many cases without visible means of support. What they want to find in each country is a Quisling who, with their aid, will become the leader of a successful party and can be depended on to be amenable to Nazi suggestions. All plans are based on confidence in a Hitler victory and they believe that if and when England is successfully invaded and the British fleet surrendered it will be possible to put a pro-Nazi government into office in every South American country. In this way the ten republics might become a cluster of puppet states dominated by Germany without anything remotely resembling an armed invasion.

In support of this program Nazi propaganda pounds relentlessly on the argument that the days of the democracies are ended. Blusteringly and cajolingly the South Americans are urged to accept what are presented to be the immutable facts of life. The world is fated to be ruled by the Nazis and it is best to be prepared for it, whether you like it or not. It is useless to resist. Those who do so only invite unnecessary suffering.

While the Nazis have gained the avowed and open support of only one prominent South American politician and party leader, there can be no doubt but that many others are listening with a mixture of interest and caution to plans for their careers as so pleasantly set forth by the Nazi agents. Groups of out-of-office politicians are to be found in every country but they are particularly underprivileged in South America.

In most of these countries where individual opportunities are so limited a political job offers the most dazzling prospects to the white-collar class. The successful political leader not only has an assured income for himself but for all his friends. No practical politician south of the Rio Grande could fail to be impressed by the efficiency of the Nazi political machine and especially those who look on the balloting and the counting of votes at an election as an unmitigated nuisance as many of them do. Considering the fact that a great many South American leaders have risen to power by the simple expedient of buying a horse and hiring an army of soldiers, it should not be surprising that many would be intrigued by the Hitler method of securing and holding power.

In fact in every South American country there are one or more unemployed politicians who watch the war news as keenly as the stock speculator watches the market reports. If the news appears to be favorable to Hitler he is more friendly with the Nazi agents who are always at his elbow with advice, encouragement, suggestions, offers to help. As the news favors Great Britain, or as he is impressed by our preparations for defense he avoids the Nazi agents or is less interested in their arguments. There can be no mistake about the fact that the people of South America ardently hope for a Hitler defeat. Nor can there be any mistake about the fact that the political leaders of these comparatively weak and defenseless nations give serious consideration as to what course they should follow if the Nazis are right about their predictions as to the course the war will follow. When and if a Hitler victory appears to be inevitable it is equally inevitable that minority leaders

will openly support Nazi ideas in preparation for the day
when there will be a position open for a local Fuehrer.
The only one who has been reckless enough to come out
openly in support of the Nazis is the erratic Senator,
Laureano Gomez, leader of the Conservative party in
Colombia, a formerly dominant party which is now out
of power.

With the open support of Senator Gomez and with the
Panama Canal so temptingly near at hand the Nazis are
devoting more attention to Colombia than to any other
country. One of their most talented intriguers has been
attached to the embassy at Bogotá as "minister of cultural
relations" and Nazi spies and agents are all over the country. A special radio broadcast is beamed from Berlin for
the Colombians' consumption. No other Latin-American
country is distinguished in this way. The broadcast has
been used on several occasions to support Senator Gomez,
and, incidentally, interfere impudently in Colombian politics. In his newspaper, *El Siglo*, the Senator daily praises
Hitler and Mussolini and as persistently attacks the United
States. In a number of political speeches he has predicted
that if the present pro-American party is returned to power
there will be a revolution in Colombia. If and when this
revolution occurs, he said, his own party would have the
active support of certain foreign powers.

No one had the slightest doubt as to what he meant.
The Axis group shares his desire to drive the Liberal party
from power and would support revolutionary measures to
accomplish this. Of all the South American countries none
is giving the United States more wholehearted support
than Colombia. President Santos in his last annual address
to Congress announced as the keynote of his administration's foreign policy the closest possible co-operation with

the United States and pledged that the Panama Canal would never be attacked from Colombian soil. While other Liberal leaders disagree with him violently on local issues they are as one in support of this policy. Obviously if a victory for the Liberal party would result in a civil war it would be because that meant an endorsement of the party's foreign policy and the civil war would be fomented and supported by the Axis powers. If there could be any doubts about the matter they were set at rest a few days after the Senator's speech when both the Rome and Berlin radios referred in laudatory terms to the great Colombian leader, Senator Laureano Gomez. Everyone in Colombia assumed that this was a semi-official confirmation that the Senator's threat was made on the basis of promises or a definite agreement entered into between him and the Nazi agents who acted with the authority of the Hitler and Mussolini governments. The German and Italian official news services have also on several occasions given the Senator reassuring pats on the back to show the people of Colombia that he had the support of interests that might be more powerful than the United States.

Some diplomats in Bogotá believe that the Nazis have promised Senator Gomez the return of Panama to Colombia with the Panama Canal thrown in for good measure. If this is true it would provide a complete explanation for the violence and persistence with which he attempts to revive the old Panama issue of forty years ago which all other leaders in Colombia have agreed to forget. When we remember that in the last World War the German government blithely offered to return Texas to Mexico it would not be surprising to learn that the Nazis should offer the Panama Canal to Colombia as a reward for wrecking all plans for hemisphere solidarity.

Even before they secured the support of the hotheaded and erratic Senator the Nazis had been paying special attention to Colombia. There is plenty of circumstantial evidence that here was one place where they had made definite preparations for military action having for its object the crippling or destruction of the Panama Canal. If the Nazi *saboteurs* and gunmen have any secret stores of arms and explosives they will most probably be in Colombia for it is in attacks on the Panama Canal that they could be most effectively used. During the years that the Germans had control of Colombian civil aviation the planes were piloted by a succession of German army officers or reservists, each one being replaced as soon as he had become completely familiar with the routes. The contract with the government gave the German Scadta line a monopoly of aerial photography with the result that there is on file in Berlin what is probably the most complete aerial survey of Colombia in existence. When control of the air lines was taken over by Pan-American the German pilots were replaced by Americans but some of them for no apparent reason have remained in Colombia. The general belief, and it is not an unreasonable one, is that they are only waiting until there is an opportunity to put their Colombian experience to use in the service of Hitler. There are many others now on active duty with the German army who are thoroughly familiar with every Colombian air field. The most distant of these is less than a thousand miles from the Canal, the nearest less than two hundred.

Present Nazi efforts in Colombia are directed toward the support of the presidential aspirations of Senator Gomez. The regular election will be held in March of 1942. His election would constitute the first big Nazi victory in South America, a victory that would send their stock soaring and arouse feverish ambitions in the minds of every unemployed politician. No one believes that Senator Gomez could possibly be elected by a popular vote and that is the way all presidents of Colombia have been elevated to office. In more than a hundred years of existence as an independent republic Colombia has never had a disputed election or a political revolution. The one bloody civil war which was fought early this century was precipitated by an attempt to infringe on what the Colombians believed to be their constitutional rights. Indeed Colombia is the most advanced politically of all of the ten republics.

But the Nazi technique scorns such old-fashioned democratic procedure as honest elections in which power is delegated to the person or party which receives the most votes. Their political methods not only legalize but approve all of the methods which have been used both by the political gangsters of North America and the political adventurers of South America. The bold threats of Senator Gomez that there will be a revolution if his party is unsuccessful indicate that he has not only listened to the Nazis but has adopted their methods as his own and will attempt to apply them in Colombia.

CHAPTER XIX

## Let Others Do the Work

THE South Americans complain, with a good deal of justice, that they have been ignored in all of the histories we study. They say that we just take it for granted that everything of any consequence happened in one of our thirteen colonies, all of which were new, raw and small in comparison with any of the Spanish colonies during a great part of the period of joint colonial history. Every South American knows about Washington but to most educated North Americans Bolivar is just a name which few of them pronounce correctly. Our histories devote many pages to our Civil War and the bloodshed which was necessary before the slaves could be freed and few of us either know or appreciate the significant fact that slaves were freed in various South American countries without bloodshed and without compensation to the slaveholders. They also say that our English ancestors and members of their generation took credit for a great many things that should rightfully be credited to the early Spaniards.

A Peruvian cotton grower who is interested in everything connected with the agriculture of his own country took serious issue with me on the history of the potato. I happened to remark on the fact that Sir Walter Raleigh had introduced the potato to Europe by taking some of the roots from Virginia to his estates in Ireland and that for that reason it was now known as the Irish potato. Just to make conversation I suggested and argued mildly that it should be known as the Virginia potato. I soon found I had not only touched on a tender spot but had introduced a subject with which my companion was thoroughly familiar and on which he had some deep-seated convictions. He insisted that the potato as known to Europe was introduced into Spain by the followers of Pizarro and that it really should be known as the Peruvian rather than the Irish potato.

When I reflected that several generations of Spaniards had lived in Peru before the first English colony was planted in Virginia it appeared more than probable that they had been the first to introduce the strange products of the New World to Europe though I had never thought of that before. At the first opportunity I looked up the facts and found that the Peruvian cotton farmer was abundantly correct. The Spaniards had carried potatoes across the Atlantic and grew them successfully long before Raleigh went to Virginia and the first to be planted in Europe came from Peru.[1] In fact in 1553, the year after

[1] The potato was developed by the Incas from a bitter wild root. It may be remarked that after Spanish occupation the agriculture of Peru declined and in spite of recent improvements has never reached the perfection of the days before Pizarro.

Raleigh was born, a book published in Seville told of a monk from Peru who introduced the plant into Spain whence it spread to Italy and Belgium. By the time Sir Walter brought the plant to his Irish estate the potato had been cultivated for several generations in these countries and their cooks had very probably learned more than one way to prepare them, which, as my Peruvian companion pointed out, is more than the English or the Irish have ever done. Having learned for the first time that the gallant Sir Walter had not been the Lindbergh of potatoes I took time to check him up on one other achievement for which he is famous and found that he was not a pioneer in the use of tobacco, was not even one of the first. Many people in Europe were smoking pipes before he set foot in the New World.

The historical facts are against him and yet there is sound reason for adopting the name he gave to the potato and for looking on him as the patron saint of the tobacco auctioneers. The Spanish were the first to discover these new products and introduce them to Europe but it took a good showman and salesman like Sir Walter to popularize them and make them important articles of agriculture and commerce. The cultivation of potatoes was necessary in order to provide food for the starving people of Ireland. The promotion of the tobacco habit was essential in order to provide markets for the principal money crop of Virginia. Sir Walter smoked a pipe as did other English gentlemen who were interested in the Virginia adventure. Others talked at every opportunity about the food value of this strange new root crop from the New World which was produced so abundantly from the soil of Ireland. The salesmen stole the show. In spite of the fact that potatoes were grown on the continent long before they were grown in Ireland they became the staple food of that country when still something of a novelty elsewhere. The Spanish were too busy collecting the gold and silver from their new possessions to bother with such comparatively unimportant sources of wealth and were content to allow their scientists to record the discovery of these and other rich discoveries in the new world.

After four centuries the descendants of the original colonists still allow others to take the initiative in the development and exploitation of their products. There was nothing else the early generations could do. During the colonial period the Spanish and Portuguese colonists were even more restricted than we were in limitations placed on individual endeavor. No one at that time had conceived the idea that colonies were of any value except to be exploited for the benefit of the rulers and persons in high positions in the mother country. Spain and Portugal monopolized the trade of their colonies, even placed severe restrictions on intercolonial trade. Trade in fact received but scant attention from anyone so long as there was gold and silver to be looted from the Indians or their slave labor could be utilized to work the mines. All these handicaps and deterrents disappeared a century or more ago and from that time on the prosperity of the people has been dependent to a constantly increasing degree on the sale of its agricultural products. As soon as these restrictions were removed our Yankee skippers began to roam the Seven Seas in search of buyers for our produce. The South American, whose freedom came a little later, had more to sell than we had. But he waited for customers to come to him and still plays a more or less passive role in what should be a matter of first concern—the development and sale of his products.

There is a long and sad list of opportunities which he missed—too long by far to recount in detail. Quinine was unknown to the world until it was discovered that Indians cured themselves of fevers by drinking a concoction brewed from the bark of a strange tree. The Spanish named the tree Chinchona, after the wife of a viceroy, who was one of the first Europeans to be cured by it, and exported the bark to Spain. It was for a time just another easy source of wealth and they exploited it as one would a gold mine in which the orginal treasure could not be replaced. The precious trees were cut down, the bark stripped from them and sold and no thought given to the planting of new trees. The production of quinine was at the time a natural monopoly and might have remained one, for South America was the home of the tree and it grew in no other part of the world.

But if it had not been for the initiative of others it appears more than probable that the trees would have become as extinct as the passenger pigeon which we destroyed with an equally reckless ruthlessness. Fortunately for ailing humanity some Dutch scientist observed that the climate of Dutch East India was not unlike that of parts of South America where the Chinchona trees thrived. Seeds and seedlings were shipped to the Far East where plantations of the trees were successfully established and it is from that part of the world that our quinine supply now comes. The successful cultivation of the Chinchona tree by the Dutch cut into Peruvian sales only enough to prevent the complete destruction of the trees and some quinine is now produced but in negligible quantity. If you buy any quinine in Lima, where its use was first discovered by Europeans, it will be an imported article. The Dutch have proven that quinine can be profitably produced from cultivated trees—very profitably indeed as shown by the quinine fortunes that have been made. It would appear under these circumstances that some Peruvian or Bolivian or Ecuadorian landowners would try the experiment of planting himself a little forest of Chinchona trees and going into the quinine business for he doesn't have to gamble with the success of the venture. Perhaps that has been done but if so, it was such a clandestine attempt as to completely escape public attention.

Rubber was another product in which South America enjoyed a natural monopoly for rubber trees grew nowhere else. The rubber trees, like the Chinchona trees, grew wild, the latex was extracted by wasteful methods with no thought of replantings. If new sources of supply had not been developed outside of South America the present growth of the motorcar and other industries dependent on rubber would not have been possible. Long before there was the present great demand for rubber British as well as Dutch experimenters managed successfully to establish rubber plantations in the Far East from which the world's supply of rubber now comes. It remained for Henry Ford to make an attempt to restore Brazil to its old position as a producer of rubber.

Two other valuable products that originated in Brazil and have been transplanted elsewhere and brought fortunes to others are oranges and cotton. The first cotton grown in our Southern States was from seed brought from Brazil. The first navel orange, the tree from which the myriads of orange trees of California sprang, came from Brazil. Any visitor to Riverside, California, can see one of the two original trees with a placard showing that it was planted in 1873. A few years ago it was still alive and still bearing fruit. The industry which has been developed in California as a result of the introduction of these trees gives employment to several hundred thousand people. For many years Brazil neglected both these natural products and it is only recently that the export of Brazilian cotton and oranges has come to represent items of some importance.

Little credit is due to the South Americans for the development of any of the many products on which their prosperity now depends. We do not now spend millions of dollars annually for bananas because the owners of the banana plantations along the tropical coast made it easy for us to purchase them. That was done by our own businessmen who made investments in railways and steamship lines and trusted to their merchandising ability to create enough consumers to make the bold venture pay and justify the investment. The same thing is true of coffee and of practically all other products. Brazilians, Colombians and others who depend on their coffee crops for prosperity do not sell us their coffee but allow us to buy it. The great Argentine meat industry and the smaller but still important meat industries of Uruguay and Brazil, were not developed on the initiative of the proprietors of the haciendas but by the English who were in search of larger and more dependable supplies of fresh meat. Later we added our contribution by establishing a number of large packing houses which market the meat and other food products of these countries all over the world.

The position of the South American is much like that of the American farmer who not only buys all of his supplies from the country storekeeper but depends on him to market his produce. And, like the American farmer, he does not make the marketing task any easier by the production of articles of commerce that are either of standard or dependable quality. The term "raw matrial" was never more appropriately used than when applied to the products which South America produces in such huge quantities and at such cheap prices.

In countries where there is such ideal grazing land and such vast herds of cattle one would expect to find a well-developed dairy industry or at least a dependable supply of good dairy products. Actually mothers living in any of these countries find it difficult to secure good milk for their children. The herds that range the pampas and grow fat on the ever green fields of alfalfa, are bred for beef, not milk and the only inferior milk that ever gets to market is that which the calf has left. Every year or so some enterprising Yankee thinks he sees an opportunity to make a fortune in the exploitation of the dairy products of Argentina or some other country. It appears reasonable to assume that with beef cattle either dressed or on the hoof selling for a fraction of the market price in other countries there should be, for example, very large supplies of cheap butter. An old Shanghai friend of mine made the trip to Buenos Aires at the same time I did with the idea of finding here a source of supply for the China Coast which would compete with the butter now imported from Canada and Australia. Like many others who had gone there on a similar mission he found the butter not only inferior in quality but of no dependable quality. There are no great herds of graded dairy cattle as in other countries and few experts in the production of dairy products. Actually the Argentine production of butter is surprisingly small. There are three cows for every man, woman and child in the country and yet the total production of butter is just about sufficient to supply each with an ounce of butter a week.

On the other hand the cheese industry is now being developed very rapidly and successfully.[2]

While the United States produces most of the world's mica we also buy that produced in Argentina and Brazil but it reaches us by a roundabout route. The mica is shipped to India just as it comes from the quarries and is there prepared by splitting and grading the sheets. No one in Brazil or Argentina knows how to do this work or will bother with it. It is shipped to us from India. Brazilian rose quartz is shipped to China where it is carved and then sent back to Brazil for sale to tourists. For a long time the sale of Brazilian semi-precious stones was greatly handicapped because of the stubbornness of the British and German lapidaries who really controlled the exports. The United States manufacturer of jewelry is just as enamored of the assembly line system as is the motorcar manufacturer. Rings are turned out in huge quantities and the stones must fit the rings. This is just the reverse of the European system of hand production in which the ring is made to fit the stone. For a long time the German and British lapidaries insisted that it was impossible to cut the Brazilian stones so that they would be of standard sizes and shapes. This is now being done and a new product made available to the American jewelers. But it was the American jeweler who brought about this reform.

The coffee growers of almost any one of the many South American countries which produce coffee might with a little well-directed advertising have created a demand for their product which would have placed it in a dominent position among discriminating coffee consumers. There is just as much difference in the tastes of coffee from

[2] Annual production of butter in Argentina is 30,000 tons, cheese 50,000 tons.

different countries as there is between the strong teas of India and the delicately flavored teas of China. In fact after drinking the strong coffee of Brazil and the even stronger coffee of Peru my first taste of Colombian coffee suggested a cup of chocolate. But it is too late now. The proportion of Colombian, Brazilian and other varieties of coffee that go into American blends are determined by the big coffee companies and it is only by producing coffees at cheaper prices that the growers in the different countries can increase their business.

Every manufacturing nation in the world has representatives in South America whose sole duty it is to buy various raw materials and all of them tell the same sad story about the difficulties they have to face and can rarely surmount in their attempts to get products that are properly graded. Mandioca is produced in vast quantities in several countries and there is always more than enough to meet the domestic demands. Little can be exported as a food product. But a very large part if not all of the surplus could be used by starch manufacturers, if the product was properly sorted and graded so that the manufacturer could be certain what he was getting. Manufacturers who purchase South American products do a great deal of sorting and grading that should be done at the point of production. Vicuña (wool) is a very valuable product of Peru, a product that would justify the most careful handling. But the owner of vicuña herds, like the owners of most other livestock enterprises, leaves the management of his flocks to his Indian peons and half-breed superintendents and often does not even bother to provide them with essential tools. The shearing is done by cutting the wool from the animal with the sharp edges of broken glass, a cruel and wasteful process. The wool is allowed to lie on the ground until the shearing is done and then gathered up and shipped with the dirt and sand and grass. It is in this condition that the manufacturers receive it.

These examples of indifferences to the salability of his own products might be multiplied indefinitely but in the end they would add up to the same total. By grading and standardizing his products the South American could take up the slack in his own production and add millions to the volume of his annual sales and secure for himself the merchandising profit which now goes to others.

Conditions of life in the past have not made it necessary for him to do this. It is idle to go back to his Latin ancestry to explain his indifferences. He has not been unlike other people in following the line of least resistance and cashing in on the bountiful gifts of nature with as little effort as possible and with no particular worries about the future. The feudal pattern of life has just lasted longer here than elsewhere.

The American farmer is often suspicious of the country storekeeper to whom he sells his produce and from whom he purchases his supplies. This suspicion and distrust are natural because the storekeeper is usually able to fix not only the price at which he sells but also the price at which he buys. The farmer is not in a position to bargain. It is natural that he should think that he is paid too little for what he sells and charged too much for what he buys. The South American is in the same position and is equally suspicious of the middlemen on whom he is so completely dependent. This is, of course, entirely his own fault. He has been content to own the land which produces his wealth and let others do the work.

Realizing that much of the work that is being done by others should be done by their own citizens, a number of governments have enacted restrictive legislation limiting the proportion of the total pay roll that may be used in the payment of foreign salaries. In Brazil no company is allowed to pay a foreign employee a higher salary than is paid to a Brazilian in the same category of employment. This amounts to nothing more than an attempt to conceal symptoms instead of striking at the root of the trouble. Such legislation would be entirely unnecessary if there were enough trained South Americans to do the work that is to be done. The legislation, which falls hardest on foreign concerns, compels the employment of the citizens of each of the countries often in positions they are not fitted to fill. The foreigner has to do the work of training them.

Any study of the question will show that if the South Americans did their share of the work that has to be done in order to find a sale for their products millions would be more usefully occupied than at present, many new jobs would be created and every country would enjoy a greater and more secure prosperity than is possible under the present system. The benefits would extend through every range of society from the Indians in the Andes who shear the vicuña with a bit of broken glass to the businessmen in every country who would, as in other countries, take over the responsibility of finding markets for their own produce and acting as distributors for imported manufactured articles.

CHAPTER XX

## *North Is North and South Is South*

HISTORIANS and other learned men account for the difference between people very glibly and convincingly, and provide a lot of textbook reasons with long words explaining why North Americans and South Americans think and act differently or do the same things in different ways. With academic thoroughness they go back to the beginning of things. Our ancestors came from Britain and Northern Europe. The ancestors of the South Americans came from around the Mediterranean. English was our language, Spanish and Portuguese was theirs. Our ancestors, we have been taught to believe, crossed the Atlantic in search of political and religious freedom while theirs crossed the same ocean, by a more southerly route, principally in search of wealth. There

[ 324 ]

were priests with the conquistadors and the gold-seeking adventurers who followed them but they were not interested in religious freedom for themselves. That was guaranteed by the Catholic rulers but they were imbued by a desire to convert the heathen to the Catholic faith. To them any other form of religious freedom was heresy. Starting with an initial list of differences like that one can put up a pretty fair argument in support of a lot of interesting theories.

All of these easy generalities are subject to a great many qualifications which put more flesh and blood into the picture of the South American and make him more easily understandable to us. Although originally the South Americans were colonists like ourselves and were ruled by kings and queens living across the Atlantic they eventually became independent and struggled as we did over the problems of self-government. In meeting these problems we had a decided advantage. As our ancestors were familiar with the machinery of the English town meeting we, according to some accounts, easily and expertly built the democratic institutions of government. As a matter of fact we were not very expert and we didn't build the machine very easily but we didn't make so many mistakes as our southern neighbors did. Their ancestors were accustomed only to the narrowly restricted civil liberties of Spain and Portugal and their conception of the ideal of liberty was not clear and well defined. It should not be surprising that they have fumbled and stumbled in their attempts to govern themselves though they have made and are continuing to make progress. Considering all of the difficulties that have been faced the South American governments are very much better than one would expect them to be. Their development has been toward the democratic ideal—not away from it. They have not achieved that ideal and neither have we. As I see it one of the beauties of democracy is that no matter how much we may perfect it there are still higher ideals to strive for.

Their governmental machinery is in most instances a replica of ours but it works differently. Those who are bold enough to raise a controversial religious issue point out that while the Catholic church has never played more than a minor part in our political life it is a factor to be reckoned with in every country south of the Panama Canal. Because of ancient fears and prejudices we have never had a Catholic president but no non-Catholic can qualify for the presidency in most of those countries. In many cases the endorsement of the archbishop turns the tide in national elections and the parish priest is too often a petty politician. Throughout Latin America the church controlled education for several centuries and has bitterly fought all attempts to separate church and state or to provide an educational system any more liberal than that provided by the Catholic schools. A cynic has remarked that education in South America with its heavy emphasis on religious instruction tends to prepare one for the life to come rather than for this earthly existence.

From a period that began a couple of generations before the founding of Jamestown environment not much unlike our own has played its part in shaping their lives. Not only environment but as with us a steady stream of immigration which over a period of decades, brought to many countries greater proportional increases in population than were brought to us. While our big melting pot has been seething and simmering ten other smaller pots in ten different countries have been doing the same thing. The mixture in each case was different and the product was different but in one important respect they were identical. Each produced men whose interests and affections were centered on the New World instead of the old. The fierce often unreasoning patriotism of the people of each of these countries is something it is a little difficult for the citizens of our great and powerful country to understand. But we make a great mistake if we do not take into consideration the fact that these people are just as patriotic as we are, just as proud of their history, just as hopeful of the future. During the generations that we were subduing the wilderness their pioneers were engaged in identical enterprise, protecting themselves against Indian raids, planting seeds where no crops had grown before and finding time to fight a good many bloody wars between themselves.

They did not endure the hardships of New England winters but they did brave the greater dangers of the tropical jungles. During the colonial period they faced problems identical with ours, had their trade restricted by the mother country, and found it difficult to sell their produce or to secure essential tools and manufactured goods from Europe. A study of the museums shows that they were compelled to develop many makeshift devices just as we did. If we forget all about the old historical and ethnological and other pedantic reasons why there should be a great difference between us and just accept the South American as he is today we find that there isn't so very much difference between us as theoretical study would indicate.

As with us and with peoples of every color or race the most important thing in life, the first duty of the head of every South American family, is, by one means or another, to secure the money with which to buy the food and shelter and clothing which life itself requires. The story of the method by which this money is acquired and the manner in which the money is spent presents a more accurate picture of the life and character of the individual and of the nation than the theories found in textbooks. The making and the spending of money provide a better yardstick, in my humble opinion, than that provided by history or the search for the survival of ancient racial traits. The average income tax return should afford any good student of psychology a pretty complete mental picture of the man who signed the report. A few thousand years from now while one set of scientists is measuring skulls from New England country graveyards another set will possibly be collecting and examining the data from copies of old income-tax returns.

When approached from that point of view, the South American becomes to me an understandable person. Let us start with the fact that practically all wealth is agricultural—that South Americans live from the products of the soil. There are of course a great and increasingly valuable number of developed mineral and oil properties, but these have been developed by others and South Americans have little share in them.[1] Production from the mines and oil wells may add to the dividends of foreign companies and the royalties collected by South American governments but on the whole the prosperity of the individual depends on the sale of farm products. It is not in the pretentious cities but as one travels about on plane or train that one sees the real wealth of the country in the great fields of grass or grain and the great herds of cattle or flocks of sheep. But the picture is unlike that which spreads such a pleasing panorama before travelers in almost every part of the United States. One will look in vain for the com-

---

[1] The tin mines of Bolivia provide an exception as they are owned and operated by natives of that country.

fortable farmhouses, the oversized barns, the broad fertile fields which the man who lives in the farmhouse owns and works.

Instead there are many huge estates, the smallest of them consisting of tens of thousands of acres, the largest having an area greater than that of some countries in Europe. There is no suggestion of comfort about the scattered houses of farm laborers—no well-dressed farmers driving to town in their motorcars. The owners of these great estates constitute the aristocracy, but it is not like the aristocracy of the old South or even of that of ranch owners of the West. The plantation owners of our Southern States built beautiful and luxurious homes where they practiced the art of living gracefully. Even though all the work was done by negro slaves the owner was rooted in the soil. The Westerner lives on his ranch, his boots are encrusted with his own mud, his face soiled by the dust blown from his own fields.

When I lived in Texas more than thirty years ago most of the ranch owners were of the first generation, that is they had by one means or another, secured possession of vast areas of land and built up the herds on which they prospered. The South American landowner, almost without exception, acquired his property by the biological luck of having been born into a wealthy family. Many of these families date back to the period of the original conquests, the era of Cortez and Pizarro. The henchmen of these conquistadores were rewarded with bountiful grants of unoccupied land which cost the donors nothing and entailed no responsibilities on the recipients. The wealth of South America is much older than ours and, unlike ours, has no tradition of personal accomplishment, no close association with the soil which produces it. Rarely does the big landowner pay his patrimony the compliment of living on it or learning anything about how to manage it. He employs superintendents and overseers who in turn employ the hardworking unromantic gauchos and the owner lives the idle and useless life of the absentee landlord.

That is the aristocracy of South America, the class from which the intelligentsia are drawn, the class who, to a greater or lesser extent, elect the officials and hold office and dominate the affairs of each country. As a class they have the snobbish and stupid pride of inherited wealth which has not yet been challenged by newer generations of wealthy men. The wealthy class has had no new blood for generations. Each year the published list of our citizens who have paid the highest income taxes reveals many new names, and always the names of men whose fathers or grandfathers were so poor that they did not even own their own homes. That would not be true in any list of wealthy men in South America. It would be difficult to find one of them whose papa or mama, or both of them, were not rich. There are no Horatio Alger heroes, no geniuses who by their own efforts have placed themselves on an economic level with the cattle or coffee barons. There is no South American, so far as I know, whose career has in any way paralleled that of Ford, Morgan, Woolworth, Rockefeller, or even Russell Sage, or Hetty Green. The few fortunes made by ingenuity and hard work have been amassed by foreigners. The Syrians, Italians, British, Germans and our own countrymen have engaged in manufacturing or merchandising and comprise the new-rich of South America. The most the aristocracy ·of the continent has done has been to conserve or to augment inherited wealth.

These differences of background cause misunderstandings. The South Americans look on us as a pushing and grasping people and are slightly contemptuous of what appears to them to be our constant slaving for material success. This is unhappily the attitude of inherited wealth in all countries throughout all times. Our neighbors do not find the same striving for the dollar or the peso or milreis in their own countries and are prone to call us "dollar lovers" which is more than a little unfair. There are few young men in South America pushing ahead in business or finance because for social rather than economic reasons there have been few opportunities.

Let us take, for example, the most common variety of business enterprises, the retail shop. With a few exceptions—a very few—these are all family affairs, just as they are in China and other countries where mutual trust and confidence does not extend beyond the family circle. A stroll through the business district of any city will reveal block after block of shops so small they are obviously one-man establishments, possibly run by the proprietor with the help of his son. Rarely do they boast more than two show windows. Even in a rapidly expanding business there is no room for the outsider—certainly no room at the top. There are always plenty of relatives to fill the managerial jobs and the outsider who is employed as a clerk or errand boy is most likely to grow old and gray in that position. The same limitation of opportunity is found in practically all business enterprises for there has been little development of the idea of stock company management or even of simple partnerships which go beyond family lines. If the South American youth is lacking in initiative it may be said in his behalf that the conditions of life which surround him are also lacking in incentive to endeavor. While it may be true that corporations have no souls they offer a big-hearted welcome to the boy of talent who has no opportunity in the old-fashioned family institution.

Under these circumstances the roads which lead to success and distinction as well as those which lead to wealth are limited in number. The ambitious young North American can train himself for one of a hundred or more specialized occupations with the certainty that there is a demand for the kind of work he is fitting himself to do. If he wants to go into business for himself he finds encouragement all about him in the presence of men who have struck out for themselves and achieved success. The imagination of the young South American is stirred by no such examples as this. The great men he sees about him are great because their fathers inherited wealth which in turn their fathers had left to them. If he is fortunate enough to belong to this wealthy class he is not distinguished above hundreds of others who are equally fortunate. If he is a poor boy facing the necessity of earning a living there are no big cruel corporations ready to employ and reward him with all the wealth and power he deserves.

The only field which provides perfect freedom of opportunity is politics; that is within certain limitations. It may be taken for granted that one must be a Catholic, be a member of the intelligentsia and have good family connections if he expects to travel far in political life. No hornyhanded son of the soil has much of a chance of becoming president of his country by the legal process of election. A scholastic degree of any sort is a distinct political asset. Pretentions to scholarship which would doom a candidate to defeat in many of our more uncultured districts bring victory at the polls to many a South American candidate. We have retained a certain pioneer faith in the homespun wisdom of the common man but the South American casts his vote for the man with the college degree. A fair college or university faculty could be organized from the personnel of most of the legislative bodies. An especially good one could be formed from the senators and congressmen of Colombia for they comprise what is without doubt the most highly educated—the most literate body of legislators in the world.[2]

One cannot escape the impression that the attainment of a degree, the privilege of adding some alphabetical insignia to one's name, plays a much larger part in the scholastic life of our southern neighbors than it does in ours. In the narrowly limited struggle for distinction this is an attainment that lifts one above the common herd. The number of college graduates who have the legitimate title of "doctor" is amazing. When I was in Lima with John Gunther he and I were the only representatives of the professional writers who were undistinguished by a title of that sort. To the Peruvians it was unthinkable that two men who earn a livelihood by writing should be so devoid of scholastic accomplishments and both of us were introduced everywhere as "doctor." I don't know what John did but I got so tired explaining I was not a doctor that I finally gave up and shamelessly accepted an undeserved honorific which was not so flattering as it might sound. One meets so many "doctors" in South America that a plain "mister" is a certain odd distinction in itself.

The way in which South Americans take up one course of study after another and hop from one profession to another constantly adding new titles and new records of

[2] Of the eleven high-ranking officials of Argentina consisting of the president, vice-president and members of the cabinet seven have the degree of doctor. In Colombia only one out of the ten in similar high positions does not enjoy that scholastic distinction.

achievement is positively dizzying to the North American
who is accustomed to concentrate on one line of endeavor.
For example, there is Dr. Manuel Prado, the distinguished
president of Peru. When he entered the university he
majored in mathematics, political science and engineering.
After graduation he taught mathematics. Not content with
being an engineer and a political scientist he enlisted in
the army and rose to the rank of lieutenant general. At
some point in his career he was curator of an archaelogical
museum and became an authority on the puzzling archae-
ology of his country. Later he managed a bank. Then,
after a period of political exile, he returned home to be
elected president of his country. His career while more
distinguished than that of others is not unique. The manager of the hotel at which I stopped in Santiago was a
general in the Chilean army. In Buenos Aires I met one of
the somewhat restricted number of young Argentine ladies
who has defied the conventions and is making a career for
herself. She took degrees in medicine and architecture and
is now designing costumes for a movie producer.

In this scramble for degrees—for what appears to be
scholarship for the sake of scholarship—education leans
heavily to the cultural side. As a result there is ample material to support the contention that while we excel in the
production of useful machines and in the organization
and management of big business enterprises we are far inferior to our neighbors in the matter of cultural life. They
are not at all backward about making claims of this sort.
I did not discuss the matter with anyone who did not
assume that this was one of the established facts about
which there could be no quibbling. Many of them also assume that we make no pretentions of culture and are content to accept our inferior position, are not in fact espe-

cially interested in such matters as art and literature. From their point of view they are correct. From our point of view their educational system is wrong because it is not practical enough. Rarely does the young man who will eventually inherit vast herds take the trouble to learn anything about a cow. He is much more likely to belong to some learned society than to a livestock association. We may as well remember that during a similar period in our national life a promising boy of good family was usually trained for the church, the law or the school. There is reason to believe that with the increased opportunities that will come as industrialism supplants feudalism, the ambitions of the youth of South America will change, just as ours have changed.

The very fine official publication *Brazil* devotes more than thirty pages to the chapter headed "Cultural Situation," a general review of education and the progress of the arts in that large, populous and progressive country. The status of agricultural education is dismissed with a vague few lines but a discussion of the literature of Brazil occupies five pages and even more space is devoted to music and painting. In the section on literature the author says:

> We are a people eminently gifted with literary talent with a vocation for spiritual matters. The Brazilian, like every Latin in general, is more inclined to spiritual things than to practical activities. We are naturally far more poets than economists. We have a more spontaneous sympathy for activities of the imagination than for those requiring a considerable application to concrete and positive things. In literature we are more easily led to poetry than to prose—and in prose, naturally more to romance than

to criticism, history or education. We are weak erudites, superficial criticizers, more romantic historians than moralists, men of letters more than humanists.

This could be said with equal truth of the residents of each of the other countries. In all of them the production of poetry is tremendous in volume. There are a large number of societies in different cities whose members meet regularly to read their poetical compositions to each other. On the occasion of holidays which celebrate the anniversary of some historical event, it is always possible for the committee on arrangements to fill in several hours with epic poems which are read or recited by their authors. With the introduction of loud-speakers thousands can be entertained in this way and thousands do stick it out for hours, listening to a performance that would dissipate any crowd at home in a few minutes. A visiting journalist some years ago made the discovery that the president of Colombia was a poet and the fact was widely publicized. It would be even more surprising to discover that a president of Colombia was not a poet, that it was not able to form interminable rhymes and metered phrases, to which the Spanish language lends itself so readily.

In spite of the great attention paid to the teaching of such cultural subjects as literature, painting and music very few graduates ever get beyond the amateur stage, and most of them appear content to remain there. Aside from members of the editorial staff of newspapers a very small number of men or women earn their livings by writing—or by music or painting either for that matter. In the field of writing this is partly due to the limited number of readers and the consequent limitations of the publishing field. Yet a number of Scandinavian writers appealing to much smaller audiences have made for themselves comfortable fortunes and gained international fame. As the Brazilian quoted above says, they are men of letters rather than humanists. With life all about them they read about it in a book. As writers they are just a little too cultured —so much so that the average man who buys books and enables authors to eat will have none of them. He buys translations of New York best-sellers.

With a natural desire for leadership and distinction the South American turns to the law for a profession which provides the easiest route to official position. In every city there are more lawyers than are needed and every year more are given diplomas. From the practice of law they gravitate naturally into politics and if successful acquire an official position which provides not only a livelihood but that much desired distinction. It would be an exaggeration to say that every South American aspires to public office but that statement would suggest a picture that is not wholly false.

Diplomatic positions are the ones that are most coveted, although they provide little opportunity for usefulness. It is rarely that a South American diplomat is called on for any great display of either energy or ingenuity. He runs little risk of a blasted career through an error in judgment and on the other hand has little opportunity to distinguish himself. His duties are largely of a routine nature. A working day of four hours or less is not at all uncommon in the diplomatic and consular offices abroad. In fact if you happen to be in Lima and want to get a passpost visa for a trip to Colombia you will find that the Colombian Consulate is open from four to six. On the occasion of my visit it was closed until almost five o'clock because no member of the staff had arrived for work.

With insistent demand for these easy diplomatic jobs every South American country has embassies, legation and consulates scattered all over the world, many of them in places where an official would find it difficult to occupy himself with governmental duties for a few hours of each week. This statement falls unfairly on some hard-working consuls who labor energetically to further the trade of the country they represent but they are few in number. In fact a great many of them are located in places where there is not only no trade but no conceivable trade opportunities that would justify the establishment of a consulate. Each of the Latin-American countries maintains a diplomatic post in all of the others and there is inevitable rivalry in the maintenance of impressive buildings and the giving of elaborate dinners. The situation is much the same as it would be if each of our forty-eight states was compelled to maintain an embassy or legation in each of the other states. The cost of such an organization would be burdensome even to the state of New York which has taxable wealth far in excess of that of any South American country.

Poverty of opportunity and the consequent desire for official positions, has made all the South American countries top-heavy with politics. Political campaigns are bitter affairs for the livelihood of a great many people depends on the outcome of the election. As it is the duty of every successful candidate to provide his friends, relatives and supporters with jobs almost every branch of the civil service is overcrowded with useless employees. A vast amount of red tape surrounds all official activities, and complicated procedures are continued because to simplify them would open the way for a reduction of the number of employees. There have been a great many governmental reforms but little if any progress has been made in cutting dead wood out of the government pay rolls. It will take a brave man to make that a campaign issue.

It is probably because of the leisurely hours enjoyed by officials as well as the midday siesta period which is observed by all that the tradition of South American languor persists. The idea of stopping all work in the middle of the day strikes the visiting North American as an unexplainably absurd procedure and he usually has to see the shuttered windows and doors before he is thoroughly convinced that this is done. Offices and shops do close for two hours at noon and those who feel the need of it have time for a comfortable nap. This is one thing the visitor always talks about when he gets back home—talks about rather exultantly for this custom strikes him as providing most convincing proof that our way of life is better. During the siesta hour, most people just go home for leisurely luncheon. The actual working day is not unduly shortened for the offices remain open with everyone at work until six or seven o'clock. The big New York executive usually manages to kill two hours at lunch but his office closes at five o'clock just the same. So far as I could observe the South American works just as long and as hard as we do.

But there is quite a gap—a gap of several generations between the highly developed business methods of the North American and the more leisurely or less high-powered methods of the South Americans. It is incorrect and unfair to think of them as being lazy or indolent but a great many of our southern neighbors see no reason why the task of making a living should be unduly complicated or why the conduct of a business should be made a kind of contract bridge game to be played for its own enjoyment. A Brazilian friend told me that too many of us were just businessmen and nothing else and never appeared to be finding any enjoyment in life except when putting over a deal of some sort. He said he believed we really didn't care so much about money as many others did, especially the Germans and Italians. It was just that business was the only game the poor fellows knew how to play. That gives us, he thought, an undeserved reputation as a grasping people interested in nothing but the acquisition of wealth. The South American can close his desk for the day full of pleasant thoughts about the fun he is going to have before he goes to work again but the North American is unhappy because he doesn't know what he is going to do with himself with all that spare time on his hands. What he really likes to do when the hours of work are over is to find some one he can talk to about business. "Shop talk," my Brazilian friend assured me, has little part in the life of the South American. When the time to stop work arrives, he stops work and thinks about other things.

Sometimes our sales managers are able to change this point of view and make a high-powered go-getter out of the South American sales agent but sometimes he rebels and just quits. He has a sense of relative values including factors which are completely ignored by the man who thinks primarily of sales quotas. A Colombian importer who had given up the agency for a well-known line of motorcars told me his story of the clash between two opinions as to what made life worth while. He had built a very fine show room and was doing a business which was satisfactory to himself as well as to the manufacturer until the latter began sending a succession of export sales managers on helpful visits to all distributors.

"The first man, when he come," the Colombian told me, "he tell me I got fine big show room and do good busi-

ness which I know already. But he say my show windows
not big enough. Much waste space because no one can
see inside. So I got a contractor and we tear out one side
of the wall and we put in more show windows, biggest
in town. First man he go away and after a few month second man come. He say my passenger car business very
good but truck business not so good. He say I should take
passenger cars out of window and put in trucks, which I
did. Third man come following year and say neon sign
not big enough. Also say only damfool put trucks in
show window where passenger cars should be. I begin to
think this is all too much trouble. Next man will probably
tell me I must paint front of my shop blue and wear a blue
shirt and if I don't I may lose my agency. So I sell my
motorcar agency and buy this shop that sells accessories.
It's my business and no one can come in here and tell me
how to run it."

The South American is always disconcerted at the
abrupt way in which the North American will start conversations on any subject he may have in mind, which is
often that of making a sale. It appears to them that the
visitor allows the least possible time to elapse before bringing out his samples or catalogue and starting on his selling
talk. According to their way of doing things the business
conversations should not be started until there has been a
little friendly chat in which inquiries are exchanged about
each other's physical well-being and possibly the subject of
the weather disposed of. The ideal approach to a selling
talk would be one in which it appears to be a natural
development of the pleasant chat in which the two were
indulging.

This is irritating to the go-getting Yankee who is accustomed to making as many calls as possible during the

business day and who usually has to make a detailed report on his activities to some one in the New York office. He frets at the delay, and when talking things over with his cronies, makes unkind remarks about businessmen who think they are at a ladies' tea party. If he keeps on doing business, he eventually falls into the ways of the country though with some misgivings and a lot of self-criticism. It doesn't seem right to be wasting all this time on useless conversation when he might be making headway with his selling talk. In the end he reluctantly comes to the conclusion that the South American custom has a lot to be said for it. When two businessmen meet for the first time the four or five minutes of casual conversation enables each to size up the other, to establish the personal relationship which the South Americans refer to as "sympatico." With that lubricant, the actual business part of the conversation proceeds much more smoothly than would otherwise have been possible and in the end no time has been lost.

In the objective and colorless handling of personal news our newspapers all violate South American traditions not only of good journalism but also of good taste. The South American reporters or copy writers have a sugar-coated if somewhat hackneyed collection of adjectives which, like plums in a pudding, they sprinkle in their columns. Brides are always beautiful, the guests at the wedding a distinguished group. If a local resident is taken to the hospital the event is recorded with a certain amount of sadness in which there is often a cheerful note because he will have the best possible attention from the very capable doctor to whom so many local residents are indebted. It is like the friendly personal journalism of the American country weekly where the announcement of a birth is not complete without the reassuring statement that mother and baby are doing well. Increased costs in the production of news-papers as well as a growing sophistication has led to our abandonment of what we now patronizingly refer to as "flowery language." But the language of our southern neighbor is full of posy-like words and phrases and to them their absence makes life a little duller.

The same exuberance of expression is found in all human contacts. When two men meet they call each other "my friend," pat each other on the back and exchange bear hugs. The newly arrived North American looks on these antics with mild amusement. But after he has made his first trip back to the States and returns and is greeted effusively and slapped on the back he finds it rather pleasant.